Community Values

in an age of

Globalization

Community Values

in an age of

Globalization

The Sheldon M. Chumir Foundation
for
Ethics in Leadership

Edited by Marsha P. Hanen
Alex Barber and David Cassels

Paperback ISBN 0-9730197-1-9 (acid free paper)

National Library of Canada Cataloguing in Publication Data

Main entry under title:

Community values in an age of globalization

"Proceedings of the symposium Community Values in an Age of Globalization held . . . Apr. 26th to 28th, 2002 in Calgary"—pref. ISBN 0-9730197-1-9

1. Social ethics—Congresses. 2. Community—Congresses. 3. Globalization—Congresses. I. Cassels, David. II. Hanen, Marsha P., 1936- III. Barber, Alex. IV. Sheldon M. Chumir Foundation for Ethics in Leadership.
BJ19.C66 2002   170   C2002-910721-0

Cover design by Sharon Abra Hanen and David Cassels

Printed at Morriss Printing, Victoria BC, Canada

CONTENTS

ACKNOWLEDGEMENTS

This book grows out of the second public symposium held on the weekend of April 26-28, 2002, by the Sheldon M. Chumir Foundation for Ethics in Leadership. Entitled "Community Values in an Age of Globalization", the Symposium brought together a group of outstanding speakers to engage with over three hundred symposium participants in thoughtful reflection and serious discussion about a range of topics of critical importance to all of us.

Because the next G8 meeting is scheduled to take place in Kananaskis exactly two months after our symposium, we undertook to publish the book as quickly as possible, so that it might be useful for people thinking about globalization issues in relation to that meeting. Any effort of this sort comes to fruition only as a result of a great deal of work by many people. Clearly, our first debt of gratitude goes to the Symposium participants whose work is represented here: Benjamin Barber, David Schneiderman, Gretchen Mann Brewin, Lynn Foster, Brian MacNeill, Margaret Waterchief, Russell Hemenway, Stephen Lewis, Robert Fowler, Naomi Klein, John Curtis, Len Findlay, Stuart Walker, Harvey Weingarten, Michael Valpy, Bronwyn Drainie, John Stackhouse and Lloyd Axworthy. Truly a stellar cast! Each of them responded with unfailing enthusiasm and generosity to our invitation to participate in our symposium weekend, and to engage with the audience in meaningful discussion of the topics at hand as well as to provide us with a text in short order, or to agree to our editing a transcript of the actual symposium tapes.

Joel Bell, Colin Jackson, Marsha Hanen, William Warden, Thomas Wood, David Taras and Ron Ghitter served as chairs or moderators of sessions, and we are grateful to each of them. As well, the program on the last day included a luncheon session arranged around discussion tables, and we have tried to capture some of the content of those very animated discussions in the Appendix. We owe particular thanks to the sixteen people who kindly agreed to facilitate one of the discussions: Cesar Cala, Peter Desbarats, Brian Long, V. Nallainayagam, Stephen Randall, Marilou McPhedran, Pat Loyer, Aritha van Herk, Anne Petrie, Michael Embaie, Jennifer Williams, Robert Ware, Diana Hodson, Madeleine King, Gajaraj Dhanarajan, Maria Kliavkoff, Roger Gibbins and Sarah Kerr.

The Symposium itself, and especially the participation of a large number of students, was made possible through the generosity of several sponsors: our partners, the Kahanoff Foundation; our patrons Bennett Jones, Barristers and Solicitors and Mawer Investment Management; and sponsors the University of Calgary, CBC IDEAS, and Nexen Inc. The Calgary Herald and Sheraton Suites Eau Claire provided in-kind sponsorship; and generous support was also extended by CIBC, Collins Barrow, Enbridge Inc., Petro-Canada, RBC Dominion Securities.

The Faculty of Social Sciences at the University of Calgary and Westfair Foods Ltd. We offer our thanks to each of these organizations.

We are also most grateful to the Symposium's co-chairs Ron and Myrna Ghitter and to the co-chairs for the closing dinner ticket committee Gary Dickson and Fran McGilvray Cooke, together with their committee. And we were immeasurably helped by Foundation staff and volunteers Sharon Hanen, Melissa Trono, Linda Van Dyke, David Hughes, Alex Barber, David Cassels and, especially, Elaine Wojtkiw, whose organizational skills made the planning and execution of the event proceed with minimum chaos and maximum good cheer.

White Iron Productions videotaped large portions of the Symposium addresses for later use, and Shelley Schwerski prepared a short video program of symposium highlights for showing at the closing dinner.

In the preparation of the manuscript for publication, we have been blessed by the capable editing skills of Alex Barber and David Cassels. Esther Drone transcribed from tapes those papers we did not have in written form, and we have attempted to preserve the immediacy and conversational tone of the Symposium presentations while ensuring that the resulting volume would also be reader friendly. David Cassels has put the entire manuscript together for the printer, with careful attention to form and detail. His technical and design skills are evident not only in the layout of the book itself, but in the execution of Sharon Abra Hanen's cover design.

Keijo Isomaa of Morriss Printing has been most generous in working through the details of publication with us and seeing to the printing of the volume. The photograph of Sheldon Chumir on the back cover was taken by Brian Harder. Photos on the front cover are, left to right in the top row: Stephen Lewis by Joshua Berson Photography, 2001; Gretchen Mann Brewin; Lloyd

Axworthy; Naomi Klein courtesy of The Herald/Gordon Terris, © SMG Newspapers Ltd; and Benjamin Barber by Mike Goldwater. Photos in the bottom row are, left to right: John Stackhouse by Cindy Andrews; Michael Valpy courtesy of Patti Gower/*The Globe and Mail*; Bronwyn Drainie by Greg Tjepkema; David Schneidermann; and John Curtis.

Finally, we express our appreciation to the Foundation's Board, Joel Bell, Betty Flagler, Ron Ghitter, Cliff O'Brien and Aritha van Herk for their unfailing support of the publication project and the Symposium from which it resulted. Joel Bell was fully engaged at all stages in the planning of the Symposium, and his involvement helped to shape its focus and content. Cliff O'Brien and Aritha van Herk have provided help and support at numerous points; and Ron Ghitter not only served as co-chair of the weekend, but also chaired the closing dinner with his usual warmth and flair.

Sadly for all of us, Dr. Betty Flagler, who was one of the founding Board members of the Foundation and a tireless supporter of all of our programs and activities as well as of each of us, died just two weeks after the close of the Symposium. A close friend of Sheldon's, she maintained her interest in the Foundation and in this most recent of its undertakings to the very end of her life. With great respect and affection, we dedicate this volume to her memory.

PREFACE

This volume represents the proceedings of the Symposium "Community Values in an Age of Globalization" held by the Sheldon Chumir Foundation for Ethics in Leadership on the weekend of April 26th to 28th, 2002 in Calgary. The program was an ambitious one, involving a roster of extraordinary speakers addressing a variety of issues surrounding the topic of globalization – what it means, its effects, both positive and negative, and the prospects for making things better in places where those effects appear to require amelioration. The anchor for the discussion of globalization was a range of understandings of community values, including questions of ways in which the overlapping communities with which we all identify can be accommodated in our representations of ourselves, our families and friends, our neighbourhoods and our broader commitments.

But just as no symposium is fully captured by what is said by the speakers, so no volume of this sort can fully express the sense of the weekend – the excitement, the "buzz", the engagement of the more than three hundred attendees. Everyone, it seemed, wanted to participate in the discussions with a view to "making a difference"; and people spoke of feeling energized by the speakers, the conversations and the atmosphere to engage more fully in positive ways in their communities. Participants ranged in age from eighteen to eighty, and there was genuine dialogue not only across several generations but across other divides as well. It was particularly noteworthy that we were able to make it possible for a large number of students to be in attendance, and their presence and involvement contributed added enthusiasm and a sense of connection that was a welcome counter to the frequent distress we hear expressed about the disengagement of the younger generation from important issues in the community and from public life. These students were anything but disengaged, and their participation was, in every way, to the point.

The Symposium topic arose through a great deal of thinking about how, at this time and in this place, the Sheldon Chumir Foundation for Ethics in Leadership could best fulfill its mandate of supporting the open expression and dissemination of ideas and tolerant discussion, and its commitment to exposing prejudice, by providing a forum for informed dialogue on important public issues that have an ethical dimension. The issues of how we should think about the forces of globalization not only in our own lives but in the lives of our communities all over the world – no longer remote from us except geographically – have exercised us all for a number of years; but the fact that the G8 meeting would be convening in Kananaskis just two months following the Symposium could be, we thought, a force for concentrating our minds.

It seemed to us that, given the location of our symposium, this particular timing would provide an opportunity to make a contribution to the debate about globalization and community that could be more focused than is usual; and perhaps this gathering could help to make a difference in people's lives. It is part of our mission to help to foster principled, community-minded values and behaviour, recognizing the significance to society of fairness to all members of the community. Symposia such as this one, together with our regular forums, our internship, our fellowships and our partnerships with other organizations are ways of encouraging ethical leadership and ethical education of potential leaders and ways of fostering participation and community-mindedness.[1]

The key, of course, to making something like this work is the quality of the speakers, and so we set about gathering a group of speakers – all of them experts in their areas of interest and committed to engaging with these challenging topics and with the audience in a way that would advance the conversation. It was truly an amazing collection of talent – a group of people whose names were so well known as to cause a rush on registrations and result in a capacity crowd for the entire three days. And the speakers did not disappoint, beginning with the Friday evening opening and Benjamin Barber's inspiring keynote address which focused on the centrality of our various notions of community in a world that has become not only globalized but interdependent, and followed by a comment on the role of legal approaches to issues of globalization (Schneiderman).

The book is organized in the order of the program itself, moving from responses to globalization that focus on what we can do in our own communities to meet those challenges (Brewin, Foster, MacNeill, Waterchief and Hemenway) to an analysis of some of the effects of globalization, particularly in the poorest parts of Africa – intended

[1] For further information about the Sheldon Chumir Foundation's programs and publications, please see our website: www.chumirethicsfoundation.ca.

to be one of the central issues addressed during the G8 discussions (Lewis). This prepared us for a consideration of disparate points of view both on the nature of the effects of globalization and on what is being done and what can be done nationally and internationally to address some of the worst of those effects (Fowler, Klein, Curtis).

The question of what we mean by "community values" and the roles that educational institutions can play in shaping those values and in reflecting them back to us was on the agenda for the morning of the final day of the Symposium. We examined changing conceptions of education and of community values, attempting to come to grips with the role of education in building ethical societies (Findlay, Walker, Weingarten). In the afternoon, we addressed questions of the responsibility of media in a democratic society and, especially, the role media can or should play in helping us to understand the forces of globalization, the challenges to democracy in developing countries and ways in which we can think about internationalization and global governance (Valpy, Drainie, Stackhouse).

Finally, Lloyd Axworthy, our concluding speaker at the closing gala dinner was asked to address a range of questions in relation to global governance, including how we are to think about ethical solutions to international conflict and the prospects for building viable international institutions that would allow us to solve some of the problems that transcend the borders of any single nation state. His inspiring address brought both hope and a resolve among his listeners to participate in appropriate action in these spheres.

All in all, it was an extraordinary weekend, as you will be able to tell both from the papers collected here, and from the introductory and concluding remarks by two members of our Foundation's Board (Bell, Ghitter). Although we were not able to capture the formal and informal discussion that followed each session, we have included, as an Appendix, notes from the luncheon table discussion groups that took place on the final day of the Symposium. These appear in the form of outlines of the issues discussed, views expressed and, in some cases, solutions proposed. The content in each case was very much a creature of the facilitator and the participants, but the reports represent some of the ways in which concerns are expressed and thoughts about moving forward are discussed. We hope that these notes may provide a basis for people to engage in the ongoing conversation that, undoubtedly, we will all continue to have about community values in an age of globalization.

INTRODUCTION

Joel Bell

It is my pleasure, on behalf of the Sheldon Chumir Foundation for Ethics in Leadership, to welcome you to our Symposium on "Community Values in an Age of Globalization."

In life, Sheldon Chumir, a close and good friend to many, vigorously debated the issues of the day with them.

In illness and failing strength, he explored how he might continue to make a difference – and considered the mandate which our Foundation seeks to advance.

The challenge he left was a large one. But, as I look out at this group, gathered to spend a weekend in discussion of issues and ideas surrounding an important societal concern of the day, I know Sheldon would be very pleased. And, we take some satisfaction in the thought that we are trying to make a difference.

Now, why does a Foundation established to try to

advance leadership motivated by ethical values take up an issue which, on its face, seems to address international governmental economic dealings and industrial and financial business activity?

Advancing technologies, particularly in communications and transportation, have greatly increased the "connectedness" among disparate and distant communities and the impact they have on one another. Such dealings affect:

– standards of living;
– health; and,
– as we have been made all too aware, society's safety.

And, "ethics" calls for individuals and communities that care about the impact of one's actions on others – and the fairness of those impacts.

So, "globalization", a connectedness beyond the bounds and bonds of our traditional civil communities, has several effects:

– it unites people of common interests and values across nation-states and distant local communities;
– it transmits problems in one community to impact on others;
– it puts heterogeneous communities face-to-face with their "otherness" to one another; and,
– it challenges the traditional social and governing institutions at local and national levels. These institutions have, in the past, "civilized" economic and other self-interests in a more or less stable, consensual manner.

So, if our "ethical" values include attention to the impact of our actions on others, more "actions" and more "others" come up for ethical attention in a more globalized setting.   Furthermore, the institutional mechanisms to address and channel these actions to civilized results must be re-evaluated as the reach of issues exceeds traditional institutional authority and creates a vacuum of institutional legitimacy. In short, how can a citizenry which cares influence international actions to accord with its community values, particularly in an increasingly interrelated environment?

We see serious and concerned people taking to the streets to lay siege to our democratically selected government leaders gathered to discuss trans-national interactions in trade and investment. We see such people pursuing business leaders gathered to explore the framework for creating greater economic value by international investment, trade and financial flows, which economic value is an essential building block for our social purposes. When we see this, we know that these globalization forces are affecting our communities and creating clashes with some community values. We know our institutional mechanisms are falling short on consensual success.

Our hope at the Foundation is to create a forum for informed and constructive dialogue among the various participants and perspectives around the relevant questions:

1.   How should, or can, we act where we live and operate, namely locally, in light of these global forces and our value concerns? This is the subject of tomorrow morning's session: "Globalization, Community Values and Democratic   Participation: Local   and   Regional Perspectives."

2.   In what ways do we wish and how can we influence these global forces at the higher levels of social organization – nationally and, through our representatives, acting internationally, in order to influence the outcome? This will be discussed in the continuation of the topic in tomorrow afternoon's   session,   substituting   "National   and International Perspectives" in the title.

3.   In between, we have asked our luncheon speaker, Stephen Lewis, to bring his social concern, domestic political background and international experience to bear. He is involved with the UN in its efforts to play an institutional role in developing a values-conscious consensus and social stability on some of the international and distant community issues. He is working with a program focussed on the African continent, a territory of particular current concern for world leaders at the upcoming Summit to be held near here. We hope Stephen will comment on what seems to be working and where we appear to fall more seriously short. How do the less powerful and less well-off fare in this process of globalization? And, what approaches should be considered to address these concerns?

4.   On Sunday morning we will ask how the educational system might prepare our communities to better handle these challenges. And, how far is it appropriate for our social institutions and governments to go in directing education to ensure a harmonious result?

5.   Sunday afternoon will turn our attention to the media as a source of influence for the stimulating of values; for community-minded discussion; for openness to divergent ideas, even in settings under challenge; for advancing democratization in a locally appropriate way or for stimulating social consensus-seeking, where traditions and institutions to that end are limited; for consideration of "otherness" with which we are faced locally and internationally.

6.   At lunch on Sunday, we will ask all participants to work with different animators to put forward ideas on the various topics of this Symposium that we will seek to publicize and use to provoke further work by our Foundation.

7.   And, Sunday evening, we have asked an interna-

tionally experienced member of our community, our former Minister of Foreign Affairs, Lloyd Axworthy, to discuss the challenges of creating institutions to harness the forces and players that are operating on the issues of international concern. These forces, and the private players in particular, operate beyond the legal power of national sovereign governments to "civilize" or harmonize their actions to accord with community values. What are the prospects for institutions to change that? How do we govern ourselves and enforce some ethical principles in a globalized setting where focussed and self-interested players work beyond the capacity of current governmental bodies to regulate?

The scope of the program is clearly very ambitious. But, our objective is to stimulate and challenge ourselves and our speakers to surface the concerns and probe directions of appropriate examination and response.

We are meeting here, close by the site of the upcoming G8 Summit where these issues come into sharp relief. Maybe some of your constructive thoughts will rub off. We will record the ideas and put them in circulation quickly to be available for the on going debate well before the world gathers here in Calgary two months from now.

All these questions are challenging. They challenge us within our local communities and in our national communities, where we enjoy a reasonable degree of homogeneity – and where democratic representative institutions (with all their defects) do exist. How much more challenging they are where we confront international heterogeneity involving some common, but often differing values; where democratic representative institutions are absent and hard to conceive of on the scale and diversity of the global setting.

The challenge increases when we confront corruption in many countries of Africa, Latin America and elsewhere which corrodes societies and threatens the realization of the benefits claimed for globalization.

Our discussion, in the global context, must reckon with many communities which need to be embraced in our solutions, but where there is an absence of democratic traditions and processes to civilize self-interested forces; where the rule of law may not always be counted on.

Since we acknowledge that we must, in a free and realistic society, allow people and organizations to pursue their self-interests within minimum socially agreed constraints, we must look elsewhere to find the social reconciling process beyond the formal legal machinery of minimum standards. But, can we count on the national governments under domestic political pressures, or on the corporate organizations focussed on economic gain, or on the communities concerned for local opportunity to relinquish immediate self-interest enough to make economic room for the growth of the less well-off economies by production and trade which displaces other self-interests? Or on private sector interests to apply minimum standards beyond those legally required which limit their own freedom of action and reduce the scale of their benefits? Can we even count on the well-intentioned national governments affected to accomplish the socially desired outcomes where international business entities understandably shop for and trade off different national environments and press against minimum standards to get the optimal deal – or where the populist bent of governments is limited?

How do we reconcile our objectives of fairness with a situation in which the power and influence of the different players is very unequal – where national governments have varying abilities to influence actions of other governments to accommodate their sometimes conflicting interests? Can we expect a fairness of result when we consider the context of a historically unique period of a single national entity, the United States, being so distinct in its power – where, although not free to act entirely independently of world opinion and forces, the choices of the U.S. to accommodate the world, or to assert its particular or isolated self-interest can have such impact on the results of any international efforts? How do we view U.S. inclinations in this regard? What can help promote the better instincts for consensual, or at least cooperative, global participation?

In historic times, this played out by conquest. Today, we aspire to harness all this in multi-culturalism and consensual harmony. But, where are the agencies or methods to animate or manage this process?

We have gathered commentators and practitioners who have given a lot of thought to these issues. We hope you will challenge them with questions:

- how do we best create the conditions of economic health and growth?
- is globalization exacerbating or reducing the disparities of economic benefit?
- are free markets the optimal mechanism or are companion actions needed to achieve optimal growth, fairness of distribution and acceptable minimum standards? Did many international successes not start with some less than freely open market mechanisms before they could thrive in open competition?
- how fast should we require the beneficial results predicted?
- what minimum standards of human treatment or environmental safeguarding should be enforced? How can they be enforced in the competitive pursuit of local growth and opportunity?
- to what extent should we protect and celebrate social, cultural and religious diversity? Where is greater homogeneity to be preferred and pursued? How do we capture the richness of diversity without the hostility and exclusionary impact of more isolated, fragmented and divisive appeals?

Tonight we have a particular treat in store. To open our discussion, we have someone who has been examining the issues and perhaps the inevitability of globalization. He has written about the pull of disparate values of open globalization, civil community and narrower, national, religious or similar passions. He has considered the mechanisms (governmental, social and technological) for consensus-seeking and decision-making in society and the problems for traditional governmental democratic methods under current conditions and, more so in the emerging environment of both globalization and more isolating passions.

He discusses democracy, community values, fairness, national self-interest, corporate motivation, aberrant actors of the international society and the mechanisms available to us to respond to the challenges.

Dr. Benjamin Barber is a man of ideas and action; a man of politics, society and culture. He brings an extensive background of thought and action to the subject of our Symposium; an abiding concern for society, community and citizen involvement; a commitment to informed and rational debate of these issues; a conviction about the importance of minimum human standards and dignity; support to social institutions of marriage, family and religion; and, a call to a sense of obligation to the community around us.

To start us off on our ambitious discussion of community, values, globalization and the challenges for all of these in the current world which includes the challenges of addressing increased recourse to terrorism, no one is better equipped than our keynote speaker, Dr. Benjamin Barber.

· I ·

COMMUNITY VALUES
in an age of
GLOBALIZATION

Benjamin R. Barber

CAN DEMOCRACY SURVIVE GLOBALIZATION IN AN AGE OF TERRORISM?

Thank you for that generous Introduction. It was so generous that I'm tempted to just ask whether there are any questions and sit down. Joel has already raised for us all of the important issues that we need to deal with. I'm going to try to give some answers; indeed, some rather opinionated answers, in part to provoke you. If you're satisfied with them we can just take the rest of the weekend off and ski.

Let me try to sketch out this evening in the brief time we have a picture of the two worlds in which people around the globe live – and the tensions between those two worlds. I think you will find that most of the issues that we want to talk about this weekend – questions of community values, how they can exist, how they can be nourished in a globalizing world – refer to these two increasingly distinct spheres in which we lead our lives. One world is old, familiar and traditional: the world of community. We know it well, and the

Sheldon Chumir Foundation, I believe, was founded to nurture and explore the values that have traditionally animated this world of communities. Most human beings, if you ask them about the environment they live in, will first of all refer to the community: the familial and kinship associations, the wider civic, religious and work communities, the recreational and cultural groups to which they belong. That is the environment in which we pray, we work, we play, we create, we educate, we learn, we raise families. That's our immediate world. And for most of human history that has largely described for most people the compass of their lives.

But over the last fifty or perhaps a hundred years there has been a second less invisible but sincerely felt environment, an environment of globalization. It has been a world of forces which we don't experience directly but which shape and condition almost everything we do experience. This is a global world that is increasingly interdependent, tied together by technology, by ecology, by the economy and now increasingly also by criminality, by disease, by violence and by terror. And that global environment, though we don't experience it directly, does shape the things that we do experience directly – our worlds of work, of religion, of prayer, of play, of art, of learning and indeed of our families. We can see today in the Middle East the way families are being literally torn apart by global forces of confrontation that lead young people to strap explosives on themselves and try to blow up other innocent people and martyr themselves. They march into the face of gunfire to be killed in the name of martyrdom. They are not reacting to the community when they do that but reacting to these anonymous but powerful conditioning global forces in which we are all increasingly engaged. The question that defines the set of issues that we want to look at this weekend is the relationship between those two environments: that immediate experience of community that we have in which relatives and friends and co-workers and colleagues and local politicians and pastors and rabbis and mullahs constitute our everyday experience; and these forces that increasingly (though we don't see them directly) shape everything that we do and increasingly interfere with, interdict, get in the way of the community experiences that go back to the beginning of time.

Now historically, the protector of community, the entity that has allowed communities to prosper over the last three hundred years, has been the nation state: the independent, sovereign, autonomous, nation state. Like globalization, the nation state is not immediately visible – most of us experience our capitals, our national governments, only indirectly and occasionally. National government doesn't really encroach on our immediate lives but it stands in the background. It protects community, providing their legal architecture; it oversees economics, defining with its laws the nature of the corporation, the nature of economic contracts. It sets limits on the role that religion can play in public or in private life, it supports the arts directly or indirectly. For three or four hundred years it has been the backdrop for the growth of local community. For better or worse, our community lives have unfolded within the nation state. Moreover, over the last one hundred years, both our communities and the nation-states in which they have evolved have been increasingly democratic. Particularly in the West but around the world as well. Democracy, the nation state and community life have gone hand in hand, evolving together, sharing similar problems and solving them through civic interactions among them. We have learned to think about the state as a sovereign and autonomous and independent entity and we have come to believe that our communities are safest, best preserved, most democratic when they are conditioned by the laws and regulations and oversight of the democratic nation-states to which we also belong. That's been the formula for success over a couple of hundred years.

Around the turn of the last century with trade already globalizing, 12 to 14% of GNP of the nations engaged in trade were devoted to exports. Interdependence was already an emerging reality. With the two great world wars of the last century, it was apparent that individual nations no longer controlled their own destinies – hence "world" wars. Not the Franco-Prussian War or the Russo-Japanese wars, but global wars where states were no longer able to dictate their fates. Their territories were vulnerable. Their populations were vulnerable and the forces that conditioned their hopes were beyond their sovereignty. These wars, the Holocaust, the new totalitarian ideologies of Nazism and Communism, the Cold War, the coming of the atomic bomb, space exploration – all of them represented experiences of the limits of the nation state, of sovereignty, of autonomy. All of them represented the limits of independence and the rise of an ineluctable interdependence. We Americans to the South, with our Declaration of Independence, proclaimed the possibility of an insular national life. Canada knew better but we Americans in the U.S. founded our destiny on the notion of an independent nation state. Independent not just of mother Britain, but independent, period. We would control our own destiny our way. If we participated in wars we did it as an export product, fighting wars on foreign soil, bringing the boys (and girls) home again when it was over to a virgin territory untouched by the horrors of war and holocaust.

Before September 11, the last time foreign troops, enemies of America, assaulted it from within was when Britain burned down Washington in 1812. From that year until September 11, 2001, no foreign enemies had set foot on United States continental soil. No wonder the United States believed Americans could forge their own destiny inside of an envelope of two great oceans separated from the world, oblivious to it. This was the great American myth – that we could be separate from the world, sovereign in our own sphere. In the United States, this myth has coursed down through the centuries, more often vindicated than questioned.

Long after the idea had vanished in Canada and in Mexico and Latin America, we in the United States still believed that when there was trouble abroad, it was someone else's trouble, not ours; and if it touched us, then we strapped on the six guns, climbed on our horses, went out, found the bad guys, finished them off, and came home again to continue our lives. Even after September 11, that was the impulse of our president from Texas, to play the Lone Ranger and seek out the "evil ones," dispatch them and come home again. Yet September 11 demonstrated even to the most powerful nation in the world that no nation, however powerful, can in an age of globalization control its own destiny, take on its adversaries and enemies alone, deal with new forces that themselves are shaped by interdependence in an entirely independent way. Globalization and interdependence have become realities so persuasive and compelling that not even the United States is in a position to defy them. The new reality is interdependence: the terrorists of September 11 were, in a sense, our brutal tutors in teaching us this lesson. The terrorists were in many ways opaque, resistant to modernity: but they grasped and exploited (perhaps better than the United States) the interdependent character of the world in which they lived. They leveraged interdependence and the connectivity between nations; they understood the global financial system, whether it was a system of world banks or whether it was the honey shops – that older system of international finance. They knew how to move their money, to communicate secretly, to use the internet and all of those new technologies that, like it or not, link us together.

There is indeed rather sad evidence that the terrorists had a better understanding of the interdependent character of the new world than the U.S. government did, because the government's response was to strike out at sovereign states, to try to find a nation state address. We acted as if it was still the 19th century and somebody had crossed the Rhine and now we had to find who they were and push them back, and so we went looking immediately after September 11 for nation-states, those, as the President said, that harboured terrorists. In fact, the only states I could immediately identify that harboured terrorists around September 11 were Florida and New Jersey. Those were not the states that the President had in mind; but it teaches a sad lesson – that the terrorists were everywhere and nowhere. They didn't have a national address. They were not about nation-states and while the Taliban certainly had helped nurture some of the cells of al Qaeda as has been demonstrated with the destruction of the Taliban regime, al Qaeda survived. It moved on to Pakistan, another one of our "allies", and from there it can continue on to Indonesia or Yemen or Sudan or indeed to Berlin and Hamburg and Brussels and Miami, because the cells move in the interstices of the new global regime, inhabiting no region in particular. If we want to understand and deal with terrorism then we have to begin to confront the character of the new interdependence, the new globalization that is that background reality and that we sense only indirectly when, for example, the air is a little polluted in a wonderful fresh place like Calgary and you realize you can't really deal with it municipally and you can't deal with it by going to the legislature of Alberta and you can't really deal with it by going to the government of Canada either because, in fact, pollution has become a cross-frontier, a global problem. And if somebody gets AIDS in Montreal you can't go to the Quebec government and say "let's put an end to this pestilence" and you can't go to Washington either, because, of course, AIDS is now a global plague and epidemiology requires a planetary perspective. The West Nile virus doesn't carry a passport and the internet doesn't stop for customs inspections.

Interdependence means that the world's state borders are porous; traditional nation-states are no longer the actors primarily responsible for the global condition because it is not within their power one by one to deal with global problems. Of course in many areas nation-states are still powerful, the primary presence in our lives, but in many others they are not. They are simply too large to deal with the things that touch us most immediately and too small to deal with global problems. The United States, the French like to say, are the hyper-power (hyper-pouvoir), but can the United States do anything about a little firm of, say, fifty or a hundred jobs that decides it wants to export those jobs to Nigeria or Indonesia? Can it control or even know what crosses its frontiers into the continental United States in container ships? Or on the internet? Our sovereignty no longer is viable because we belong to an international system defined by new economies and new technologies that put our destiny beyond our control. Sovereign power simply isn't what it once was.

This brings me to the central feature of the new globalization which gets to the issues that Joel raised for us concerning the role of community in a globalized world. Globalization has in fact evolved in a peculiarly asymmetrical form. We have globalized our market institutions – markets in capital, markets in goods, markets in commodities, markets in labour, markets in currency – but we have hardly begun even to think about globalizing our politics: that civic and democratic envelope of free institutions in which, for the last four hundred years, capitalism has grown up and been bounded, and in which markets and their contradictions have been tempered and moderated. We have, as it were, ripped capitalism and capitalist markets out of that civic envelope of institutions that make it relatively productive, relatively efficient, less unjust than it would otherwise be, less Darwinian than it is in its naked form, and we have set it loose in an anarchic global environment where there is no analogous envelope of democratic and civic and political and legal institutions to be found. We have surrendered to anarchy, conspired in creating not a new world order but a new world disorder.

Why do so many peoples who aren't part of the Western world find globalization so dangerous, so pernicious? Because to them it looks predatory, because to them it's a Darwinist jungle, because their experience of it suggests not order but anarchy, not growth but exploitation. They don't have the experience of living under a capitalist system that's closed in on all sides and limited by the law and by regulation and by the moderating influence not just of a capital state but of civil society and its myriad communities. More perhaps than the democratic state, democratic civil society in its local community manifestations has been crucial in tempering capitalism's impact on equality and justice. The church or the synagogue, the family, the philanthropic associations, the civic associations of local communities, have been the crucial arena in which capitalism has played out its entrepreneurial, competitive, rather Darwinian but nonetheless productive and efficient form of social organization. And it is the synergy between the two that saves us from capitalism's contradictions and at the same time allows us to enjoy its many benefits. This evolving synergy took three hundred years to develop, but we have almost overnight, in effect, abolished it in the global realm. Put bluntly, we have in effect globalized most of our vices and almost none of our virtues. Think about it: what's really global today? Crime. The syndicates that control drugs and prostitution and crime are global. Disease, plagues, HIV, they are surely globalized. The problems we have with our environment, with the oceans, with the atmosphere are all global in nature. The exploitation and misuse of women and particularly of children have been globalized. Who are better seen as the true victims of globalization than children? They are always first on line in paying the costs of globalization. Look at the children on the streets of Brazilian cities, homeless, sometimes murdered so their organs can be farmed and sold in North American and European cities for medical operations. That's not hyperbole: it happens. Or look at the sex trade in Asia where eleven and twelve and thirteen year old boys and girls are offered up as virgins on the Internet to organized sex tours that help define the new international tourism. Look at the role of children as proxy warriors. Why do the old guys like Arafat and Sharon carry on and on and on and the children keep dying? Why do so many thirteen and fourteen year olds do the killing for the forty and fifty years olds? and the ones who get killed, who you see at their feet, are also thirteen and fourteen and fifteen? We have watched the age of the so-called suicide bombers get younger and younger, we have watched girls join the boys, and preteens beg to join the teenagers.

What is to be made of this? Does this reflect an anarchic global system of weak states and evolved chaos in which the most defenseless segment of our population is left unprotected because the civic and political and legal institutions that protect them within nation-states simply do not exist? The kids are without protectors. Certainly the market cannot protect them. That is not its job, which is to secure profits. That's what it's supposed to do. But that's exactly why we require other global institutions. Within nations, communities are children's best protectors because communities are the venues for family and church and civil association. But globalization often means the wrecking of communities, their growing irrelevance in a world of forces beyond their control. As Manuel Castels has shown in his remarkable trilogy *The Network Society*, increasingly the communities, the traditional communities, even those patriarchal communities that we don't approve of anymore – at least they protected the children. They are being annihilated as a function of the new globalization –

not incidentally but as a result of that globalization – and in the place of those communities we have found nothing to do their job.

In a word then, market capitalism stripped of the civic envelope is another term for anarchy. Anarchy, quite literally, means the absence of government, the absence of archons, the Greek word for governors. And the global regime right now is not a world order as we so often call it but a world disorder. To frame the questions that need to be asked properly, one must say 'What's happening nowadays with big banks in the world disorder?' ' How are investors faring in the world disorder?' 'Do you think children can survive the global disorder?' For the world system is disorderly, anarchic, without legitimate governance mechanisms. There is power but it is undemocratic; there are those who would master it but they lack all legitimacy. The asymmetry this creates goes to the heart of the dangers we face. Because it's not just that in the global sector there's no democracy, there's no civic oversight, there are no political and community institutions. It's that those global and anarchic forces are themselves making war on community and making it harder and harder for us to preserve our communities whether it's in Calgary, or Detroit, or Bogotá, or Damascus.

Community is under assault because we are undone by these global forces which we cannot control. How do we normally control the communities in which we live, the villages and townships and municipalities, the provinces and states? Democracy has been the answer. We organize ourselves to oversee our institutions through choice and elections. We make the decisions about what we want, how we want our communities governed, how open, how closed. We don't always make wise decisions but in the democratic nations we make the decisions. But the decisions about the global environment are not being made by anybody in particular because there is anarchy.

There certainly are people who are powerful and in an anarchic jungle, just the way there are certain animals that are more powerful than others in the real animal jungle. In the global market jungle, banks and investors and multinational corporations play the role of the most powerful animals but they don't really "govern" even as despots because they are at war with one another as well. The consequence is a world that isn't even very good for corporations and businesses. The global environment attracts capitalist investment. It attracts people out of what to capitalists appear to be the confines of democratic states. They believe they will find more working room, more profit, freer situations in the global environment. But it turns out that capitalism doesn't do very well there because in the absence of democratic oversight it once again falls prey to its own contradictions. Capitalism is an ideology rooted in entrepreneurial competition. That's one of its great strengths. Yet left to its own devices it tends toward monopoly and the destruction of the competition it requires. The great guarantor of competition has been not markets but the democratic state which, through its regulations, has assured a relatively fair playing field. In the United States towards the end of the 19th Century, after the Civil War, the great capitalist behemoths that grew up produced robber barons who exploited the American people and diminished competition and expropriated resources. They created huge monopolies in oil and coal and steel and railroads and, in time rubber and then automobiles. And only with that great Republican Teddy Roosevelt who recognized that the vaunted capitalist system was not working very well – not even for capitalism let alone for democracy – did the state develop countervailing institutions of oversight and regulation that saved capitalism from its own contradictions. We needed a more aggressive and interventionist state and in time, with President Wilson and the second Roosevelt, we caught up to what the Canadians and the Germans under Bismarck had understood much earlier: is that for capitalism to be productive and fair, it must be contained within a democratic envelope. Capitalism produces goods more effectively and efficiently than it produces jobs, even though Henry Ford understood that without jobs there's no income for the consumers to buy all the things that capitalism produces. But again it's been the democratic state that helps assure that jobs are also produced so that there will be consumers to buy the goods of capitalism.

Now in the international marketplace, we are back to 1880 and an anarchy of outlaws both in the suites and in the streets. It's John D. Rockefeller in the oil fields. It's global robber barons, not because they're bad men but just because there's nobody to watch over and regulate them, because there's no effective international rule of law, because we haven't begun to recreate around them that civic and legal envelope for which Roosevelt reached at the end of the nineteenth century. What do we do about it? I have some suggestions but perhaps this ought to be your agenda as well, one of the things that will be a subject of conversation this weekend.

How do we create a global order in which both our local communities that still give life and pleasure and creativity to all of us can be preserved and at the same time that permits us to produce something like a global community because only at such a global level can we address the challenges of globalization? Is community itself a stretchable and elastic enough entity that we can talk meaningfully about a global community? It's an interesting question because that is right now precisely Europe's problem. Can there really be a European community? It's called the EC, it's called the European Community, but to many residents of the continent it feels more like a technocracy – an economic market, to be sure, a financial and currency association, a defense alliance: but a community? Not yet. It's easier to talk about the Euro than the European, though Jean

Monnet began with a dream of the European. Perhaps that is why countries like Denmark already part of the EC have had difficulties with Europe, and why countries like England still on the outside are so ambivalent about membership. Perhaps that is why Jean-Marie Le Pen is getting more rather than fewer voters because even on the left, many populists feel that whatever else Europe is, it's not yet a community, a civic community in which they feel an active participatory citizenship. Unfortunately, nobody has worked very hard to make it feel very participatory. They worked hard to create a technocracy of appropriate rules, to create a common market, to create a common currency. Yet at least among the younger generation of Europe there was an appetite for common citizenship and common identity as well: where was THEIR Europe? So instead they have identified with the pop culture of North America. With MTV and Hollywood and the NBA because those felt more cosmopolitan to them than the idea of Europe. Before then we even think about a global community we may have to think about what it might mean to forge a real European community.

This raises a central question about community itself to which Joel referred in his opening remarks: the question of whether communities are closed or open, democratic or hierarchical. The term community is itself ambivalent and ambiguous with respect to these characteristics. Community can mean "us versus them," and be closely associated with terms that suggest exclusivity such as solidarity, fraternity, sorority – us defined in by defining others out. Some of the most vicious wars today are being fought in the name of one community asserting itself against another community. What kinds of local communities can we nurture that will allow us also to be part of a national community and a global community? Multiculturalism, we know, is part of the answer, but of course multiculturalism comes in two parts: there is the "multi" suggesting variety and pluralism. But there is also the "culturalism" part, suggesting solidarity and singularity. As members of the multiculture African-Americans seem to resonate with variety and difference, but measured against Polish and Italian Americans, they are an exclusive and unique group whose differences pit them against other hyphenated Americans. The "multi" in multiculturalism looks outwards, the "culturalism" looks inwards. Each of the multicultural components of a multicultural country may themselves see themselves as distinctive parts of a fragmented nation at war with their fellow citizens. The Québecois, no they say, they are not Canadians but fragmentary Canadians with their own identity; the Cree say, no they are not Québecois but fragmentary Québecois with THEIR own identity...and so forth all the way on down. The parochialism of the idea of community in a globalizing world is then a problem for those who talk about 'global community.' Can the idea really be extended globally?

We are going to have to create some new global civic entity, whether it is captured by the idea of community or not. There has to be a new global civic envelop for global capitalism. For there is no going back. The anti-globalization movement it isn't that. "Anti" was the name the cynical media used to create an oppositional image for the movement, not the name chosen by those who created the movement. The aim of the movement was not to reverse or take back globalization but to redirect and reform it. Globalization is the reality, whether we are talking about jobs or diseases or weapons or crime or investment or terrorism. We have to find a way not to bring markets back inside the nation state but to extend democratic and civic and community organizations out into the world to re-envelope the forces – whether of the market or of criminal syndicates – so that we can bring order to the anarchy that currently defines their relations. We have to domesticate global anarchism the way we once domesticated American anarchism in the post-Civil War Wild West. We have to extend our civic ideals outwards. We have to find the way to use the NGO's that right now represent one form of civic organization inside of nations to create genuinely transnational entities that become a home for global citizenship.

A global order is not just about law and legislation, a world federalism. It is also about global civil society and global citizens. We have médicins sans frontières and terroristes sans frontières and capitalistes sans frontières: but where are the citoyens sans frontières? The strongest and safest container for anarchism, for the disorders of the human soul, is not the law but community. For it is within the institutions of the community that citizenship is forged and it is citizenship that is the key to forging a democracy. Without global citizens, no global democracy.

Alexis de Tocqueville noticed when he traveled around the United States in the 1830's that it was not the federal government that endowed young America with a new and fresh sense of liberty, but the towns and municipalities. Freedom in America is local, he wrote: municipal. Near where people live and work. Speaker Tip O'Neill said the same thing a hundred years later when he insisted all politics is local. No one is born a citizen of the United States or of Canada or of Russia or of China. People are born in Calgary or Trenton or Montpellier and they begin to think about Alberta or New Jersey or Provence only later, and come to recognize their connection to Canada or the United States or France only later. We begin life locally and our experience with democracy and citizenship starts locally too and only later does it extend out as we come to understand that, in order to control our localities and our municipalities, we have to control forces that move beyond them. In time we move out to the province and from there to the nation; and now, because of the proximity of global forces, we begin to recognize we must think globally as well.

In fact, democracy in the modern world is beset by a

powerful contradiction which globalization has exacerbated: participation is local, but power is central. We participate most easily in our townships and localities, but the power that shapes are lives is located in distant capitals and beyond. Once upon a time power and participation overlapped in municipalities and provinces. In ancient Athens power was local and community was local and citizenship was local and participation was local. Autarky and the lesser scale of politics meant citizens could control their world from their villages. But in today's world while we can participate here in a forum like this over the weekend – many of you are from Calgary and most of the rest are from elsewhere in Canada – but the levers of power that affect the issues we want to talk about are where? In the Indonesian rain forest, being cut down to make matches for Japanese smokers? Up there in that hole in the ozone layer, (the consequence of pollution) where dangerous radiation is seeping through to OUR towns? In the African hot zone rain forests where some new disease may be crossing over from animals to humans and where no local doctor we go to when we get infected have ever been? In distant war-zones whose outcomes affect us but whose causes are beyond us? The forces that impact our communities are simply way beyond the control of those communities – even our national communities. Farewell sovereignty.

This brings us back to where I began: the United States is no longer in a position to govern the forces that govern it. Unless it finds ways to collaborate and cooperate with other nations to create forms of local as well as global civil societies. Local as well as global law. One of the great ironies of the United States today is, at the moment that we're out to catch and prosecute and bring to justice international terrorists, we have refused to ratify and become a member of the new international criminal tribunal which would be the perfect instrument to do it with. How crazy is that?

Caught up, as we arc, in the myths of the 19th Century, the great and good but increasingly obsolete myth of independence proclaimed in the Declaration of Independence, it is hard to recognize the new reality. The reality of interdependence. We still want to do it our own way, do it all with our own soldiers, impose our own unilateral solutions – as if our sovereignty were still unlimited and invulnerable. As if September 11 had never happened.

The challenge today is then to find ways to move beyond the 19th Century concepts of sovereignty, of nation-states, of Declarations of Independence – concepts too many nations still believe in. America, Russia, China, Egypt still play with the idea of independence, still cling to the belief that they can be powerful. But the era of independence is over, even for the most powerful nations. We need new ideas as "smart" as the bombs we drop in place of policy. We need a new Declaration of Interdependence to displace and replace that Declaration of Independence that has not just been America's founding document but the envy and a model for people all over the world who want to create their own democracies. Even today new states and transitional states proclaim their independence as if it were 1776 or 1789 – most recently in East Timor. What a charming, what a disastrous mistake. For the reality we face is the reality of an ineluctable interdependence. What is required is a resonating new Declaration of Interdependence to symbolize our entry into a period when democratizing globalization is not a dream of idealists but a necessity for realists.

Let me conclude with a kind of provocation – a Declaration of Interdependence to which communities, individuals and states might actually subscribe. Would this be the beginning of the fashioning of a global community? Try this out:

A DECLARATION OF INTERDEPENDENCE

·   recognizing that technological innovation, pandemic disease, crime syndication, ecology, new telecommunications systems, evolving weaponry, market economics and an expanding pop culture of pervasive consumer brands have rendered traditional territorial frontiers increasingly porous if not irrelevant; and

·   recognizing that the self determination and sovereignty that once defined nation-states are no longer feasible in a world where networked transnational systems dominate the affairs of nations and where nation-states are no longer the primary actors in many international affairs; and

·   recognizing that governmental institutions and policies founded on national autonomy and sovereign independence are not only likely to fail in achieving their ends but may also compromise or even undermine those ends while endangering other peoples and states and the public goods and rights of human kinds as a whole; and

·   recognizing, finally, that as individuals living in the 21st Century, we have both rights with respect to and responsibilities in connection with a global entity, even if it does not yet have a structure or a constitution and even when the interests and goods of other communities to which we belong may sometimes be in tension with these global interests and goods...

We the people of this smalling world do hereby declare our interdependence both as individuals and legal persons and as members of distinct communities and nations and do pledge ourselves citizens of one world. Acknowledging herewith our responsibilities to the common interests and public goods of humankind as a whole and pledging to work both directly and through the nations and communities to which we also belong, to secure the rights of every person on the planet and to foster democratic policies and institutions expressing and protecting our human commonality while at the same time guaranteeing free spaces in which our distinctive religious, ethnic and cultural identities are protected from political, economic and cultural hegemony of every kind.

Might such a pledge, such a declaration, offer a starting place for those who, though still touched two hundred years after a glorious document was signed that pledged 18th Century men to the idea of freedom being protected by independent sovereign states, are ready to embrace interdepedence? Might not this be an opportunity to recognize a new global reality in which liberty can no longer be protected, social justice can no longer be protected state by state by state by state, but can prosper only when we fashion a common community as broad as our common humanity? Only when we acknowledge that we all dwell on a common planet where the fate of the least prosperous will become the fate of those who are most prosperous? For in this new era, no nation, however powerful, is likely to survive in the long term unless the weakest are also permitted to survive, when no child however well educated and promising her environment is, is likely to grow to old age unless children in the poorest communities around the world are also given the opportunity to do so. These are not byproducts of some new moral injunction but are mandates of necessity in a world that has become one, whether we like it or not.

David Schneiderman

THE DIFFICULTIES OF LOCAL CITIZENSHIP IN AN AGE OF ECONOMIC GLOBALIZATION

This essay is about the possibilities for local citizenship in an age of economic globalization. By economic globalization, I am referring to the rules and institutions identifiable at the regional and transnational levels – the North American Free Trade Agreement (NAFTA), the World Trade Organization (WTO), and bilateral investment treaties (BITS) – mini NAFTAs of which there are over 1,700 (UNCTAD 1999). By local citizenship, I have in mind engaged citizenship practices occurring below the level of the nation-state – what are called sub-national politics. These might be at the level of the province or state, municipality or township, hall of worship or public square.

In an age of economic globalization – when the range of political alternatives seemingly have narrowed and political action appears futile – where are those places where "alternative futures" might be imagined and pursued? We might want to consider politics at the local level – at the level of local community – as such a place. I want to draw here on insights made by British political scientists writing in the early part of the twentieth century – the so-called 'political pluralists.' The pluralists argued that the national-state is merely one among many associations and groups to which an individual might belong. It was not at the highest levels of government that politics was experienced, but on the shop floor, in municipal government, or in the halls of the university (Laski 1919).

I should admit at the outset that the exercise of political authority at local levels is not necessarily a panacea to economic globalization. Though smaller political units potentially are better able than large ones to narrow the distance between ruler and ruled, they are less capable of responding to decisions taken by large non-state entities, like transnational corporations. And sub-national units may offer political orientations fully consonant with the dominant values of economic globalization. But sub-national units – states, provinces, and municipalities, etc. – also provide important sites within which to explore political alternatives. This is particularly significant at a time when national governments are dominated by what Bourdieu calls the "right arm of the state" (1998, 95). This is the branch of the state concerned with promoting trade and investment, a goal to which all other units of government are made subordinate. It makes sense, then, that local government will provide important openings to pursue oppositional forms of politics.

The problem is that these forms of local resistance too often will run up against legal rules and institutions – what I call the constitutional order – of economic globalization. Resistance often will be prohibitory – that is, illegal or unconstitutional at the national or transnational level – or prohibitive – that is, too costly to pursue. I want to review briefly three instances of local action aimed at resisting the values of economic globalization and, in doing so, to explore the difficulties that this constitutional order poses for local community action.

The first concerns the state of Massachusetts' Burma 'selective purchasing' law. The law required agencies under state control not to purchase goods and services from firms that conducted business with the brutal military regime of Myanmar, formerly known as Burma. The National Foreign Trade Council, a consortium of U.S. businesses, challenged the constitutionality of the Massachusetts law in U.S. courts (Greenhouse 2000). Thirty-four of the Council's members were on the state's restricted list of companies doing business in Burma. The European Union and Japan also filed claims with the World Trade Organization that the law violated the 1994 Government Procurement Agreement which forbids states from using non-economic criteria in bidding for government contracts. The U.S. Supreme Court agreed that the state law was unconstitutional as it conflicted with existing federal law regarding Burma (Crosby 2000). Because it used differing (and perhaps more effective) means than the federal law, the state purchasing law interfered with the President's ability to "speak for the nation with one voice." While the Court did not deny to states the capacity to pursue foreign policy objectives through government procurement, these kinds of state or municipal laws likely will be much less effective, though it is well documented that U.S. based companies benefit economically from the abuse of human rights in Burma (Stumberg 2000). Interestingly, this decision, (like that in Bush v. Gore) is at odds with the general orientation of the Court, favouring state's rights (Tushnet 2000).

Sub-national resistance to the parent-state also was part of the dynamic in a second controversy. This concerned a hazardous waste facility near the town of Guadalcazar, in the Mexican state of San Luis Potosi. In

1993, the Metalclad Corporation of Newport Beach, California purchased an operation that had been closed down in 1991 following concerted local action. The earlier operators improperly stored industrial waste and failed to contain leakage into local water supplies, so the site was shut down by the Mexican federal government (Wheat 1995). Metalclad reopened the hazardous waste facility site, with the active encouragement of the central government. The local populace were mobilized in opposition. The site, after all, had lived up to its name – it had proven to be environmentally hazardous. Despite the support of the federal government, Metalclad eventually was denied a municipal construction permit and later, the State Governor issued an Ecological Decree freezing further development in the area.

Metalclad promptly sued for damages under NAFTA. Chapter 11 of NAFTA grants to investors an extraordinary range of rights, including a right to compensation in the event that an investment is so impaired that it amounts to an expropriation (Art. 1110). Metalclad claimed that state and municipal actions were tantamount to an expropriation – though these actions would not qualify as such under NAFTA-compliant Mexican law. An arbitration panel agreed with Metlaclad and awarded the company $16.6 million U.S. in damages (Metalclad 2001). This decision was appealed to a Canadian court (the site of the arbitration), and the panel's award was trimmed back somewhat. It is extraordinary that the NAFTA panel issued its ruling without giving any weight to the community interests at stake. Community resistance to the site was characterized as irrational or protectonist. Exercises in local citizenship, according to the Metalclad panel, are tolerated only to the extent that they do not disrupt expected returns on investment.

The last example concerns events in the town of Cochabamba in Bolivia – Bolivia's third largest city.

Cochabamba's water system was leased to a consortium, Aguas del Tunari, led by San Francisco-based Bechtel Enterprises. The costs of this privatization plan, to no one's surprise, were passed on to the citizens of Cochabamba. Water rates almost doubled – according to one observer, in a city where the minimum wage is less than $100 U.S. per month, many families saw their bills rise by $20 U.S., almost a quarter of their monthly income (Schultz 2000; Finnegan 2002).

The citizens of Cochabamba took to the streets in protest. A general strike shut down the city for four straight days in January 2000. The government of Bolivia agreed to a price roll back with local leaders, but subsequently responded by sending in police and military troops for two days in early February, then by declaring martial law in April 2000. More than 175 protestors were injured, two youths were blinded, and one 17 year-old, Victor Hugo Daza, was killed while walking home from a part-time job.

After four months of protest, the government of Bolivia terminated its contract with Aguas del Tunari and retook control of Cochabamba's water utility. Aguas Del Tunari is now suing the government of Bolivia under a Holland-Bolivia bilateral investment treaty. Aguas del Tunari, conveniently, incorporated under Dutch law in order to take advantage of investor protections available under that treaty.

In each of these instances, local community action was prohibited – as in the case of the Massachusetts law – or was made prohibitively expensive – as in the case of Metalclad. This will also be the likely result in the Bolivian case. Exercises in citizenship that give rise to these kinds of claims for compensation simply are not sustainable.

What alternatives exits, then, for local community action to resist economic globalization? Well, they remain few. One course of action gaining ground – an example of which is the Massachusetts 'selective purchasing' law – is the consumer boycott. Consumer activism provides an increasingly important site with which to resist corporate power. There are, however, some significant limitations to this course of action. First, in order to have voice, one must have purchasing power. Second, the history of consumer boycotts suggests that, once corporate actors respond, movements can quickly disperse. These are strategies with due dates. More telling, perhaps, is the fact that consumer activism is a permissible form of resistance because it is entirely consistent with the values promoted by economic globalization – citizens are preferred to be viewed as consumers rather than as volatile political actors.

Arundhati Roy writes that we should "support our small heroes." In order to do so, I suggest we might begin by dismantling some of the rules and institutions that are obstacles to effective and responsive local self-government. Perhaps what the twenty-first century has in store for us, Roy writes, is the "dismantling of the big. Big bombs, big dams, big ideologies, big contradictions, big countries, big wars, big heroes, big mistakes." "Perhaps it will be the century of the small," she suggests. "Perhaps there's a small god up in heaven readying herself for us. Could it be? Could it possibly be?" Roy writes, appropriating the corporate sloganeering of McWorld: "It sounds finger-licking good to me" (1999, 12).

Bibliography

Bourdieu Pierre. 1998. *Acts of Resistance: Against the Tyranny of the Market*. New York: New Press.

Crosby v. National Foreign Trade Council (2000) 530 US 363.

Finnegan, William. 2002. "Letter from Bolivia: Leasing the Rain." *The New Yorker*. 8 April. 43 53.

Greenhouse, Linda. 2000. "Justices Overturn a State Law on Myanmar." *The New York Times* (20 June) A23.

Laski, Harold. 1919. *Authority in the Modern State*. New Haven: Yale University Press.

Metalclad Corp. v. United Mexican States (2001) 40 International Legal Materials 36.

Roy, Arundhati. 1999. *The Cost of Living*. New York: The Modern Library.

Schultz, Jim. 2000. "In the Andes – Echos of Seattle" at "www.democracyctr.org/onlinenews/water.html" (accessed 9 April 2001).

Stumberg, Robert. 2000. "Preemption and Human Rights: Local Options After *Crosby v. NFTC.*" Law & Policy in International Business 32: 110-96.

Tushnet, Mark V. 2000. "Globalization and Federalism in a Post-*Printz* World." Tulsa Law Journal 36: 11-41.

United Nations Conference on Trade and Development (UNCTAD) 1999. *World Investment Report 1999:Foreign Direct Investment and the Challenges of Development*. New York and London: United Nations.

Wheat, Andrew. 1995. "Toxic Shock in a Mexican Village." *Multinational Monitor*. 16 October (10) at "www.essential.org/monitor/hyper/mm1095.07.html" (accessed 13 March 2001).

· II ·

GLOBALIZATION, COMMUNITY VALUES AND DEMOCRATIC PARTICIPATION:
Local and Regional Perspectives

Gretchen Mann Brewin

Good morning everybody. Wasn't it a treat to see all that lovely snow when we arrived? But the sun is going to shine today, I'm sure of it. There is hope – not only for the weather in Calgary and the flowers but also for the prospects of democratic participation in this era of globalization.

May I first say a warm and heartfelt thank you to Marsha Hanen, Joel Bell, the Foundation and the whole team for their inspiration for this Symposium. You have gathered a wonderful array of talent and expertise to tackle a complex and confusing topic. It is indeed a pleasure to be part of such a group.

Last night we heard some stimulating ideas from Benjamin Barber and David Schneiderman. That's quite an act to follow. All I can say is that I'm glad I'm not also following Stephen Lewis – that would be a bit much.

Just a couple of bits of personal history. You heard about city council and Mayor – at the provincial government level I was a backbench MLA, then the Speaker of the House for a couple of years, then Minister of Children and Families, then back to being a backbencher when I retired. I grew up in Ottawa – Stanley Knowles lived at my parents' house in Ottawa – as a child and a young adult, Parliament had a romance about it. But as an adult local politics were more attractive – at that level one could follow, and make immediate decisions about, what was really going on. I wanted to deal with and help solve community issues. So, after a term on the Scarborough Board of Education, I found myself drawn to city council work when I moved to Victoria . And I must say that after my years of experience on council and at the provincial level, I have not changed my mind.

Those of us who were here last night heard about another way of looking at municipal/local governments and communities – that they may well be the front line in the attempt to contain this "behemoth" of globalization. There is something about local government that can temper those difficult pressures, demands and issues. As a model of governance, and as a model of democratic participation, the municipal level offers the most local control. Public participation can be vigorous, channels of communication and decision-making are much clearer, action can happen immediately, and intervention by the public can happen between elections. All of these elements are, I think, crucial to effective participation. Such elements are much less evident or easy to access at the federal or provincial levels. Geographic distance, degree of complexity, and the length of time between elections are just a few of the frustrations with the decision-making process felt by a large proportion of the voting and non-voting public.

Traditional approaches are no longer acceptable: the public is demanding greater and greater accountability and processes that respond more quickly, both in communities and in legislatures. People are saying, "We want to be part of how the decisions are made – not just to be consulted, or briefed." So how are we going to go about doing that?

At the municipal level, it is already possible to go to a city council meeting, pass a note to a council member in the middle of a debate, and say, "I've got extra information for you". The debate can be halted while the new information is reviewed. You can't do that at the federal level or at the provincial level. The issues are essentially sorted out in the government caucus, or at Treasury Board, or in Cabinet. Provincial legislatures and the federal Parliament have become pieces of theatre. People have roles to play and they essentially put on performances for the cameras located in the House and in the halls. The legislation is written by the civil service and presented as a done deal. If you, as a lowly backbenchor on either side of the House, want to influence a policy direction or a piece of legislation before it gets tabled in the House, it's a pretty involved process or crusade. And it is many, many times harder for the community to have an impact.

Mulroney's Free Trade legislation was but the first step in the major shifts of power away from elected bodies. Globalization is the deeper manifestation of the changes we are seeing at all levels of our society. Despite the fact that fewer and fewer decisions affecting our lives in our communities (other than negatively) can be made at any level of the democratic process, there are issues that can only be dealt with that way. So we can't abandon it all. I think the impact of globalization has been to make an already difficult job almost impossible.

At the municipal level, community groups and neighbourhood groups can have an impact. I live in the city of Victoria, the capital of British Columbia on Vancouver Island. The city of seventy-eight thousand people is surrounded by thirteen municipalities. (Amalgamation is of interest to the city only!) I live in the neighbourhood of James Bay, a community of 11,000 which has a particular story, a particular ambience, and most definitely, an attitude. For twenty-five years, services have been organized and delivered to the people in that community in a way that doesn't happen in many other places. Legitimized by the provincial government many years ago, the James Bay Community Project delivers some social services and health care, the latter through a clinic with four salaried doctors and a nurse practitioner. It's very successful, there has always been a waiting list for new patients. Over 19 other groups work with the Project to respond to community needs and facilitate solutions to issues like housing, tenants' rights, rezoning, parks and the need for other amenities. People are elected to the board of the Project and one of their jobs is to find the resources needed to support the work of the community. Participation develops experience, and as more and more people get involved in the issues, more are interested in being candidates for election to public bodies while others continue to develop expertise to achieve community change.

So what has happened in Victoria and James Bay, then, around globalization issues? What do we see in this community? What's been our experience? Well, Victoria's downtown has a number of the international name-brand shops. We have "big box" stores in a couple of the outlying municipalities, chased there because in other areas, especially the city of Victoria, the public objected. We have lost paint, lumber and fish packing industries in the Inner Harbour; six tank farms are gone. All have been replaced by residential and hotel developments. Ownership is increasingly off-shore. We have beaten these trends in one aspect only – food. Our very own grocery chain began in James Bay, I believe, when Alex Campbell took over a major food chain's outlet and began Thrifty Foods. Highly successful, many more stores have opened on Vancouver Island. Still, we can ask legitimately, "where does our food come from?" Good as they are, Thrifty's sells very little local produce or goods. Like most folks these days, most Victorians have little or no idea where our food comes from, but we are proud of our local entrepreneurs.

In what way then has local council been able to 'temper' the overt problems presented by globalization issues? On the one hand it doesn't look like there's been much to prevent anyone from setting up shop anywhere anytime. Well, without going into each case in great detail, many details were required to be decided before anyone could proceed to open their enterprise. Many were, and are, turned down as was the case of the "big box" stores. There's no doubt that off-shore/out-of-town ownership creates communication complications. The city of Victoria has had a number of examples of developments requiring much long distance negotiation, for instance with the formerly CP owned Empress Hotel and Cadillac-Fairview, to get acceptable projects. The city is involved in such activities all the time. What is an important factor here is the involvement of the community through the several public processes in place, to participate and thus influence the final decisions about our city.

It is still true that no matter how much vigilance a council exerts, global entities like Jacob or The Gap or Polo Ralph Lauren or Guess or any of the other multinational companies could disappear tomorrow with a single decision of head office. We have been left with job loss and empty store fronts in the past and may be so again in the future. We don't have much control over some of that, but we can help to contain some of it.

Municipal governments are strong; they are responsive to the community; they are effective in carrying out their mandate. You *can* beat city hall. But there's another aspect of this that intrigues me. Last night Benjamin Barber pondered aloud whether the nation-state as we know it is about to become extinct. Is it then to be replaced, perhaps, by the rise of some kind of city-state system? Is this not history repeating itself? In the Greek model, the inevitable inter-city squabbling led to a uniting of them all into nation-states. Still, acknowledging their strengths and fundamental democratic nature would go a long way to encouraging residents and citizens to continue to pursue democratic and participatory values for all aspects of civil society.

Municipal governments and local community groups are also involved on the international stage.

Through sister city programs many, many cities are seriously connected to other cultures and communities. Regular exchanges of officials, business people, students, sports teams, and yes, even residents take place. Victoria has four such relationships with cities in China, Japan, Russia, and New Zealand. The Sister City group is a regular committee of Council which is empowered to develop ways to enhance these relationships and to recruit members of the community to participate in their work. I have often thought that much more could be made of these attachments, especially the more community based ones. Formal and informal dialogues could happen on a range of topics of interest to each city, ideas exchanged, collaboration undertaken. I think of the environment, economic systems, democratic values and citizen participation as just a few possibilities. A new power base could indeed be born.

The Federation of Canadian Municipalities is another municipal outgrowth that has done some impressive work bringing Canadian cities together to discuss issues of mutual concern and, naturally, lobby senior governments on behalf of the needs of local government. It also connects with similar bodies in other parts of the world – enhancing already existing international connections and developing new ones has been an important part of its work. Not many years ago their Africa 2000 Program linked many smaller communities in Canada to small communities on that continent. It was an impressive and ambitious exercise and I believe a successful one. I know that many in Alberta and British Columbia participated, learning and sharing a great deal. What other agencies can we encourage in this work? How can we encourage more collaboration as we all struggle with issues that are no longer just our own but increasingly global?

There is another way in which international/local interface offers an avenue, a forum, where we can begin to talk about one aspect of the issues Benjamin Barber discussed. Much concern has been expressed about the nature of the protests taking place, primarily at the sites of meetings of groups like WTO, GATT, IMF and the G8. I believe the protesters have a role to play. They are the outward manifestation, if you like, of the deep and real concerns about what globalization is doing to our communities, our workers, and our environment. They are telling the rest of us about the canaries in the mines. We need that. While some of us don't like dissent, and no one likes the violent element that seems to accompany it, we must find a more positive way for the legitimate pursuit of other possibilities and choices to be heard and discussed.

Perhaps civil society, through local government, could provide that much needed venue. It's discombobulating right now. We are in the midst of a huge transition – old and familiar ways of doing things just don't work any more. In ten, twenty years, our world will be quite a different place with different institutions and ways of doing business and politics – at least part of me hopes so. But where to begin? Let's elaborate on the collaboration that is already In place, the friendships and cultural exchanges that have already begun. The strengths of municipal governance with strong community input offer some hope for a reasonable and even exciting journey into the future.

I believe that all is not lost, though, for our provincial and national government institutions. I talked already about the problems – the distance these bodies have from voters and from the participation that voters are beginning to demand, the theatricality of the debates, the inability of the community to effect change once legislation is created or to learn about it before it's launched. Let me offer two examples of change in British Columbia – one real and one largely symbolic. The 'real' one is a piece of legislation created in the mid-90's entitled 'Initiative, Referendum and Recall'. The purpose of this Act is to allow citizens to do three things: first, put forward an idea for legislation; second, request a vote of the population on a particular idea; and, third, recall an MLA who may have broken a specific set of rules as laid out in the Act, and force a by-election. Also outlined in the Act is the process by which the opinion of the voters is to be collected. To date only the recall section has been tested – several times in fact – and it was only partially successful in one situation when the MLA in question resigned before the vote was tabulated: goal achieved from the public's point of view.

The second, largely symbolic change has been the opening of cabinet meetings to the public and television cameras. BC'ers are treated to a series of carefully scripted announcements from ministers on topics of interest. The audience doesn't see them in the cabinet room because it's too small to accommodate all the members and the media and they certainly don't see cabinet discussion as I recall them! But it *is* an opportunity to see those elected members together; somehow it seems slightly less secretive.

Benjamin Barber also discussed the growth of a different kind of regional approach than provinces or states. The Georgia Basin Initiative could be described as one such regional approach. The name comes from the body of water and its tributaries, drawn from the Fraser River, Puget Sound and southern Vancouver Island. The Province of British Columbia, with the states of Washington and Oregon and the cities of Victoria, Vancouver and Seattle, is involved in an exercise to consider the impact of the tremendous population growth expected in the Pacific Northwest in the coming years. Issues like transportation, air and water pollution and the pressures of development on the environment of the Georgia Basin watershed are just a few of the concerns on the table.

In addition to this actual initiative there has been talk from time to time that a region called 'Cascadia' (comprised of British Columbia, Alberta, Washington, Oregon, Idaho, California and several others) might have the ninth greatest economy in the world. Perhaps not surprisingly, not much more than talk has come of these ideas. Reconfiguring our known world that much is likely a long way off.

Let me share a little story that predicted the change that has taken place in the ability of our federal and provincial governments to respond to real needs of the people of our communities. Back in 1988, in Ottawa, it was Christmas Eve and like Calgary, it was snowing like crazy that night. Brian Mulroney's Free Trade Bill had just passed into law in a very, very acrimonious debate. Two MPs got into the elevator. One, a Mulroney supporter from Ontario, turned to a burly NDPer from Manitoba, grinned hugely and said – and if you don't mind the crudity – "now you socialists are f**ked." No longer can government – as we in Canada have become accustomed to expect – provide for the needs of the community. No longer can it be an interventionist government for good. Indeed our experience most recently has seen the negative impact of government interventions – cuts to health care, social services and the environment to name but a few. Is this what we can continue to expect? It may well be so. Our needs are going to have to be met differently – we turn to our families and our neighbours and our community for that response. My community of James Bay is in a pretty good position to act; is yours? Let us begin the discussions to get going on this new and exciting journey.

We need more collaboration among communities, and I believe a good beginning is the development of new ways of connecting, including making use of one of the most powerful tools available today – the internet and the computer. Techniques are now available to us through technology that allow communities to be connected as never before in history. I don't think the Seattle protests came about simply because the people who gathered all had the same idea at the same time. I think just as money can be moved in an instant with a single key stroke, so too can information and ideas swing around the world in an instant and stimulate all of us into creative new ways of working in our communities and neighbourhoods, at home and internationally. Therein lies hope, a focus for our energies, and for recruiting others to participate in what could be a very exciting period in our history.

I will close by saying that, despite all the 'big box' and international brand name stores in Victoria, there is still no Starbucks in James Bay!!

Brian MacNeill

The topic today is "Globalization, Community Values, and Democratic Participation". I would like to make a few comments on each of those three areas, then conclude by discussing what I think is the main conclusion and response that is required.

Globalization:
The globalization.com website defines globalization as "the process of denationalization of markets, politics and legal systems – the rise of the global economy." The website also quite correctly identifies globalization as a matter of heated, but certainly legitimate discussion and debate among international organizations, governments, academics, labour unions and individuals concerned about the impacts of these changes on local economies, human welfare and the environment.

Having said that, however, I do think the key point that too often gets overlooked is that globalization is already occurring, and is inevitable. No single organization or nation is capable of stopping it.

It is probably the biggest force for change in our world today. We now live and work in a world of disappearing borders, where space and time have shrunk, eliminating natural barriers to competition. What happens in one part of the world swiftly affects economies located elsewhere.

A key driver of this change – and a major reason

why the change is inevitable – is technology. With just a few strokes of our keyboard, we can order products, download information or carry out business transactions quickly across borders – at any time, anywhere in the world.

In our energy industry in North America, globalization has been the case for many years now, and it's increasing. Our ability to grow our business and provide shareholder value is constantly shaped by international commodity prices. As enterprises, we are required more than ever to compete globally by reaching out across borders to tap new markets and new customers.

It's not a bad thing, and it's not particularly scary. It's just a fact of life, and it's happening whether individuals want it or not. On balance, I find it a positive development.

Democratic Participation:

In the 2000 federal election, in a country of over 30 million people, 5.25 million voters selected the winning political party as their governing choice. And 8.25 million voters chose not to vote.

In the 2001 Alberta provincial election, in a province with a population of 3 million, the winning political party received just over 627,250 votes. Almost 900,000 eligible voters chose not to vote.

In the 2001 Calgary civic election, in a city of 900,000 people, the winning mayoralty candidate received 62,745 votes.

Voter turnout in Canada and elsewhere in the world has been declining in recent years. Clearly people are disenchanted with politicians and with the political process. Citizens have to be re-engaged. Not voting is an abdication of individual responsibility and does nothing to improve government and decision-making in our country. Not voting hurts our communities.

Community Values:

Over 6.5 million Canadians volunteered in 2000 – a 13% drop since 1997. While 26% of Canadians volunteer, a small minority of Canadians do most of the volunteering – 80% of all charitable donations come from only 20% of donors, and 72% of all volunteer hours dedicated to building communities is contributed by a mere 8% of volunteers.

Contrast this with the extraordinary growth in the charitable sector – 80,000 registered charities. Is our sense of community and philanthropic spirit declining? Should we be concerned by this evident trend? I think there are plenty of examples, at least here in Calgary, of a strong sense of community and a strong base of volunteerism.

The real concern should be that the bulk of donations and much of the volunteerism is coming from my generation: what is needed is for those of us with strong senses of community and philanthropic values to pass these values to the next generation of leaders.

So my call to action is that we need to create this legacy of opportunity now. And the way to do it is through education and leadership development.

The Implications: Continue to Develop Leaders:

How can my generation create a succession plan? How can those closely involved with the sector encourage and engender participation? What mentorship strategies can we create now with my generation to ensure we support the next generation of community and philanthropic leadership in Canada?

All three of the subjects we are touching on today – globalization, community values and democratic participation – require sound and inspired leadership. Leadership to ensure globalization benefits all of society, not just further widens the gap between haves and have-nots. Leadership to ensure that the next generations continue to make community a priority, and understand the need to contribute to their communities. Leadership to rejuvenate the political process in this country and rebuild democratic participation by citizens.

All of these challenges require leadership, and leadership requires education, training and mentoring. Organizations everywhere today are concentrating on seeking leaders, not managers. Leaders are needed as agents of change to guide organizations to success. It's not a matter of being trendy or progressive; it's a matter of survival in a world marked by rapid change. Leaders are a competitive advantage.

In a world of globalization and uncertainty, we have to look aggressively for opportunities to change, adjust, innovate, if we truly aspire to be effective leaders. We require an appetite for change and life-long learning. Our learning starts with a formal education. And after we graduate and walk in through the doors to our first job, it never stops. That, in my view, is the true key to developing leaders – instilling a commitment to life-long learning.

It's essential that we continually strengthen our educational institutions, and do so in ways that help our students to maintain their edge – to increase their knowledge capacity and be successful in the new global economy.

I believe there are three opportunities that I consider to be priorities. First, teaching students to learn how to learn – which is part and parcel of life-long learning. Second, addressing financial barriers to education and identifying ways to keep the brightest and the best in Canada and in Alberta. Third, building new business-education partnerships and coalitions to sustain and improve our educational institutions.

Let me conclude today with a quote by Sir John Browne, the internationally respected Group Chief Executive of BP. He described, I thought very well, the kind of people we need as leaders of the future. What we don't need, he said, is clones.

We need people with a common understanding of the need to deliver what's been
promised – but then we need real human
beings, each one of whom will deliver in a
different manner – meeting the targets,
working to common standards, but not dehu-
manized by a deadening uniformity.

So let's work together to keep the passion and commitment to learning and leadership strong in our organizations and in our communities.   We have the power to
empower others, and to help develop "real human beings."
Our efforts will certainly be worth the result – strong and
sustainable leadership for our communities, our businesses, our governments – and for our society overall.

Reverend Margaret Waterchief

I thought about my talk, and even while I was preparing it I kept asking myself what I was supposed to present because globalization is very new to me. I won't speak for my people. I have a daughter who's finishing her Masters in social work this year, and she is very much involved in that type of work. And I was just wishing that someone like her had been asked rather than me. But I'm the one that's seventy years old and have some wisdom – and experience!

I once read a book, which I picked up at the World Council of Churches Conference in Canberra, in '91. It's a book written by Anne Pattel-Grey: *Through Aboriginal Eyes*. I often wish that I could use that title, because I have worked amongst my people as a leader, as a tribal counselor. I've been through residential school, I was active in the Anglican Church Women. And I've been in politics too, of course; so I think I could put a lot into that book. But I guess this opportunity is just as good to point out some of the things that are on my mind.

I truly believe that we do have a lot of young people who are very well educated. We have doctors now, many teachers and nurses – a lot of well educated native students. They probably have all the information on globalization. But I would still say the majority of us have no idea of what's going on, and are not really preparing. And so I strongly feel that we need to be brought up on that information, through more education. But I also feel that to create a better working relationship between Aboriginal and non-Aboriginal people we have to start at a very young age. At CUPS (Calgary Urban Project Society) they have begun the One World Child Development which will very well serve this purpose – teaching the infants about some of the things that us older Aboriginals should have had as part of our education, rather than being completely lost because we were not involved in the curriculum of the education of the day. Some of us even lost completely our history because of that.

We have sitting amongst us (Calgary City Councillor) Madeleine King. She and I had lunch together one day and, as mothers, we started to talk about how little our young people know about each other. And even us adults, we can live side-by-side in towns, as neighbours, but we never bother to visit, or to inform each other about our ways of life, our culture – and just how we're doing. So I would present that as a challenge to those of you who would take an interest in learning more about us – the Aboriginal people – because we have much to teach.

At that luncheon meeting we decided that it would be a good thing to have a conference for the young people, to get together, to learn about each other, to exchange information about their culture, and just to have fun together. So we chose a campsite for that, and there was fifty per cent representation by Aboriginal youth, and fifty per cent by non-Aboriginal youth. And it's amazing how well they got along, and developed relationships, in just those two or three short days. It was just amazing. We need more of that type of program for young people.

There is still (I hate to use the word) discrimination in the workforce; but I suppose that happens in any place where you are a part of the minority. I come into a place here this morning, and maybe there is an Aboriginal person sitting amongst us, but I have yet to see that person. So I would challenge you to involve more of the Aboriginal people. Learn from them; get them involved in decision-making too. This would go a long way toward creating a better society. More *practica* could be created within the workplaces for our students; they could work during the summer. I also suggest job shadowing. And don't be afraid to offer your support to our students as they strive to reach their goals. And of course there's always the resources of all kinds that are needed. This would lessen the uncomfortableness as we approach a place like this. It would make us feel more comfortable.

A lot of the time we don't say anything when we're in a crowd of people. And I guess basically what that's about is that we don't always jump in with our own opinions right away; we listen first. And many times the silence means, "out of respect I'm waiting for others to express their opinions." Sometimes it has to do with the translation of one's language into English. So we need to respect listening, and being silent, and to provide times that encourage other people to express their opinions.

I would have to say that a condescending attitude is very bad – it's a "no-no". And I, personally, have experienced that, as many of the older generation have experienced it – because in our day we were told what to do, when to do things. And so today, we tend to resent that condescending attitude. In my five years of work at the Calgary Urban Project Society, in dealing mainly with people with addictions, I have found that the only way to get through to a person is by showing love and respect, acceptance of that person – equality – regardless of who they are or where they've been. That brings to mind the baptismal vow in the Anglican Church: to respect the dignity of every human being.

Just a reminder here that the American system of democratic government is really based on the principles and ideas of the Iroquois Confederacy, as I have read, which consisted of the Huron, Cayuga, Mohawk and

Iroquois. These principles were there to help keep peace amongst the nations. Each nation was known for different strengths, and their ideas were used for everything, including commercial values. And always the credit goes to other people, and not to the person themselves. The Blackfoot Nation, and all our nations, had a system of government based on religion, which the Europeans neglected to study or respect. A so-called Christian faith was used to destroy the system. It was replaced by paternalism such as the Indian Act, which governs our way of life as Aboriginal people. I'm so glad to find out, before I got much older, that this kind of religion is not Christian. Jesus did not say to strip a person, a nation, of everything and make him just like yourself. The Christian faith I practice today teaches me to speak out against injustice, just as Jesus did when he tackled the authority of the day.

Our systems of traditional government guaranteed the protection of every man, woman and child. How wonderful it would have been if this system of government had been combined with the principles that Jesus proclaimed as the true Christian faith. I'm sure we would not have such a high rate of Aboriginal people in jails across the country, infant mortality, children in jail, homelessness, unemployment – the list goes on. But I have no animosity towards anyone. These are mistakes of the past – they can be made right. But first there must be forgiveness, and a letting go of the past. You of the present generation have no control over what happened in the past. Hand in hand we have to move on, and begin planning a better future, for our children, and their children.

To the non-Aboriginal: don't hate us for living on tax-free reserves, using taxpayers' money to educate ourselves and our children – which is a statement I've so often heard. We pay taxes too; I personally pay taxes. Some reserves have gas and oil, rich farmlands, and I'm sure a large part of that resource goes into the general pot that educates our children – yours and mine.

To the Aboriginal people: let go of the past, and let us seek ways that we can live side by side with our non-Aboriginal brothers and sisters in harmony and peace.

Lynn Foster

I must say that I find this title, "Globalization, Community Values and Democratic Participation: Local and Regional Perspectives," a bit daunting, ranging as it does from the global to the local. However, it parallels the conference that we are organizing, the G6B, representing the group of six billion people in the world, many of whom have some disagreements with those eight guys who are having a meeting in Kananaskis in June that will cost Canadian taxpayers at least $350 million.

I know that the term 'globalization' has come to have a very negative connotation, but, in reality, it simply means 'of the world', a completely neutral term. The word that should be used is 'corporatization', or, the taking of power by corporations whose objectives are to make money for their shareholders. While I know that not all corporations are exclusively absorbed by the profit motive, unfortunately, there are too many whose devotion to profit precludes other considerations, such as fair compensation to local people whose lives are disrupted by development, fair treatment of workers and protection of the environment. It also seems that there is a huge disparity between how many corporations function in Western societies and how they function in the developing world. In the developed world, there are laws, and means to enforce them, about such items as compensation for loss of property, minimum wage laws (too low, I should add, but at least they exist) and some protection for the environment. In the developing world, too often these laws either do not exist or the power of the corporations grossly exceeds that of the governments. Even in the developed world there are trade laws that enable corporations to sue governments who do anything that results in a lessening of their profits, like attempting to protect the environment.

The conference that we are organizing is not opposed to the concept of globalization; we are opposed to the abuse that corporatization has caused in too many countries, in too many communities. We are opposed to an economic order that allows 75% of the world's population to live in underdevelopment. We are opposed to an economic order that allows extreme poverty for 1.2 billion people and is growing. We are opposed to an economic system that, in 1960 gave the richest nations revenue that was 37 times that of the poorest, and is now 74 times larger. We are opposed to what Shell did to the Ogoni in Nigeria, to what Talisman is doing in Sudan. We are opposed to the fact that the net worth of three individuals, all of whom reside in the United States, exceeds that of the 48 poorest countries in the world combined. We are opposed to free trade; we are not opposed to fair trade. We are opposed to forcing Third World countries to lower or eliminate their trade barriers, while the First World keeps theirs -- does the phrase "softwood lumber" ring any bells? We are opposed to a world in which two billion people have no access to low cost medications and 2.4 billion lack basic sanitation. Remember, the total population of the world is six billion. We are opposed to a world in which the powerful slaughter the weak with impunity.

Our conference hopes to condemn what needs to be condemned while, at the same time, encouraging what needs to be encouraged. There are a number of items on the G8 agenda that need to be encouraged and monitored. Debt relief is one. Although the G8 countries have promised $100 billion for debt relief, only a minuscule amount has actually been delivered. Why? Because the countries either cannot or will not, engage in the structural readjustment demanded by the international financial institutions. This structural readjustment demands that countries cut their spending on the health, education and social needs of their citizens, but not on the militaries. Obviously, military might is needed to keep people under control when their basic services are slashed, plus these countries buy their weapons from the G8 countries. Debt relief is a good concept, but its implementation needs vast changes.

A second commitment that needs to be encouraged is that every child in the world will have at least a primary education by 2015. Today, 100 million children, two-thirds of them girls, are not in school. Although this commitment was made in 2000, Canada's 'plan' was only released on April 24 of this year. To date, to my knowledge, nothing has actually been accomplished. There is a commitment to 'finding global solutions to environmental threats endangering the planet'. I don't think I need to say much about the Kyoto Accord. There is a global fund to fight HIV/AIDS, malaria and TB, which has approximately one tenth the money needed to make any significant impact on these diseases.

So, how does all this global doom and gloom relate to community values and democratic participation? Well this is, of course, my opinion but I really feel that most Canadians, most Calgarians, care about their neighbours. We care that others are forced to live – no, to barely exist – on two dollars a day; that children die from hunger and easily preventable diseases; that corporations get away with dumping toxic waste into local water systems; that Third World countries are forced to destroy their infrastructures and that billions of dollars are being wasted on increasingly sophisticated weapons with which countries can slaughter each other's people when these billions could be used to solve all of the world's problems in the areas of health, education and poverty. These things are not consistent with our Canadian values, but the $64,000 question is, what can we do about it? Well, we certainly cannot solve all of the issues in the next week. We can, however, do the following: educate ourselves about the issues, read not only the mainstream media but make an effort to find alternative media to give us information the government does not want us to have; choose an issue that has some meaning to us, something that we can relate to, something that makes us feel angry; find others who agree with us and join the activist movement.

In closing, I want to quote from the G8 communiqué issued in June 1999,

> The challenge is to seize the opportunities globalization affords while addressing its risks, to respond to concerns about a lack of control over its effects. We must work to sustain and increase the benefits of globalization and ensure that its positive effects are widely shared by people all over the world. We therefore call on governments and international institutions, business and labour, civil society and the individual to work together to meet this challenge and realize the full potential of globalization for raising prosperity and promoting social progress while preserving the environment.

Wonderful words; but, my friends, it won't happen unless you and I, we, the people, learn about what really happens, and learn to come together as local citizens of the world, to demand that corporations and governments live up to their responsibilities to the people.

I would like to invite each and every one of you to join us at the G6B, to engage in local, democratic participation in global issues; to help find effective, practical solutions to the issues and to be part of a long term campaign for peace, justice and equality: Canadian values.

Russell Hemenway

I'm going to add a couple of more sentences to that very nice introduction so that there will be no misunderstanding as to exactly from where I come. I spend most of my time running the National Committee for an Effective Congress. I noticed, when Colin first mentioned that name, a few smiles on a few faces in the audience. It always manages to get a good chuckle out of some people who know about the government of the United States, when you talk about an "effective" Congress. But they're the same people, I might add, who would be filled with laughter if they knew they were going to be spending the weekend discussing ethics in leadership and public affairs.

But anyway, that's what I do. We're the largest citizens' committee that concerns itself with Congress; we're one of the oldest – organized in 1948, 54 years ago, by Eleanor Roosevelt. Eleanor Roosevelt called herself a "Liberal Democrat." Others called her a "bleeding heart liberal" and some called her a "knee jerk liberal." I'll answer to any of those names.

What do we do? We're supported by about 70,000 Americans. Our charge is to try to elect the best men and women from our communities to the Congress of the United States, to the Senate, and to the House of Representatives. We maintain a large store of information, the largest data bank of electoral and demographic data in the country on a precinct by precinct level. A precinct is our smallest political subdivision. There are approximately

200,000 precincts in the United States, and we can tell you a lot about each and every one of them, in terms of how they voted over the last decade and about their demographic makeup. From this data we are able to produce highly sophisticated campaign technical services which our candidates find invaluable in running a modern campaign. If our candidates were speaking here, they would say that it's the National Committee for an Effective Congress that often makes the difference between victory and defeat in close races. It's a challenging job that I do, but it's not where I started in politics, which is what I'd like to speak about.

The late Tip O'Neill, former Speaker of the House of Representatives, was very fond of saying that money was the "mother's milk of politics" and after fifty-five years in politics, I find absolutely no reason to disagree with him. Any discussion of ethics in leadership and in public life, or democratic participation in the political processes, quickly brings you to the subject of money and its influence on public values. We might take a moment to look at how elections are financed, and the sources of that mother's milk that flows so copiously in our political affairs. When I started as a political activist there was little or no public disclosure as to who financed elections, and how political money was spent. Some of you may remember the days when most political money was in cash, and in plain white envelopes. It was generally understood that Democrats received most of their financing, and financial contributions, from rich liberals and from the trade unions. And the Republicans were supported by big banks, big oil, big steel, big railroads, big coal, big anybody-who-didn't-like-government-regulation, and who especially didn't like to pay taxes.

When the 1971 Campaign Finance Reform Act was passed, the *New York Times* editorialized that President Nixon should give me and my colleagues a pen for signing, because without us there would have been no bill. The most important thing about that 1971 law, other than the fact that we wrote it, is that it was enacted at all. Incumbents hate reform; they got to where they are in the present system, and they don't want any change in the law that's going to give a challenger any advantages at all. So their rhetoric about reform is very lofty but they certainly don't want any part of it – and particularly Republicans, who have a tremendous money advantage over Democrats. They're the ones who have the access to the large corporate money and to special interest money, and they just don't want to give up that advantage.

That law, in 1971, really opened the door. And that law made possible all the subsequent reforms, including the law that passed three weeks ago which President Bush signed reluctantly, and without ceremony, before he flew off on another fundraising trip to raise as much unrestricted soft money as he can before the law takes effect on November 6th. Again, the principal importance of this new reform bill is that it passed at all and it would not have passed without the Enron scandal. It certainly is no panacea. But it will somewhat limit the number of destructive negative television advertisements in the last weeks before election day; it will also limit unrestricted soft money in federal campaigns; and it will increase the financial support of state and local political party organizations which should lead to greater citizen participation and involvement, which is the subject that brings us together today.

It also means that the fight for reform will go on, which is most significant. Had it been defeated – and believe me, the President, his entire staff, the Republican leadership, used every trick in the book to defeat it – had they defeated it, it probably would have been the end of any reform until we had another scandal of the magnitude of Enron, or Watergate, or the savings and loan scandal. But the fight will go on to balance the enormous advantage that incumbent office holders have over our challenge candidates to achieve full and timely public disclosure of campaign money and to establish a federal election commission that will have the power and the will to enforce the law.

April is tax time in the United States and in Canada. Every year at this time our news, and your news, is replete with stories of tax cheating. Secret corporate offshore bank accounts, off-balance-sheet accounting scams, and some huge multinational companies that pay no taxes at all. There are endless accounts of individuals – both rich and not so rich – who go to extraordinary ends to avoid, and to evade taxes. Now, ladies and gentlemen, these stories take a terrible toll. The general public, already disenchanted, and convinced that our system protects the rich, and that politicians have little concern for ordinary folk, find their cynicism deepened by these scandals like Enron, Watergate, Iran-Contra disclosures, savings and loan rip-offs, and the many instances where our government has raised lying to an art form. The fifty per cent of Americans – and I was astounded to hear the Canadian voting figures that you discussed, I assumed that Canadians voted in larger numbers than we do – the fifty per cent of eligible Americans who don't bother to vote or participate in any way in our democratic process, use as their excuse that their vote really doesn't matter. That there's no difference among the candidates, and that "you can't fight city hall."

Survey after survey shows that this negativism among Americans is growing apace, especially among the poor and the less educated, precisely those groups who need government most. If democracy is to flourish, and not flounder, we must find a way to attract our best men and women from our communities to public office. Now those men and women, the best among us, the future leaders on whom we count so much, will probably get their start as young people working in a community organization. That's where I started. Politics was very personal in those days. We rang doorbells. We asked the person to sign a petition to get a candidate on the ballot. We asked to come in, and gave them personally a piece of campaign literature. We talked with them about the issues: what was best for our community, for our congressional district, our city, our state and our country. It was a personal identification, face-to-face contact. A precinct worker, walking the precinct, meeting voters. Today if you ring a doorbell in New York City, the person is liable to call 9-1-1.

One would think that the 2000 Presidential election would have proved once and for all that our lives and our futures can rest on a handful of votes. Every vote does count. We've got to find a way to reach out – not to just any-body, because mediocrity is not good enough. You can't run a system as difficult as democracy with mediocre lead-ership. We must find the best. Ask yourself: when was the last time that you read in the newspapers or heard on the telly a story about ethical behaviour, of high moral conduct, and goodness? The sad fact is that we are deluged with news of misfeasance, malfeasance, dishonesty, calumny, corruption, conspiracy, greed, avarice, and every other evil doing. Not-yet-elected people, elected people, formerly elected people, appointed people, public officials, business people, professionals – everybody is included. Nobody escapes. Now, this avalanche of wrongdoing prevents sto-ries of good works, ethical and moral conduct, and human decency from getting much attention.

It should not surprise us that this constant bom-bardment about antisocial and felonious behaviour has given rise to a self oriented "me generation", too cynical to sit on a jury, or to vote in an election, or to write a postcard to their government representative. Someone described our time as one of "acquisitive individualism". It's not a bad description. Of all the threats to this 200 year old experi-ment in democracy, public apathy is among the most seri-ous. Our keynote speaker, Ben Barber, is a highly respect-ed political scientist and writer. He's a leading exponent of the interdependence of public education and democratic participation. I'm one of his many acolytes. If we're to find a route to the restoration of pride in public service, respect for elected officials, understanding of rudimentary civics and government organizations, and the importance and rewards of good citizenship, public education must play a major role. I think it was Winston Churchill who said "Democracy is the worst system, except for all the others." Someone should say that it's a great system, if all of us participated in it. Unfortunately the current trend is moving the other way. After September 11th Americans have professed a greater interest in civic life. This crisis, hopefully, will intensify the participation of individuals in society; perhaps it will even make us better citizens and temper our demands for instant gratification.

One question that we've been asking this weekend is: "Can the democratic process, can democracy, be made to work in international affairs? Do relations and problems among nations lend themselves to resolution through democracy and ethical leadership?" If we look to history, the answer is probably no. Despite Ben Barber's call for a Declaration of Interdependence, whenever nations have been asked to cede sovereignty, and to give up real power to a multinational body, their rhetoric has been lofty, and their actions negative. World War I, the war to make the world safe for democracy, led to the proposal for a League of Nations. The United States Senate shot it down, and it failed. Our next best chance for international order was after World War II. We struggled mightily at the San Francisco Convention and produced a United Nations with each great power getting a Security Council veto, rendering it useful, but toothless. Read the deliberations of this founding conference. Things haven't changed much. If you want to be inspired, read Canada's great leader, Lester Pearson's comments at the conference.

Also, when it comes to abrogating treaties, your

wonderful neigbour to the south, the United States, acknowledged to be the greatest power on earth, really takes the prize.

Global warming? Needs a lot more study. Sorry. We can't endorse the Kyoto accords.

An international Criminal Court? Well, maybe that's for others, but not for the United States.

And by the way, let's drop that ABM treaty while we build some Rube Goldberg missile defense system that may lead to even greater global destabilization.

I'm afraid that global order founded on democratic principles and institutions, continues to be a dream, But, we should note that our global population has reached 6.2 billion people. When I was born, by the way, it was less than 2 billion, to give you some indication of what we've been doing in our spare time. All the demographers, with no exception, project the population of the earth to level off at around 10 billion people in the near future. So we'd better get our act together. Powerful nation-states warring over finite resources evoke a future that no one wants really to contemplate

I want to add my salute to Joel Bell, Marsha Hanen, and their staff for the wonderful job they've done organizing this conference. To make the whole thing work they've had to impose time limits on all of us. Someone decided that I should be the "cleanup batter" on this panel. Had I come first, I would have said that I take the time constraints that you've imposed very seriously. If you exceed them, you're cutting into the time of people from whom we all want to hear. But because I've come last, I'm now cutting into your time, and that makes me feel even more guilty; so I think I'll just stop. I look forward to the Q and A period.

· III ·

GLOBALIZATION:
Promises and Problems

Stephen Lewis

Thank you immensely – that was an extraordinarily generous and deliciously hyperbolic introduction and I appreciate it immensely. I am forced by way of confessional only to make one observation which some of you have heard me make before. I am extraordinarily discombobulated by the reference to honourary degrees. The truth is that I spent an infinite number of years at four post-secondary institutions of celebrated higher learning and managed never, but never, to acquire a degree. I therefore spent my entire adult life lusting after degrees through the backdoor since I was unable to acquire them through the front.

I'm obviously delighted to be here. It's always a pleasure to leave the pre-Paleolithic philistines of central Canada and to come to this crucible of enlightenment. But I want, if I may and if you will permit me, to enjoy the usual feckless banter to which I am addicted, although I will not resist what Bob Fowler described as my touchingly socialist predilections during the course of these remarks. I have and he is entirely right in the use of the adjective, I have but thirty odd minutes I'm told. No one covers globalization in thirty minutes; indeed I can barely clear my throat in thirty minutes. So I want you to bear with me if I address the subject matter with what can only be regarded as unseemly rapidity.

Let me begin by providing a context by way of anecdote. In 1988 when I was at the United Nations I remember a quite vivid luncheon which was convened by another quite well known Canadian, Maurice Strong, who was then active in the interstices of the United Nations system bringing people together. And on that occasion he invited a number of diplomats from the developing world to meet with the then managing director of the International Monetary Fund, Michel Camdessus, to discuss the entry into the Uruguay round of international trade talks. It was an extraordinary lunch. During the course of the lunch, two ambassadors in particular, one of them from Singapore – a fellow whom Bob and I know very well, Kishore Mahbubani and the other from Ghana – a fellow Victor Gbeho who subsequently became the foreign minister and now sits in the Ghanaian Parliament. They took Camdessus on, told him that what he was saying was palpable nonsense, told him that the developing world would be marginalized by the trade talks, told him that there was not the slightest suggestion that there would be an opening to trade anywhere internationally once the trade talks were consummated and that all of this would marginalize further the least developed countries of the world. Camdessus, with that exquisite combination of intellectual blandishment and intellectual fraud, not to say intellectual fabrication, assured them that they were entirely wrong, that the Uruguay round would usher in the panacea for the developing world. I remember it vividly because it was heated, acrimonious and therefore to my ears a delight.

The truth is that the Uruguay round was exactly as Mahbubani and Gbeho said it would be. It was a desperate disappointment for the developing world by and large and most emphatically for the least developed countries, whose position in the international trade regimen was more and more marginalized and that is clearly the process that has been set in place again in Doha, Qatar last November when we jump-started the new round of trade talks through the World Trade Organization. And there is not the slightest suggestion that the major wealthy countries of the world are going to open their borders to the kind of acceptance of the products and commodities of the least developed countries in a way that will make any appreciable difference whatsoever. And what is so interesting about it all is that this so called triumph of globalization, which focuses strongly on trade and aid, is now understood to be fundamentally flawed even by its protagonists, even by those who welcome the large measure of globalization to which the world regularly refers. It has been an excellent experience for the rich countries and for transnational corporations. It has been a lamentable experience thus far for the uprooted and disinherited of this planet. Kofi Annan, at the millenium summit, talked about the disappointment of globalization. Even at the World Economic Forum when the celebrated aristocracy of capitalism, and I use the world descriptively rather than pejoratively for the first time in my life, the aristocrats of capitalism at the World Economic Forum got together and attempted to traduce numbers of non-governmental organizations, understanding that they better bring them into the talks because globalization simply wasn't working as they thought it would be working.

The president of the World Bank Jim Wolfenson admits openly now time and time again that something went terribly wrong with globalization. When the *New York Times* reported on the Monterrey conference last month in Mexico, dealing with financing for development, they reported it under the analysis headline "Monterrey Globalization Has Come Up Short" – a recognition that all of the expectations we have – that a combination of the liberalization of trade and shifting aid patterns and celebrating the activities of multinational corporations and giving greater and greater strength to the private sector – that all of this would somehow usher in an era of romanticism and plenitude for the least developed nations of the world, and something has gone very wrong. And then there appeared a document recently, one of the really first rate documents that's appeared in the last few years. The Macroeconomic Commission on Health which was chaired and authored in large measure by the formerly Harvard economist Jeffrey Sachs but was commissioned and has the imprimatur of legitimacy conferred by the World Health Organization, in which Jeffrey at the opening puts it pretty well and he puts it as everyone now sees it.

> Globalization is under trial, partly because the benefits are not yet reaching hundreds of millions of the world's poor, and partly because globalization introduces new kinds of international challenges as turmoil in one part of the world can spread rapidly to others through terrorism, armed conflict, environmental degradation or disease as demonstrated by the dramatic spread of AIDS around the globe in a single generation.

Let me then rather speedily deal with some of the items which are raised. Number one, globalization certainly doesn't appear to be able to deal with poverty. 1.2, 1.3 billion people on this earth still live on less than a dollar a day. Over three billion still live on less that seven hundred and fifty dollars a year. It was the United Nations development program and their human development report that pointed out that the twenty five richest people in this world have income and assets worth four hundred and seventy four billion dollars – greater than the entire gross national product of Sub-Saharan Africa, and I draw reference to Sub-Saharan Africa because necessarily it forms the backdrop of the G8 summit which is forthcoming and will be the subject of much of the discussion undoubtedly this afternoon. This month, the World Bank published its world development indicators for 2002 and pointed out that the millenium goals for the year 2015 involving cutting poverty in half, involving universal primary education, involving a reduction by two-thirds in infant mortality rates – that all of these goals would probably be beyond the capacity of most of the least developed countries to achieve and certainly not achievable by almost all of the countries on the African continent.

There were two crippling factors given evidence from Wolfenson and from the Bank. I want you to understand that these are not the maniacal spasms of a left-winger. These views are rooted in the observations of the establishment. I mean, Jeffrey Sachs can barely sit at the same table with me let alone endorse any of the absurdist views which I so willingly embrace. I want it therefore broadly appreciated that I am now speaking of people who have, as a result of observing what is going on with the human condition, come to conclusions which are frankly irresistible and the crippling factor which is acknowledged by all is that the alleged marginal openings for trade have not occurred. Indeed, the developed world is now spending three hundred and fifty to four hundred billion dollars a year simply to protect agriculture through subsidies alone, thereby dooming all of the agricultural export and commodity export of a number of countries and, as everyone here knows, official development assistance has been in catastrophic decline. It's interesting that the subsidies to agriculture from the rich countries represent six to seven times as much as all of the official development assistance in any given year. The decline is quite calamitous. That target, which was fashioned by one of our own former Prime Ministers, Lester Pearson, of .7 per cent of GNP – seven tenths of one per cent of gross national product has never been reached, has not even come close to being reached by any of the G7 countries. Indeed the average is now roughly at .22, less than a third of where it should be. At this moment in time official development assistance amounts to something like fifty-three billion dollars a year. If the .7 target were reached by the countries of the world which agreed on that objective collectively in 1969, it would yield close to a hundred and seventy-five billion dollars a year today, close to two hundred billion dollars a year by 2005, and we would be able to do everything all of us want to do to make this a more just and civilized international community and are frustrated from doing by the nature of the environment in which we work.

Africa – this is incredible to me – I always look at these figures and I wonder: can they be true? – Africa, the continent in greatest need saw its official development assistance fall from 17.2 billion dollars in 1990 to 12.3 billion dollars in 1999. Even the good performers in Africa who are always celebrated by those who pretend to be the cautious analysts – the Ugandas, the Tanzanias, the Mozambiques, the Ghanas – all of their official development assistance fell year by year over the last couple of years as they so desperately required it. Monterrey promised another ten to seventeen billion dollars overall, upping the ante three to five years from now by that amount but still a relative pittance compared to the target and to the need. Non-oil commodity prices in Africa are down thirty-five per cent since 1998. So much for the liberalization of international trade. Income per capita is down in Africa from five hundred and fifty two dollars a head in 1991 to four hundred and seventy four dollars a head in the year 2000. School enrollment is down, particularly for girls. One out of four girls are not even in primary school on the continent at this moment in time. Everyone says Africa requires a growth rate of roughly seven per cent a year in order to achieve the millenium goals of 2015. It's hovering somewhere between 2.6 per cent and 3.1 per cent with no possibility of achieving the target.

Even HIPC as it's called – the highly indebted poor country debt initiative – is in trouble as recently evidenced by a report from the World Bank and the IMF yea this very month. An initiative which was supposed to emancipate forty-one countries from the yoke of debt in order that they could turn the money over to poverty reduction, and one finds now that for many of these countries they are still spending on debt servicing more than they spend on health and education combined. I want to ask, because it seems to me not illegitimate to ask: How is it possible that we can reach the year 2002 with the extraordinary riches which this world embraces and see an entire continent of six to seven hundred million people treated in that fashion?

Forgive my speaking for a moment about my own country. We've had a pretty dramatic decline in official development assistance since 1993. We're now down to .26, .27, .25 – it depends on the year. When the Prime Minister of Canada says that he will increase foreign aid by eight per cent a year for a number of years thereby doubling aid by 2010, eight or nine years from now, that would bring us back to where we were in 1985 under a Conservative administration. Now I'm the only person you'll ever meet who's indebted to Brian Mulroney, so I can speak about this quite confidently and it has always bemused and bewildered me that the Pearsonian legacy should have been so much more authentically conveyed by a Conservative administration than it has been by Pearson's own successors.

We are promised a five hundred million dollar special fund for Africa. That may be what we will end up spending on the G8 summit in June. I noticed that the Foreign Minister refused to say that it would be less than that. Most people now see three hundred million dollars as a legitimate figure to use in relation to the G8 summit. I think five hundred million sounds a little high although, God knows with the present situation what it will rise to, but the juxtaposition does cause one a twitch, a pause. Five hundred million for Africa, five hundred million for the summit, I must say that on occasion people could feel that things were faintly out of whack. I am encouraged however to see that the Honourable Paul Martin has indicated that the budget surplus this year may rise yet again to something like eight billion dollars – undoubtedly that will make an immense difference. I wanted to ask Bob Fowler at lunch but I never did and I won't do it from the public platform because it would be gauche, why they don't just have a video conference. It works extremely well. It's much safer all in all for those who are anxious about international terrorism and my suspicion, and I am a democratic socialist and therefore my arithmetic capacities are not to be given credence, but my suspicion is that it would cost less than Kananaskis.

I must say overall that I think there's an astounding moral delinquency where official development assistance is concerned. What globalization is doing on this front is to sanctify poverty, inequality and injustice and I want to tell you it leaves me in a perpetual rage. There was a time in my life when I would have moderated or subordinated my rage. I'm sixty-four. I'm inching into my dotage. I see no reason now to compromise with the feelings that course through me.

This brings me to the second point I want to make which flows in part from what Jeffrey indicated and that is that globalization certainly can't deal with conflict. Just take a look at the Middle East, think about Afghanistan, think about the Balkans, think of Cambodia, Sri Lanka, East Timor, Colombia,   Burundi, Sierra Leone, Liberia, Democratic Republic of the Congo, Angola. Think, if you will, of Rwanda. Think of the hundred days between April the sixth, 1994 and early July, 1994 when eight hundred thousand people were slaughtered in the full view of the world and the world raised not a finger. It was that magnificent Canadian General Romeo Dallaire who begged the security council for additional troops to at least diminish the slaughter if not contain it entirely and, thanks in particular to the position of the United States of America and France on that Security Council, not only didn't he receive the additional troops he wanted, but the few troops that were in the country were further reduced in number. It is almost inconceivable that, as recently as 1994, you could watch eight hundred thousand people slaughtered in a country and the world simply be a passive observer. If that doesn't tell you about the intensity of subterranean racism towards Africa, I don't know what will.

As a matter of fact the only moment I've seen latterly of sort of ethical imperatives came with the resignation of the entire Dutch cabinet because of what had happened with the Dutch forces in Srebrenica. It's quite a commentary. It occurs to me, as subversive, as inappropriate as this occurrence may seem to be, that no one anywhere thought of resignation when the United Nations report on Rwanda by the former Prime Minister of Sweden, Ingvar Carlson was tabled. We're in an odd, odd place in this world where insufferable depravity occurs, where we watch a descent into dementia and somehow the globalizing of our activities, that precious phenomenon of the global community, can never be sufficiently engaged to do anything about it. And it leads me to the third point I want to make which is that globalization certainly can't deal with disease.

I spend my life these days in and out of Africa dealing with HIV/AIDS. The figures, as all of you will know, are overwhelming in Sub-Saharan Africa. There are more than twenty-eight million people now infected out of close to forty million people worldwide. There were three million four hundred thousand new infections last year. Two million, three hundred thousand people lost their lives, went to their death. It is increasingly a gender based pandemic. Fifty-five per cent of the infections are now women. In the country of Botswana, for young women and girls between the ages of fifteen and nineteen the prevalence rate is twenty-six per cent. For young women between the ages of twenty and twenty-four the prevalence rate is forty-three per cent. For women between the ages of twenty-five and twenty-nine the prevalence rate is 51.2 per cent, which means that one out of every two women in that age group has effectively been served with a death warrant. It's an extraordinary thing that's unraveling the continent, that's shredding its infrastructure, that's taking a human toll that is almost impossible to convey. The single most vulnerable group now are the fifteen to nineteen year olds and girls in a number of places on the continent in that age group are six times as vulnerable as boys. And then you've got thirteen million orphans. Everywhere you go on the continent you have orphans. These lovely abandoned kids who are orphaned at such a young age. Orphan care in Africa consists of grandmothers looking after six, eight, ten, twelve children in many instances, and when the grandmother goes, who's coming up behind, and then you get the phenomenon of child headed households. Usually little girls, ten, eleven, twelve years of age looking after their siblings. They live in the most impossible of circumstances and there is very little food and they have no money for school fees.

God there are ironies in this life which just drive me to distraction. You know in the 1980s and the early 1990s most of these countries didn't have school fees, but when the structural adjustment programs of the World Bank and the IMF were imposed on Africa in that period of time one of the things which the Bank in particular embraced was user fees, and one of the conditions which was imposed on African governments in return for the loan were school fees. Now the Bank says, with that simple, dismissive arrogance to which from time to time international financial institutions are given: "We don't believe in user fees anymore. We were wrong." I've heard that said publicly. In fact I've heard it said structural adjustment is dead. But the consequences linger on horribly for these countries who are subject to the policy and now you have school fees all over the place which children who are orphaned by AIDS can't pay and therefore can't even have one environment which would give them some sense of place, some sense of hope, some sense of self-worth, some sense of friend-ship.

But I have to tell you, as impossible as the whole sit-uation is and it truly is, what I've learned in visits to Cote d'Ivoire, Burkina Faso, Nigeria, Rwanda, Uganda, Kenya, Zambia, Namibia, Botswana, South Africa, all of it over the last ten or eleven months, is that we know exactly what to do. This is what curdles my molecular structure. We know exactly what to do in this world. It isn't as though that pan-demic can't be stopped in its tracks. We know about what is called voluntary counselling and testing so that there are centres in a country where people will know their HIV sta-tus. We know how to prevent mother to child transmission. There's a little drug called nevirapine. A mother takes one tablet at the onset of labour, one tablet during the course of giving birth, the child takes a liquid equivalent and trans-mission is cut by up to fifty-three per cent. Imagine the number of lives you save of kids who are born to HIV pos-itive mothers. We know about anti-retroviral treatment and all kinds of people are trained to provide it in many parts of the continent and yet less that four per cent of those on the continent who would be entitled to the treatment, that is, whose so called CD4 counts and viral loads require treat-ment intervention through anti-retrovirals – less that four per cent of those people who are entitled actually receive it.

We know there are inspired prevention programs. I just came back last week from looking at a program called Love Life which combines an extraordinary advertising campaign with services on the ground, particularly for youth, funded by the Kaiser Foundation at a level of ten million dollar a year for five years which is really raising consciousness throughout the country. A few weeks ago I was in Ethiopia, sitting down with the Patriarch of the Ethiopian Orthodox Church. Ethiopia – this is really interesting – is a country where there's virtually no level of literacy at all so print material doesn't do any good and where, and I think this is the only country in Africa this is true, where radio reaches only twenty per cent of the population. So how do you get the message out to a population which has three million infected people? Well, the Patriarch of the Ethiopian Orthodox Church said to me I have three hundred and fifty thousand priests and, if it were possible to do a training program for which we need a little financial support, we could bring the message to every community. Obviously there would be some questions about the message which may or may not concern numbers of people but the awareness, the consciousness raising would be a far greater benefit than any deficiency inherent in the message itself.

Bob Fowler and I were talking about something that we'd jointly seen in Ethiopia in a little town called Alwassa outside of Addis Ababa in the south, where the World Food Program has been training its own truck drivers who truck the food, because the truck drivers are one of the high risk groups. They've got commercial sex workers, migrant labour and truck drivers as the three target high risk groups on the Sub-Saharan African continent and these truck drivers were engaged in an educational session sponsored by the World Food Program so that the individual truck drivers would get up in a crowd of people and talk openly about the fact that they were now using condoms and they now understood how to protect themselves and their partners. It was extraordinary.

All over Africa these undertakings are evident. We know how to do peer counseling where young people use music and dance and theatre and art and songs to convey messages – messages which are so bold and vivid and straightforward that they'd take your breath away. We know how to do home care at the village level. Everywhere on the continent – this is what is so wonderful about Africa that so few people in the Western world understand – that at village level, community level, grass-roots level, you have tremendous sophistication particularly amongst the women and you have networks and you have community based organizations which, if they could enlarge the work they do would make a tremendous impact in stopping the pandemic in its tracks. There are problems of infrastructure, there are problems of delivery, there are problems of human capacity but none of that is stifling. What is stifling, what drives me crazy is the absence of resources.

Let me take you to page four of Jeffrey Sachs' struggle. He says: "The problem is that these interventions don't reach the world's poor. Some of the reasons are corruption, mismanagement and a weak public sector but in the vast majority of countries there is a more basic and remediable problem. The poor lack the financial resources to obtain coverage of these essential interventions." He goes on to say that the key recommendation of the commission, the key recommendation, is that they should have the resources. The high-income countries would simultaneously commit – as the low-income countries use their own budgets to the outer extremes – the high-income countries would simultaneously commit vastly increased financial assistance in the form of grants especially to the countries that need help most urgently which are concentrated in Sub-Saharan Africa. And then in the only place in the book where he uses bold italics it reads: ***"They would resolve that lack of donor funds should not be the factor that limits the capacity to provide health services to the world's poorest people."*** What Sachs is saying is that with twenty-seven billion dollars more per year by 2007 and thirty-eight billion dollars more per year by 2015, you could defeat AIDS, you could defeat tuberculosis, you could defeat malaria, you could set up research and development institutions. You could improve the infrastructure so that the diseases emerging globally, which are creating havoc for the entire country, could be stopped in their tracks. He's asking for .001 of gross national product, i.e. one penny for every ten dollars of official development assistance that comes from the West at that level would go to health. That's all it would take and it would save eight million lives a year by the year 2010.

And he wants to turn – I want to mention this because it speaks to the nature of globalization – he wants to turn the existing economic paradigms on their heads. That's one of the most fascinating pieces of this work. There is an assumption, there is a prevailing conventional nostrum that economic growth will simply deal with your health problems and your poverty problems and Jeffrey says: Nuts. We now know from all of the studies we've done and all of the empirical evidence that we have assumed, we now know that the disease burden, that's the phrase he uses, the disease burden of so many countries is so great that, until you deal with the issues of health you will never get to economic growth. So you are talking about it at the most elemental human levels. You're talking about the need to be a decent globalized community, the need to respond to this tremendous vulnerability of the human condition and if you will forgive me and I will wend my way to an appropriate close, I want to quote just a couple of further items.

The world has made solemn pledges to address the crises of diseases of the poor but has not yet taken strong enough practical steps to implement them. With millions dying unnecessary and tragic deaths and with global institutions under stress, a scaled up war against disease is vital for the legitimacy of globalization. I don't know how globalization is ever going to embrace that legitimacy but it's clearly not now in evidence and in his last page, 110, he says: "There is no excuse in today's world for millions of people to suffer and die each year for lack of the thirty-four dollars per person needed to cover essential health services. A just and farsighted world will not let this tragedy continue." I embrace Jeffrey because at the moment he has the single greatest international influence on these issues, on numbers of governments and the United Nations system where he is an adviser to Kofi Annan. I smiled at the felicitous turn of phrase when he said recently in a speech "My simple message today is that people are dying because they are too poor to stay alive."

God I remember being in South Africa at a little palliative care centre with a young woman in her twenties. I went there with a fellow named Farid Abdullah who ran the Western Cape AIDS program for Cape Town. It's so bizarre constantly to encounter particularly young women in their twenties who are infected and fighting like crazy to stay alive and they lose, they lose the battle and you know a year or two from now they'll be gone. And we went upstairs to this lovely young woman In this palliative care centre. She had three young children. She'd been expected to die within two or three days but she was lasting three or four weeks because she had some food, she had some care and I said to Farid, "Farid, you know with anti-retroviral treatment this woman could live another two or three years." And he said to me "No Stephen, she'd live another seven to ten years or more." And you think to yourself, why do these kids have to be orphans? Why does this woman have to die for the absence of a drug whose prices are now low enough that the world could afford to subsidize the treatment?

Everywhere you go you see these lovely orphaned children who attach themselves to you as though there were some kind of indelible welding to your physical person because there is such a sense of abandonment and such a sense of need. For the first time in my life I've come home from Africa and said to my wife Michelle, "Have you ever thought of adopting?" You just want to sort of embrace the whole continent because these kids are being robbed of absolutely everything in their childhood. What happens when these youngsters themselves have children without the parenting, the nurturing, the love, the affection that grows with a child over life. What happens to antisocial and delinquent behavior as these kids take to the streets? It's expected that there'll be up to thirty million of them by the year 2010. Why does the world sit by and watch it happen? You want to know the *reductio ad grotesqueum*? I was in Namibia in a little Catholic AIDS centre and they took me out back to show me an income generating project. And the income generating project consisted of a group of men making paper maché coffins for infants. Coffins about this long and they were putting on the silver handles and they said to me in a combination of anguish and pride, "We can't keep up with the demand."

I want to know, I want to know what's wrong with this world. I want somebody to tell me what price this globalization we all talk about. What's gone wrong? What is it about our inability to respond to the human condition? Kofi Annan has asked for seven to ten billion dollars per year for a global fund to fight AIDS and everybody agrees that that's the minimum. The global fund has raised from governments two billion dollars over three years. The government of Canada has offered a hundred million dollars over the three years. Juxtapose that again to the cost of the forthcoming summit. Am I totally deranged or is something wildly out of whack? Have we managed to be converted to financial architecture, to deficits and debts and taxes and all the arithmetic folderol at the expense of the human condition? I'm not even going to deal with globalization's inability to cope with the environment. I want to simply say that globalization is failing. The twin pillars of trade and aid are failing and there is no sign of change.

Africa is coming to the G8 summit next month with what it calls NEPAD. The new economic development program for Africa, the new economic program for African development. And they will ask the G8 countries for a considerable swath of financial support. I don't think they're going to get it. I don't think there's any evidence to suggest that we will approximate the genuine needs of the continent and that's why I want to tell you I have a tremendous regard for the protest movement that pulsates around this world. I share a lot of the cynicism and anxiety about political behavior, although I have to say I honour politicians as a rule. My own experience was profoundly appealing, reassuring, meaningful. I don't disparage politicians witlessly, gratuitously and irrelevantly, but I worry about what is going on internationally, as you worry. And the assumption of the changes and the benefits that globalization would bring to humankind are all being damaged, eviscerated by policies that are so insensitive, so distant, so immovable, so self-important and yet around this world there are groups of people, young people everywhere who know that there is a profound injustice, who know that human rights are off the rails, labour rights are off the rails, environmental rights are off the rails. They may not have etched every single platform of a mandate but they understand that what is happening now is profoundly wrong and needs an antidote and they're prepared to find the time to carve that antidote out and I'm with them. I'm with them in every sense as they fight the present trends because there is no ambition more noble than to create a more just, decent, caring, international society. We're off the rails. It's time to put us back.

· IV ·
GLOBALIZATION, COMMUNITY VALUES AND DEMOCRATIC PARTICIPATION:
National and International Perspectives

Robert Fowler[1]

It's a pleasure to be here with you this afternoon, and it certainly is a pleasure to be talking to you about such important issues and in the company of such an important panel. I hope, certainly, that any of you who know me would know that I'd rather give Stephen's speech than mine. You also will know that even if I were in such a position I couldn't possibly match tongues with Canada's finest orator. So I will hide behind my bureaucratic grayness and not rise to the occasion; but Marsha and Joel, it was bad enough to put me up against Stephen, but then to squeeze me between him and his daughter-in-law is really a little much, and I look forward to inviting you to a conference soon. We are in this country indeed blessed that we have such a family as these guys come from where we have such articulate, effective, intelligent, ethical spokesmen who believe so deeply in what they are doing and what they are saying and are making such a big difference around the world. I have had the pleasure of working with Stephen for ages. It's always inspiring. We've both been ambassadors at the United Nations and we each approached the job somewhat differently, but very much from the same ethical perspective I think, and certainly Stephen made a big difference that I felt every day that I was at the UN ten years later.

It was very nice of Stephen not to ask me from the podium to juxtapose the cost of the Summit with Africa and I'm very glad he didn't do that. So I will probably get into

---

1 This chapter is prepared, with minor editing, from an audio recording of the Symposium proceedings.

that area anyway as I proceed with my remarks, but let me just start a little bit in that direction. You know, we all said to each other as we watched the second plane hit on September 11th, that our world was changing, and I think we have to come to terms with the fact that it changed, and that running our world and managing our world and doing the things we have to do to bring some order and reason to our world did change that day. And organizing meetings, particularly meetings that bring together the eight highest value targets in one place for the first time since those events – doing that is going to be different than it has been. So this Summit is going to cost what it costs, and I don't mean to be fast and loose with your taxes, but the reality is, and I challenge Stephen to say he really believes that he thinks the world can be run by video conferencing and by long distance telephone chats. It cannot be. The General Assembly can't be run that way. The Security Council can't be run that way. Our dialogue with Africa can't be run that way. Stephen and I have been crossing paths all over the African continent for the past many months. It is grueling. Stephen goes to South Africa for a day and then he goes to West Africa for a day. For each of those days he puts 40 hours in on an airplane, and it is appallingly taxing. And why do we do that? Why don't we just give them a phone call? Because we can't do it by phone. We can't change the way the West, the rich countries, deal with the poorest countries by phone. We can't set up a new partnership with Africa by video conferencing and I would argue, we can't have al Qaeda condemn us to having meetings on American aircraft carriers. So these meetings are going to be expensive. They're going to be very expensive and I don't know how expensive they're going to be because I don't know at the end of the day how many soldiers and how many policemen are going to have to be assembled against what kind of a threat because that threat is con-stantly evolving. So I regret to leave that sort of bottom line

– that it will be expensive.

Yes, the government of Canada put 500 million dollars aside in December, and at the risk of blowing our own collective horn a little bit, I think that's had a hell of an effect. And half a billion Canadian dollars in December and a whole bunch of very intensive, very high profile discussions on Africa in the meantime has had, I think, somewhat of an impact on those remarkable decisions that were announced around the time of the Monterrey conference. Stephen mentioned the numbers to you and he mentioned them to you in a context that suggested that they weren't enough. By the way, I don't think they *are* enough, but they are an awful change from what was. You know the Americans increased their aid by 50 per cent, pledging the equivalent of 80 billion additional Canadian dollars over the next 10 years significantly for Africa. Whether it was because one or the other was playing I can do anything better than you, the European Union at their Barcelona Summit meeting pledged that they would raise the average of the EU aid performance from .33 of GDP to .3. They would bring everybody in the Union up to .33 which would have the effect of changing it from .33 to .39. That then brings 27 billion additional Euros into play for ODA over the next five years. That's obviously assuming certain growth projections, etc. At the same meeting, Mr. Chrétien pledged to add to the existing CIDA budget plus 500 million, eight per cent compounded a year indefinitely and, by my calculations as I do mortgages, that tells me that our aid budget will double in the next 8 or 9 years. That's good news. That's good news for those of us who care about the Third World and the ever widening gap between them and us, particularly in Africa.

Is it enough? Is it Jeffrey Sachs' $27 billion U.S. for AIDS right now? No it's not, but is it a truly significant change in the way we collectively pledge not to allow that gap between rich and poor to become utterly unbridgeable? Yes, I think it is. So what do you juxtapose? Yes, there were half a billion dollars in December. Yes, this Summit's going to cost a lot of money. You heard Stephen's numbers about the ravages of AIDS in Africa. I don't know, Stephen, did you get into the fact that malaria's ravages are far greater? That 2,700 children below the age of 5 die of malaria every day? Africa desperately needs our help and huge volumes of it. There are interesting abstract discussions to have about the absorption capacity in Africa, about just how much our renewed attention to Africa can make a difference to African lives, given the enormous paucity of African institutions to absorb change; but I certainly hope that the new partnership that I'm going to tell you about will help fix that too. That is, that it will help ensure that Africa is well placed to absorb these significant, new commitments and yes, of course, the pitch I will be making is that if we get this right, if these new monies are used properly, that more will come. That is certainly, I believe, the case with respect to the global health fund that was kicked off at Geneva last year with, as Stephen puts it, only two billion American dollars, three billion Canadian dollars. The fund only came into existence on January 1st, and I think it is this week that the fund is looking at its first tranche of $650 million U.S. – expenditures which certainly, I expect, will begin to make a difference on the ground. But is two billion or three billion enough for AIDS in Africa? Of course it's not, but it's a start; and if we use it smartly then I suspect more will come quite soon.

Now, getting into the stuff of my talk to you today, Ms. Klein and I obviously will approach the Community Values and Globalization theme set to us by Marsha and Joel from slightly different angles, but I would be very surprised if they were diametrically opposed positions; but I'll find that out. She sees a very dark side in globalization, and from reading her book and from reading her articles she certainly has broadened my own understanding and helped me comprehend why I feel so damn angry every time I see a Benneton ad. I didn't know why it got me so angry. It did, and I thank her for doing that. Certainly my family would be quick to attest that the thought of getting me anywhere near a pair of Nikes is inconceivable, but I didn't know that Michael Jordan was paid more to advertise Nike than Nike pays people to make Nikes, and that is a startling fact, and it does suggest to me that our values are somewhat screwed up. I thank her for that as well, and I'm using just a couple of examples, Naomi, that I picked out of what I'd seen.

My current job is to prepare the G8 Summit which will end precisely two months from today, 120 kilometers west of here in the Kananaskis Valley. I hope by then it might have stopped snowing, but it is a remarkable site. I had a meeting there in the early nineties, and certainly our visitors from the NATO constituency at that time had their collective socks knocked off by its beauty. It is the perfect place to have a different kind of Summit and that's the kind that Mr. Chrétien has instructed me to prepare — not just a Summit done differently. I am, of course, daunted by the fact that I know he's been to eleven of these, and therefore when he says he wants it done differently, he knows what he wants done differently. He wants to get away from all the pomp and circumstance and the long, black cars and the constant moving and the protocol orders which confuse the meeting and diminish its effectiveness. He wants leaders to be able to talk – talk collectively, talk individually, talk in groups and deal with the essential, important, overriding issues of the moment and he's instructed me to ensure that the Summit deals only with those issues. No classic, bureaucratic, Christmas-treeing of the agenda; no sneaking your item on the agenda so that you get the staff and the funds to fund your favorite program over the next year. He wanted to simply get rid of the tired communiqué, which had become an exercise in anti-communication, certainly from my perspective. The communiqué would go on for pages and pages and pages as, indeed, did the Monterrey consensus declaration. I counted one sentence of 272 words, and only bureaucrats can write like that, but nobody can read it. Indeed Mark Grossman, the political director in the State Department, said at about four o'clock in the morning about a year ago, at the end of a long communiqué drafting session: "Wouldn't it be wonderful if more people read the communiqué than wrote it?" So we're not going to have one of those.

Instead we're going to have a chairman's statement of some kind which will recap in a very few paragraphs what they talked about. Not what they might have talked about if they'd had time or whatever, but simply what they talked about. In addition there will be other deliverables (in communication speak) at the time of the Summit, the most significant of which – indeed what Mr. Chrétien insistently calls the centerpiece of the Kananaskis meeting – will be the Africa Action Plan. I wear three hats with respect to the Summit. I'm the housekeeper. I'm very happy to say I don't have to deal with security but I deal with the two bits of policy. I deal with the regular Summit stuff – it's called "Sherpa", and I deal with the Africa stuff and there's a separate group of Sherpas for the first time in twenty-seven years of Summitry that leaves aside a separate group of personal representatives to prepare this African agenda. Those of you who know me will know that I have a long attachment with Africa. I feel deeply about it and I feel particularly privileged to be able to do this job at this time, at a time when, I would argue, Africa is close to simply falling off the international agenda.

I left the UN 18 months ago and at that time you would hear normally reasonable people opining privately on the edges of meetings that, maybe, we should forget about Africa for a while. Africa has issues. We can't get it right in Africa. The peace and security agenda seems intractable and impossible; AIDS poses a whole new set of problems that are taxing our systems beyond endurance. Maybe we should just simply leave Africa alone for a couple of generations and let them work out these issues and we'll get back to it. A marginal development investment in Thailand or Bolivia produces much better results and so maybe we should concentrate there with the limited resources we have available. I hope you will know from the way I set that up that I don't agree with it. I think it would be ethically indefensible to do something like that and Mr. Chrétien has made it very clear that that will not happen. Indeed within days – a very small number of days – of the horrors of September 11th, he made very clear that Africa would remain the centerpiece and would not be squeezed off by the other items on the agenda. Let me remind you what the other items are.

I said the focus will be simple and the items are going to be economic growth, terrorism, and Africa. Economic growth and terrorism will not be allowed to squeeze Africa off the agenda. I think most of you will agree that we're facing a slightly better situation with respect to the global economy than we were six months ago. Growth rates in most G8 countries, but not all, are back to quite respectable levels and indeed the prognosis is that they will slightly improve over the intervening weeks and months. With respect to terrorism – and I don't propose to get into it in any detail, but obviously if anybody was interested I'd be happy to answer your questions – there is a huge amount of activity going on out there. We have four groups of Ministerial meetings dealing with different aspects of terrorism, from getting hold of terrorism finances, to dealing with bombs on airplanes, trying to come to terms with the 68 million containers that wander around our planet each year, and indeed improving intelligence and improving information flow. Obviously leaders will want to take stock of what all that means and give some direction for the future to our bureaucracies to pursue this new and world-changing threat.

With respect to Africa, the leaders appointed African Sherpas, that is personal representatives, to speak for them on and vis-à-vis Africa, and our mandate is to prepare a concrete plan of action for Africa, very much directly in response to what was adopted by African leaders last June in Lusaka as the New African Initiative, and which has since transmogrified into NEPAD, the New Partnership for Africa's Development. Why did the G8 leaders say yes to NEPAD? Let's face it: they and the rest of the world have managed to not notice a withering array of "fix Africa" proposals. Certainly my own bookshelves groan with them and why is this one different? What was it that caused them to say, "OK, let's see if we can make this one work together in a new partnership with Africa?" It really is different. For those of you who've read it, it is eminently readable, it's 200 paragraphs, it's 50 pages and it says things very differently and says very different things than have been said in the past. It looks forward, not backward. I'm not saying there's no point in looking backward. Africa's history is not a happy one and a whole bunch of people outside Africa have had their part to play in its unhappiness, stretching way back, and much more recently. But it doesn't do Africa an awful lot of good to endlessly worry about why that was, and of course NEPAD does cogitate upon that a little bit. But what this paper does is to commit African leaders to owning Africa's present and future – to taking charge of it and becoming accountable for it and becoming responsible for it. It commits Africa's leaders to forming first and foremost a new partnership among themselves: the original request for partnership is among Africans and only secondarily with Africa's friends outside. It acknowledges that things have not worked very well in Africa, and it acknowledges that there is no foreseeable amount of Official Development Assistance that's going to make Africa significantly better.

In other words there is an acknowledgement that it is up to Africans to change the way they govern, to change the way they deal with their own people and to make a difference directly in a manner that is accountable to their people. Most significantly, and particularly for those of you who have dealt with Africa politically as Stephen and I have in the General Assembly, Africans are not militarily powerful. They're not economically powerful. But in multilateral organizations they are politically powerful. They can slam fifty-three votes onto the table and that is a big block of decision-making in multilateral organizations; and they have been remarkably effective in imposing political discipline on the way they use those votes. That's the power they have. What that has done, though, is that it has imbued a sense of, on the upside community, but on the downside, sameness in the way Africans deal with each other and the rest of the world. NEPAD acknowledges that the fifty-three countries of Africa are not the same. They have different problems. They have different kinds and qualities of leadership. They have different constructions of civil society. They manage the relations between the governed and governing differently and, not to put too fine a point on it, there are very different qualities of governments in Africa. They have committed themselves, most markedly, to setting up a transparent peer review process that will assess those differences in Africa, that will point out first of all for them to see where are the problems, what are the lacunae?

At the meeting of the 15 leaders who are charged with implementing NEPAD, they decided in November in Abuja, Nigeria to mandate the economic commission for Africa that is led by the remarkable Ghanaian K.Y. Amoako, to create this peer review process. A month ago they approved in principle that process and they expect to adopt it formally two weeks before the Summit in mid-June.

They're not doing it for us. It's not a present for the Summit. It is an earnest of their intention to deal straight up and effectively with Africa's problems in a way that they all can see. Now many people are skeptical. Many people out there are saying the Africans can't do this. I think they can. The ECA, the Economic Commission for Africa which is, as you'll be aware, a UN organization, has done much of this before. They already measure, for instance, financial administration in Africa and they rank (I think they've only got to 36) – they rank 1 to 36 the way countries manage their finances in Africa. This will be a big wrenching change for the Organization of African Unity, and it will breed all kinds of new tensions and jealousies and concerns, but I will certainly argue that it is *sine qua non* to moving forward with this new partnership.

We in the G8 are concentrating, as we prepare this Africa Action Plan, on a fundamental paradigm shift in the way we do business in Africa, which is very controversial. I'll outline it for you. In addition, we're concentrating on five main sector areas for particular attention. The paradigm shift is selectivity. I began my professional life teaching in Africa and my first job in the government was with our aid agency which was then called the External Aid Office, now CIDA. Even today within CIDA, the debate I'm going to out-line to you, the essence of that controversy, was present then, is present now. Put very, very grossly there is a dynamic tension in CIDA between the missionaries on the one hand and the pragmatists on the other. The first includes the people who believe that the job of aid, that the job of development, that the job of the West, that the con-science and the resources of the West ought to be devoted to the poorest of the poor, ought to be devoted to alleviat-ing, relieving the suffering of those who most need that assistance. I would argue that in the main that has gov-erned the administration of Canada's aid effort over the past 40 years – and it hasn't worked. It is a nice thing to do. It's a decent thing to do. But as I wander around this country, and I've done an awful lot of it over the past month, people ask me continually the same question. They say, "I would be willing to be more generous vis-à-vis Africa and vis-à-vis aid generally if you could show me that it works. Show me the country today in Africa that is better off than when we started 40 years ago."

There are two. They both sit on a large pile of diamonds. Aside from that, answering that question is very difficult and there are lots of reasons why it's difficult, population being the first one. Massive population explosion in Africa has outstripped our efforts to deal with the fundamental problems of development in the continent, but of course that's not all. The bottom line is that virtually every fundamental trend line, every indicator with regard to life in Africa is trending downwards at the moment, and I am quite convinced that if we continue to do the same as we've been doing, we will not change the direction of those trend lines despite those significant additional billions I have mentioned. I would go even further – if we did much better, if we had met that Pearsonian goal from 1969 and we'd all met the .7, I am still not sure that we would significantly impact those trend lines. In the NEPAD, the African leaders understand that in order to achieve what the buzzwords call 'sustainable development', in order to create growth in the area of 7 per cent that will allow those lines to shift, Africa needs investment. It needs a great deal of Official Development Assistance. It needs a lot more than we're now providing but it also needs investment. It needs jobs. It needs commercial activity. It needs to engage in the multilateral trading system, the multilateral financial system; yes, indeed it needs to become part of our globalized system. In this discussion we're having about communities and globalization, I think I should point out what the first paragraph of NEPAD says. In effect, if I can use the New York vernacular (and I spent 10 years living in New York) what the first paragraph of NEPAD says is: "Globalization, we should be so lucky."

There is no globalization in Africa. Africa is marginalized utterly and completely from a globalized system. They say it's all very nice for you guys to be able to pick and choose or at least attempt to pick and choose among what you like and dislike about globalization and its process, to comment on its ills and its failings and its vicissitudes but we don't have that option. We don't have any globalization in Africa. We're not part of the system. So the first element, the fundamental paradigm shift in the approach that we're taking is selectivity, that is, that we will form a partnership with Africa, all 53 countries of Africa, with each of the 800 million people in Africa, and we will worry about the fundamental issues of their lives particularly, say, as they are impacted by the challenge of the millennium goals.

And you'll recall in September 2000, we all signed on to a whole bunch of brave promises that I hope very much we will be held account to. We have promised to reduce the number of people who will go to bed hungry each night and that means by taking 400 million people off the hunger rolls. We said that we will achieve universal primary education by 2015 and Stephen talked to you about how far short we are falling from that goal in Africa today, particularly with regard to girls but also in all three levels of education. Africa is the only area in the world where enrolment in all forms of education is declining particularly among women and girls. We will have this partnership with Africans with respect to health and we spent a lot of time today talking about AIDS and malaria and tuberculosis and a hundred diseases that a very few of you in this room have ever heard of, and you'll be aware of the 90-10 paradigm: 90 per cent of the world's medical research efforts are spent on 10 per cent of the world's maladies. So we will do all those things. Gender, equality, education, health, people fleeing from floods and volcanoes, from wars which continue to beset Africa, indeed impact on one African in five. So we'll do those human things. But we will migrate our development assistance and we will devote a significant portion of those new monies I talked to you about to those countries that demonstrate that they are individually prepared to live up to the NEPAD premises. That is, those countries that are prepared to accept the challenge that they have set for themselves and to provide adequate governance and adequate trust to their own people.

This is significant. Canada at the moment delivers a little over half of the development assistance to Africa that is provided by Denmark, Denmark with a population the size of Toronto. Denmark provides it to 9 countries in Africa and we provide it to 48. We can't do that anymore. It simply doesn't work, and I think Stephen suggested that most countries in the G8 follow our pattern. Instead, what we've got to do is to stop constantly reinforcing and rewarding failure which we have done again and again over time. We have simply suspended disbelief. We instead have to start rewarding success and creating examples In the first instance for other Africans to follow, best practices to demonstrate, to defeat Afro-pessimism in Africa. To convince Africans that it can work, and yes, not incidentally our own taxpayers, that it can work.

Getting to the very specific issues, and briefly, we're going to concentrate specifically on peace and security. I mentioned that if we don't deal with peace and security, we're not going to deal with the most fundamental issues that impact Africans. Secondly we're going to deal with governance. Governance in all its parts described as widely as you can, political governance, economic, financial, fiscal governance, administrative governance and judicial governance – the way countries manage themselves – and to try to make that better.

Thirdly we're going to deal with knowledge and

education. Knowledge is a little larger, knowledge in health, knowledge being a little bit more than education. We're going to talk about distance learning and we're going to talk about distance health and we're going to talk about bridging the digital divide and hoping that we can help Africans skip a few of the generations of mistakes that we have made in that regard. We're going to talk, of course, in that context also, about achieving our millenium goals of universal primary education in Africa and that within the next 13 or 14 years. On the health side, Stephen has spoken as only Stephen can speak about the AIDS pandemic and the enormous challenges it represents. Stephen, correct me, I think that within five years the number of AIDS orphans in Africa will be the equivalent of half the population of Canada and these in circumstances where there are, of course, extremely limited facilities to deal with them. There are a number of countries in Central and South Africa whose GDPs will be reduced by 40% over the next few years as a result of the ravages of AIDS. There are many, many more statistics, but I haven't time to tell them all to you.

So in addition to knowledge and health, we will deal with trade and investment. Africa, with almost 12 per cent of the world's population, accounts for 1.6 per cent of the world's trade, and falling. Stephen spoke to some of the reasons why that is the case. He talked about the enormous agricultural subsidies provided by countries, principally in the G8 and the EU, a level of subsidy that is equivalent to Africa's GDP. The principal exports Africa has are agricultural exports, and how can they possibly compete in such an environment? Trade: Canada has the highest restrictions to trade from the least developed countries in all the G8 right now. Almost 60 per cent of imports from the Third World, that is, the 48 poorest countries in the world, encounter a tariff or a quota coming into this country and Mr. Chrétien has committed to changing that now.

Investment is vital, is key; and what we're trying to do is help countries in Africa through the establishment of an enhanced partnership, by migrating development assistance towards the countries that have demonstrated that they can live up to that NEPAD premise, to try to help them to become places where investors will invest. In other words, if you were the CEO of a Canadian corporation and you went to your board and said, "I've got a good idea; let's invest 800 million dollars in X country in Africa," what would it take to get you not fired? What would it take for you to be able to demonstrate due diligence with respect to that investment? What would you have to be able to tell your board about the circumstances that pertained in that country that would convince them that it's worth risking your shareholders' money to do that? And obviously, and I'm sure that Naomi would point this out if I didn't, obviously that has to be intelligent, humane and reasonable investment and should correspond to all the existing codes of conduct and guidelines that apply in the OECD and very particularly here in Canada and probably then some.

Finally, agriculture and water. The proportion of collective aid that goes to agriculture has fallen over the last 10 years from 26 per cent to under 7 per cent today. Finally, water. One African in two has no access to clean water. Women in Africa spend 25 per cent of their time carrying water, mostly dirty, to nourish their families, and in most cases to make them sick.

So those are the five areas that we will concentrate on. Stephen made a passing reference to debt and what we are or are not doing about it. The HIPC Initiative was indeed a G8 initiative begun four years ago at the Summit in Cologne. It ain't nothing, Stephen. It has written off two thirds of the debt of 22 African countries, eliminating 40 billion dollars worth of debt. It may not be enough, but it is a good start.

Now I must stop. but I wanted to give you an idea

of what that Africa plan was all about. Needless to say, I'd
be happy to take your questions.

Naomi Klein[1]

There are a lot of concrete and specific criticisms of the G8, and here in Calgary there are a lot of people with axes to grind: you are going to be hearing about everything from Plan Columbia to the Middle East. But there is something deeper underlying all of the critiques, particularly from young activists. It is really almost an emotional feeling that I think we need to confront; an emotional feeling that when the leaders of the eight richest countries in the world get together, nothing good will come of it. Anyone who hopes to lead in future has to come to terms with where that profound cynicism is coming from.

I think a lot of the cynicism comes from the perception that we all agree. I have found this over and over again in debates about globalization: you will have people from all sides getting together and basically agreeing that everything is wrong and that we need to fix everything and it is all going to happen really, really soon. I think if there were more debate and more honest disagreement, more ideological disagreement, there would be less cynicism, frankly.

There is a gap – and it isn't just the gap between rich and poor – it is the gap between what is said and what is done, that is driving people to the streets.

I find this rebranding of the Summit as a kind of "retreat" interesting. In Kananaskis it is almost as if Roots has taken over: "We're going to have a G8 Summit, but it's going to be like camp." It is all very woodsy and Canadian. It is true that I did write a book about branding, and I know

---

[1] This chapter is prepared, with minor editing, from an audio recording of the Symposium proceedings.

it is not what I am supposed to be talking about here today, but it does seem to me that it is an incredible branding opportunity for Roots. (You know Roots did the leather jackets for the APEC Summit. They were kind of embarrassed about it after Suharto... Nobody wants to talk about that...) But Kananaskis is a branding opportunity, and as something of a branding expert, I would like to propose a new slogan, an advertising slogan for the G8: "Rules: We make 'em. We break 'em." And we could have this on the backs of leather jackets and those horrible hats, berets.

Ambassador Fowler talked about the need for these meetings to bring order to the world. But I think it is the order that people don't like. I think the order isn't working. And it has to do with the incredible sense of double standards that come out of organizations like the G8. And I am going to come back to that, to the "We make 'em. We break 'em" motto.

But if I could just build on [Stephen Lewis'] incredible speech, I think that many of us here were extremely moved and felt...maybe like joining the protests? Anyone? Anyone? I don't know if everyone here is ready for that, but I would ask you to bottle that feeling and think about it when you hear young activists in Calgary talk about how they can't get a place to have their meetings; to have their convergence spaces; to put up tents; to express dissent – because there is plenty of dissent to express. And we need dissent. And think about [that feeling] if you see those young activists getting beaten, and tear-gassed.

Activists were getting treated like terrorists *before* September 11th. I respect that you were up against a new world order after September the 11th, but the reason why it rings hollow for a lot of activists is because this crackdown started before September 11th. Anyone who was at APEC '97 can tell you that. And in Genoa *before* September 11th a young activist named Carlos Giuliani was shot dead. And at a school, at midnight, while people were sleeping, the activist convergence space was raided by the police, and they were beaten bloody and dozens were hospitalized.

I'm not an Africa expert, but I have to say that the dynamic of talking about Africa just in terms of aid and trade and of bemoaning political corruption, rings a little hollow to me. And it rings especially hollow to me here in Calgary because I keep thinking about Talisman, and the fact that we have more than just charity and good will at stake here. This is very much related to that other goal of the G8, which is growth. Because the quest for growth and short-term profits all over the world has often worked in ways diametrically opposed to human rights. And we owe, not just out of the goodness of our hearts, we owe not just aid but *reparations*; reparations for what we've taken, reparations for slavery, reparations for faulty policies. It is not charity. There are many ideas coming out of the developing world about alternatives, and those alternatives have to do with debt cancellation, with slavery reparations, with opposition to privatization. There is a huge amount of disagreement in Africa from social movements over the NEPAD plan, because one of the reasons why people at the G8 are so excited about it is that it puts forward more public-private partnerships as the solution to Africa's problem. That is, it creates more opportunity for growth, for *our* companies to invest in water, to invest in transportation.

During the anti-racism conference in Durban in August, the headlines were hogged by debate about the Middle East. But alongside that debate, there was a kind of consensus that emerged out of Durban, which was that you can't talk about racism without talking about privatization. There was a general strike that took place in South Africa, timed with the anti-racism conference, to talk about economic apartheid that was being enforced through precisely these types of privatization programs that are putting water and electricity out of the hands of millions.

I feel like it is important to talk about good intentions, but particularly when we are talking about the G8, we need to talk about power. Power is the "elephant at the table." Nobody wants to talk about power, eh? But power is there. And power is what the G8 is about, and power is why people are going to be in the streets. There is a profound feeling that what is going on is about a *consolidation* of power, often illegitimate power.

I like the framing of this conference, "Globalization and Community Values." But I want to change it a little bit because I never know what "community values" mean...I think what we mean by community values is what is valuable to communities; how do we decide [what's valuable], and are we able to act on it, most importantly. What is happening in the movements that are often called 'anti-globalization' is that there is an interception going on – direct action – because there is such a gulf between the needs of communities, basic needs, and what globalization is delivering. And into this gap we are seeing things like, in South Africa, the Soweto Electricity Crisis Committee, where unemployed electricians are reconnecting their neighbours' electricity, after it gets cut off.   By the thousands. Reconnecting their water.

I just came back from Argentina. I was in Buenos Aires for five weeks. And I saw an incredibly disturbing example of this [interception] a couple of days before we left. As you know, Argentina's a little bit like Canada in the sense that it is very rich in natural resources, a very large country, not such a big population. One of their largest exports is beef. And in Argentina right now, as they continue to produce huge amounts of food for export, people are starving and 50% of the population live below the poverty line.   We've seen images of people looting supermarkets and so on.   But something happened before I left which was somehow even more symbolic. A huge truck carrying the live cattle for export jackknifed on the road between Rosario and Buenos Aires. The cattle went free, they were roaming around on the road, and these kids – twelve, thirteen years old, from nearby shantytowns – saw that these cows were free, these cows that were about to be exported, and they swarmed them and they slaughtered them on the road. The images on the news were of kids running away with sides of cattle. They were "interrupting the trade flows"...This has happened in India with shipments of grain being intercepted – grain for export – because people are so hungry.

There is this incredible crisis of legitimacy going on. It is a global crisis. It is why there are protests outside of G8 meetings, WTO meetings, APEC meetings; but somehow it is accelerated, it is in fast-forward in Argentina. And it is affecting absolutely every single institution, simultaneously. The banks, for instance, have done something interesting: they have broken rule number one of capitalism. I mean, Rule Number One of Capitalism – and this is why I say that the slogan of the G8 should be "We make the rules. We break the rules", because they don't even respect their own rules, not just on agricultural subsidies or on drug patents, but on the most basic capitalist principle of all – respect for private property. Banks like Citibank and Scotiabank have taken their money out of the country at the same time as people in Argentina don't have access to their life savings, and are locked out of [the banks], watching their life savings devalue, cut in half, every day.

You have a total crisis of accountability with relation to the courts who have been complicit in all forms of corruption. And of course you have an absolute crisis of accountability, of credibility, of faith with politicians. In fact there is really only one politician in the whole country who feels he can walk down the street and go to a protest or go to a neighbourhood meeting. And he's a guy who has everybody's respect because he gave up his pension and started selling books – a guy named Louis Samora. This country went through four presidents in two weeks in

December. And the slogan on the streets is "que se vayan todos" – everybody out. Which is kind of a sweeping demand. You hear this slogan chanted not just outside government offices at every level – federal or municipal – but also outside the banks, outside the courts. It is a crisis in representative democracy. There's a sense that you can't trust powerful people with anything, because they'll steal it, whether it is your vote or your money. And of course the IMF is the ultimate example of the rupture between what is valuable to communities – little things like food, housing – and what we call globalization, particularly because the conditions that the IMF, even in the midst of this crisis, are placing on the possibility of new loans, involves further cuts to the public sector. It involves, for instance, eliminating the provincial currencies, which are coupons that are being printed because there is no money. And if they do this, then it means the entire public sector, including the police, simply won't get paid. You can see why the government has been a little bit reluctant: they've had enough problems on their hands without not paying the entire public sector.

I find the debate about globalization difficult because I don't know what globalization means. In fact the more I learn about it, the less I know what it means. It is not a new phenomenon: Canada was founded in an act of globalization and free trade. I like to redefine globalization as a belief that has been globalized, and that belief is that what's good for business, will be good for all of us, eventually. And often, because that is not on its own the most popular idea, [globalization] is often bundled with things like air travel, the internet, internationalism, so that it seems more palatable. It seems like opposing gravity – you must be nuts! It takes on an air of inevitability when we bundle it. It is helpful to unbundle [globalization], and talk about the sets of polices that are actually in dispute.

The reason why I went [to Argentina], is because Argentina was held up as the kind of the jewel of Latin

America. It was the model child of the IMF and the World Bank, it did everything right and believed in this core ideology that what is good for business, what is good for investors, will be good for everyone, eventually; that the role of government is essentially to act as a lubricant for trade and investment, and to set the conditions, the optimum conditions, for that trade and for that investment. Which involves cutting taxes; which involves creating opportunities for investment through privatization; opportunities for growth; and basically getting out of the way, as much as possible, and taking a payoff along the way. What has clearly happened in Argentina is the opposite. First, it started off being bad for some, then it was bad for many, and then it was bad for everyone, including business.

You have a country with layers upon layers of social exclusion...The birth of the movements that we saw, the 'cacerolazo', the people banging pots and pans that eventually overthrew the De la Rua government in December, comes from the 'piquetero' movement, which is an interesting phenomenon. It is unions of unemployed workers. It is a way in which the labour movement in Argentina has found – and it comes from the workers themselves – to deal with the phenomenon of being discarded from the global economy.   Pierre Pettigrew once said that the difference between the new economy and the old economy is that in the old economy you had the phenomenon of the exploited, and in the new economy you have the phenomenon of the excluded (i.e. people who have just been told their services are no longer needed, that they are off the economic map). By its very nature, it is difficult to organize people who have been discarded, because they don't have factories to shut down, because they don't have services to withdraw. And one of the ways in which you respond to being excluded is you start moving.   Then you don't even necessarily have communities to organize because communities of excluded people are mobile communities. The piquetero phenomenon is one of the ways people are finding to respond to the phenomenon of exclusion, of mass exclusion.

It started with the privatization of the national oil company, which used to employ 58,000 people and now employs, I think, around 5,000 people, and displaced whole communities. The piqueteros thought, "Okay, well, we can't have a picket in the traditional sense 'cause we don't have jobs. We're not going to block people from getting *into* the refinery, but what we can do is block the roads to keep the oil from getting *out*." And these 'piquetes', these roadblocks have become the bane of every successive government's existence in Argentina because they aren't just a one-off, day-long picket. They often last for as long as a month. They become sort of tent cities; whole communities move into the streets and are finding new levers.

The middle class in Argentina before the current crisis really hated the piquetero movement; they thought of them as terrorists, much like protestors are treated in Canada, at the moment. They were a terrible inconvenience. They would shout out of their cars "get a job," and "who are these people," and "they're jeopardizing the country, they must just be lazy" and so on. There was a lot of racism in the responses to the piqueteros. Now, what has happened is that this process of exclusion, of discarding huge groups of people, has reached deep into the middle class in Buenos Aires. And that has led to a reconciliation between the piquetero movement, which is largely rural and suburban, to the centre of the 'Paris' of Latin America, Buenos Aires. There are these meetings, neighbourhood assemblies every night in the city, it is almost like the country is in group therapy. People get together and they talk about how they used to see one another, and how they used to disparage each other. Now the middle class protestors have the 'cacerolazos', which are the people banging their casseroles. (We saw some of that in British

Columbia recently, against the Campbell government... that's another form of globalization.) The slogan now is, "Piqueteros and cacerolazos, the struggle is one." How do you create one country instead of two? Well before this crisis, there was kind of a truism that in countries like Argentina and Brazil there were actually two countries; and so the question is, "How do you create one?"

The exclusion has now reached the country as a whole, we are now seeing Argentina just written off. At conferences like Monterrey, Bush stands up and says he's not going to be sending any more money to Argentina until they get their house in order, and they are tired of throwing money to corrupt regimes; and he says this *while* the Enron debacle is going on. The irony was not lost in Argentina, I can tell you. The whole country has, sort of, 'disappeared'; and partly because it isn't strategic at the moment, from a military point of view, in the war against terrorism. But the phenomenon of being 'disappeared' is a very powerful concept in Argentina. During the military coup, 30,000 people disappeared; they don't say that [the people] were killed because the bodies, in most cases, were never found, and the government never admitted that it actually happened. They are still called "the disappeared." I met somebody in Argentina who said to me, "You know, in Argentina first the people disappeared, then the money, and then the country."

It is easy, I think, to shake our heads and say, "well, that's there and that's different." But I had a feeling that we were seeing *our* future, that we were seeing a process, our process, in fast-forward and that *because* it was happening in fast-forward people were reacting. Whereas we are experiencing this in slow-motion, so we don't have that instant reaction. It is like the old story about the toad, when it's dropped in boiling water it knows to jump out.

I know that Ambassador Fowler has a difficult job. I thought it was interesting that he talked about counting the days, not to the start of the Summit, but to the end. I would too, if I were him. But we do have our own crisis of faith here; it is not just Argentina. I'm sure that as you cross the country consulting with NGOs, with activists of different kinds, I'm sure that you've encountered this crisis of faith that I'm talking about: where there is some kind of social contract that has been broken, that brings people to the table in good faith, to think that maybe they could work something out with their elected representatives. I want to try to shed some light on this because I think, particularly when you're meeting with young activists, you are dealing with a generation of young people who have never seen the government do anything particularly positive. Who have never been part of a process of inventing something new and ambitious and exciting – a health care program – or have never seen any of the commitments, a real sense of causality between politicians standing up on a podium saying, "We have to deal with this crisis," and it actually happening. Look at our incredible failure to deal with homelessness in Canada. Look at the number of reports that have been produced that all agree it is a national crisis, and yet it grows every year. This is where that sense of "nothing good can come of this" comes from, I think.

And it also comes from the experience of criminalization of dissent. I still find it shocking (and I can't believe that my politicians don't) that when you meet eighteen-year old university activists here in Calgary, they will take it absolutely for granted that if they go to a protest, they should take a bandana soaked in vinegar. Because they think that when you go and express dissent, you get gassed. That's what they think. And they don't think that hypothetically; they think this because it has happened to them, many times.

After APEC '97 there was a process, an investigation...I remember after APEC we were shocked at the treatment of those young protestors. I'm still disturbed by how desensitized we've become to it. But after APEC, when we saw the footage of Sergeant Pepper saying, "Get out of the road!" and then immediately spraying all those students from UBC, there was a sense of "How could this happen?" This was un-Canadian. And there was an investigation, there was a process; and a lot of the activists took part in the investigation that eventually led to the Hughes Report. I think that they can be forgiven for asking once again, "Where is this causality? When you do engage, when you do sit at tables, when you do negotiate, even when you come to agreements, what does that lead to?"

I don't envy you having to be up against this well-earned cynicism. But there is a generation of activists who have been treated as enemies of the state for daring to express dissent. Let's remember that Kananaskis was not chosen because there should be some sort of spa-like atmosphere for G8 meetings. It was chosen to get away from the protests. It was chosen after Genoa, it was chosen before September 11th, and it was seen as a slap in the face to this movement; part of a larger pattern, of the WTO meeting in Qatar, for instance.

[This movement] is not against trade; it is against the trade-offs. It is against all the trade-offs that are being asked of every country – not just Africa – to make ourselves trade-friendly, investment-friendly. We saw three million people in the streets of Italy protesting against a new law, a new workplace casualization law. In Ontario, it is focused on cuts to health care and education, on homelessness, on safe water. In Brazil, much of it is focused on long delayed promises of land reform. As I said, in South Africa it focused on privatization of water and electricity. These are the trade-offs. This is why, often, when you get into debates about globalization, the defense is growth: "growth is good." If you can show that trade is leading to growth, then you've basically won the argument. This is how Mulroney defends the record of NAFTA and the free trade agreement; he says, "Look, 43% of our GDP is now exports. Look at the amount of money that's been made." And that is exactly the point; he just doesn't get that that is exactly why people are in the streets. They are in the streets because there has been a huge amount of growth of profits, and nothing has been built with it. And that was during a period of incredible prosperity, now we're in a period of contraction.

So that's community values: what is valuable to communities, and this gulf between globalization and what is valuable to communities.

Power. Ambassador Fowler recently said that summits aren't about ceremony or protest but that they are about ideas. I wish that that were true, but I think that the G8 Summit is about power. I think it is about consolidating it, and often abusing it. This is a three-pronged agenda: war on terrorism; growth; and NEPAD. What we're seeing is that the war on terrorism around the world is being used. I'm not saying it's not real; I believe it is real, but I also believe that it has become a kind of brand, 'the war on terrorism'. I've come back to brands. You have brand extensions where [the thinking is], "Oh, I could use this brand. I could use it on Iraq. I could use it in Colombia, I could use it – hey, I could use it in Venezula get rid of that guy Chavez. I could use it wherever." It is sort of like a multipurpose brand extension. It is just like verging, you can extend it whichever way you want. Then sometimes it gets pirated, copyrighted by Sharon. And you're like, "No, that's our brand. You can't use that brand. Give us our brand back. I'm still using that brand." Obviously, it is not a value neutral war, because there are going to be a lot of people on the streets who feel that the war on terrorism is being used against them. It is becoming a war against people, a war against dissent.

You also, fundamentally, have a crisis of faith in trickle-down economics, in growth itself. The entire discourse of "how do we create more growth?" is precisely what is being questioned. I see all kinds of alternatives, a lot of them *do* involve looking backwards and then forwards. Fundamentally, what we are seeing is a desire to reclaim the commons, reclaim the public sphere, but not just to defend it in a static way, defend unaccountable state bureaucracies, in many cases. But to think about what it actually means to have a public sphere, and what does public mean in terms of accountability and participation.

Part of the problem we face is the incredible seductive power of all-knowing systems. I feel, with regard to the war on terrorism, that we are caught between two fundamentalist approaches to the world, and I think the same was true during the Cold War. Often, history is told as wars between great all-knowing systems, imperial powers of various sorts who believed they had it all figured out. They have a set of elegant rules that they can enforce with cookie cutter uniformity around the world; whether it is state socialism, whether it is capitalism, whether it is neoliberalism on a global scale, whether it is an imperialist version of Islam.

There is something interesting about people who believe in rules so much. They become fundamentalists when they love the elegance of a system, the promise of a system. If you just create growth, then it will all trickle down, and we won't actually have to set standards because they will rise on their own and it will fit together perfectly. The problem with believing in a system like that (if you believe in it with true faith) is that, when presented with evidence that the system is not working – and this is how you tell the true zealots – they will tell you that you haven't enforced the rules strictly enough, that you need a stricter enforcement of the rules, a purer enforcement of the rules. The problem is that women's ankles are showing in Afghanistan; or the problem with Argentina (and people are saying this now) is that there are still a couple of things they haven't privatized yet. An MIT economist wrote an essay in the *Financial Times* (it was reprinted in the *National Post*) and said, "They still haven't privatized" – and the only thing he could think of was – "the ports." They have privatized absolutely everything else.

This is fundamentalist logic. Among the alternatives that are emerging is an activist alternative that is fundamentally anti-fundamentalist. Now what does that mean? It means that there isn't going to be a one-size-fits-all alternative presented on a silver platter for everyone to examine and say, "Hmm...let's see if these rules will work everywhere." It is precisely that arrogance that is being rejected. Instead, there is a kind of a renaissance in participatory models of democracy, looking for a higher-impact kind of democracy. Not the democracy of voting every four or five years, but a kind of democracy that's woven into every aspect of our lives. In Canada, and around the Summit, we are seeing an explosion of independent media. I know we have people here from Indymedia who are developing, not just alternative media, but a kind of media that allows for everyone who reads indymedia to post to Indymedia, to participate in the production. We are seeing this desire for participatory economic and resource management on Vancouver Island, with ideas for community forests, community fish lessons. These are ideas that are never taken seriously at forums like the G8. It is a desire for a deeper kind of democracy. The problem with one-size-fits-all models is that they can only deal with a few players at once. So there is a tendency to centralize power – not just internationally, but even nationally – so that you only have to deal with a few players. Genuine diversity is the enemy of these one-size-fits-all models because you can't contain it. It is like herding cats.

I'm just going to end by talking a little bit more about what is going on in Argentina. In Argentina, I believe we are seeing the first revolt against neoliberalism. It is not a revolt against one political party. It is not a revolt against one regime. It is a revolt against a system: whoever gets put forward as the next president just gets thrown out. The question is: if you can oppose that, what do you propose instead? That is where there has been a power vacuum. If you drive around Buenos Aires at night, you'll see something very interesting. I didn't know what I was seeing at first. You see clusters of people on street corners – this could not work in Canada, except maybe in the summer – you see clusters of maybe 200 or 300 people meeting on street corners, meeting in parks, meeting in the oddest and strangest places. The busiest intersection in the city has a roundabout in the middle; it is just a big piece of concrete and a monument. But on Tuesday nights between 8 and 11 there are 300 people in that little roundabout, surrounded by traffic. I thought, "What are they doing there?" And then I saw them go like this [gestures with her hand]. They're voting. They are voting.

There are 200 of these neighbourhood assemblies that have sprung up since the first president stepped down on December 20th. They come from a desire to start over. When every institution has failed, the only thing left is talking to your neighbour. People say, "This is strange. I haven't talked to my neighbour in 30 years." They are talking about not paying the external debt. They are talking about having referendums on important issues in the country. They are talking about placing their politicians under very short terms, with the ability to recall them. But they are also talking about (and *doing*) filling the gaps of the crisis: setting up community kitchens, creating trading clubs to trade goods and services, instead of using money (which nobody has). Even, in some cases, taking over factories, which has started to happen because capital has fled – there are all these empty factories and so they are taking them over. They are making clothes; they are baking bread. It is not a Marxist revolution where the workers demanded the means of production. The boss has left, and they are, like, "Well, no one's here."

These "assembleas" have their weekly meetings, and then they also meet once a week in a big park, and then they have national meetings where representatives from each of the assemblies attend. It is a very new form of participatory democracy. They are hoping it will turn into the type of participatory democracy that has taken hold in Brazil, where you have the PT (which is now leading federally in the polls) introducing something called participatory budgeting where, instead of just electing politicians and letting them run things for a few years, people are demanding the right to vote on every line item in their budget.

The last night that I was there, I noticed that there was an assemblea – one of these neighbourhood assembleas – that met on the steps of the National Congress. I went and talked to them. I said, "Why are you meeting here?" (It is as if you were to have a neighbourhood meeting at the White House.) I said, "Do you want to go *in* there? Is that what you're saying, that this is an alternative to that?" They said, "No, no. We don't want to go *in* there. We just want to keep an eye on them."

In Brazil, there is a movement of landless people – called the MST – that reclaim large pieces of unused farmland, because the land reform process in Brazil has been so negligent. They just take over the land and they start planting; the same process is going on in Thailand, but on golf courses. But they did something interesting about a month ago. They had one of their land reclamations, but they reclaimed the farm of the President of Brazil. [President] Cardoso was saying, "This is a terrible security breach." – it looked like a revolution – and "What does it mean for people with masks and pitchforks to be taking over [my] vacation home?" They said, "Well, we don't want the power. We just want the real estate."

It is a theory of power that is not interested in just

seizing power. This crisis of faith means that there are no longer many people who believe that just changing the people in power is going to make any difference. They have seen it happen. Now, they are talking about radical power dispersal.

I think I'll end there.

John Curtis

When one looks over the entire sweep of human history, from the paleolithic to neolithic period some 10,000 years ago, to the post-neolithic period 5,000 years ago when the foundations of our agricultural, urban and political systems were laid, to the scientific-industrial age from 1600 AD onward, one realizes that today most of us around the world benefit from a vast richness in terms of material wealth, ideas, technologies and experiences arising from what we generally think of as globalization. By and large, developed and developing countries as reflected in the New Partnership for Africa's Development (NEPAD) and the Monterrey Consensus of this past March agree with this overall favourable view of globalization as does the public. In most every public opinion survey that I have seen, a majority of citizens feel that "globalization has had a positive impact on our well being."

Think of the United States today, the recovery of Europe since 1945, the rise of post-war Japan, Korea, the coastal regions of China, Southern India, parts of Latin America, never mind this country including this province, the poorest on the Prairies during the first part of the last century to the richest now. This change for the better since about 1600 is the net result of globalization.

Nevertheless, there remain very serious problems in the world economy and with respect to globalization in particular: globalization appears to me to be "in the dock" on three essential counts:

• Globalization is said to be, in the words of Salman Rushdie, an attack on "the world's precious localness: the Indianness of India, the Frenchness of France."

• The system of international governance that has been put in place to "manage" globalization, including importantly, since 1995 the World Trade Organization and its linchpin the Dispute Settlement Body, is said to undermine democratic governance at the nation-state and even local levels with regard to issues ranging from socio-economic frameworks and environmental policy to water quality and zoning regulations in our cities.

• Globalization is said to have resulted in the determination of the fate of economies having been ceded to unregulated and unaccountable forces of global capital, which have pitched one economy after another into financial and economic crisis and, in extreme cases, into political and social chaos.

Also standing accused are the principal drivers of globalization – which include international trade and investment – and the socio-economic theory, which supports it, which might in shorthand be called the "Washington Consensus."

Since most of the world's ills can be shoe-horned into one or another of these charges, a defence of globalization, its drivers and the theoretical framework that supports it must involve either denial of the world's ills or finding an alternative scapegoat to take the blame. And, indeed, there have been many who have risen to the bait and offered defences of globalization along these lines, citing statistics to show that never have so many people been as well off and citing human error and policy failures to account for the failed states and crises.

This is, in my mind, how the debate on globalization has unfolded. This particular framing of the issues thus leads to the gridlock in which governments and the international institutions that they have created, especially since World War II, and public groups now find themselves. Is there another, more fruitful way, to address these issues? I think so.

Allow me to make three observations that might help take the debate down other paths.

First, although all societies are faced with rapid change, the sense of cultural diversity under threat is hard to square with the historical evidence of the survival of distinct cultures under the ever-widening scale of our governance arrangements and even under the most extremely adverse circumstances. The world has seen survival of suppressed cultures (e.g. Greek culture under centuries of Ottoman rule), of stateless cultures (Basque culture and language), of purely local cultures (ranging from the persistence of features of cities such as the distinctively different arrondissements of Paris to regional dialects and accents), and of specific elements of particular cultures under different influences (Chinese guanxi has survived the Cultural Revolution on the mainland, British rule in Hong Kong, Portuguese rule in Macau and American influence in Taiwan). In short, cultural features – which might be thought of as cultural DNA – have persisted and often thrived.

At the same time, we see the proliferation of certain elements even within very distinct societies mixed in with "traditional" elements of those societies. The combination – or better, recombination – of elements of cultural DNA from different societies does not create necessarily a new homogeneity – rather it creates novelty. A useful example is provided by one of the most widely used foods, especially on this continent – the pizza. Flat bread seasoned with olive oil and native spices was a common food of ancient Mediterranean people such as the Greeks, Romans and Egyptians. However, the pizza as we know it today originates from the old word pastas and new world tomatoes brought to Europe by the Spaniards and combined, so the story goes, by an Italian baker named Raffaele Esposito, who created a dish for the visiting Italian King Umberto and his consort, Queen Margherita, that would best represent the colours of Italy: red tomato, white mozzarella cheese and green basil. The further evolution of varieties of pizza as it was introduced into national cuisines world-wide through combination with other elements resembles specialization in nature – proliferation of types rather homogenization.

This proliferation of types is best evidenced by the flourishing of wildly different subcultures within the most media-saturated and largest in scale nation-state of the world, the United States itself.

Moreover, insofar as the emergence of mass media provided the basis for a "shared experience" that served to create a perhaps unprecedented degree of homogeneity within nations and to a lesser extent internationally a couple of decades ago, the continued proliferation of media in recent years, especially perhaps in the case of television, has fractured that powerful signal into a kaleidoscope. The era when most North American households were tuned into Ed Sullivan to see the Beatles North American debut are gone. The audience is scattered across hundreds of channels and/or tens of millions of internet websites.

It remains the case, nevertheless, that community values are unavoidably buffeted and disrupted by evolutionary change. Globalization and intense media feedback accelerate, intensify and modify the direction of normal-course generational change. The fact that the current elites – essentially greyed baby boomers – who rejected some twenty or thirty years ago the values of their own parents' generation but now are concerned, as all elites are, with preserving community values is scarcely surprising. However, the only way in which particular sets of community values can be preserved is to put them in formaldehyde. Living systems change, they often grow in size; this is simply inescapable.

Second, there are many threads in the weave that is globalization. Of these, one of the least objectionable must be trade. This is so on at least two major counts. First, for most people, and especially for those in comparatively smaller nation-states, variety of consumption – choice – depends on trade. Second, for most countries – and this again applies particularly for smaller states – trade introduces competition which reduces what we economists call producer surpluses and expands consumer surplus. Since foreign direct investment is in large measure an alternative to direct trade – especially in the case of services which must be delivered through a local establishment – the same points apply in large measure for investment as well.

Accordingly, the degree to which trade and investment have taken the brunt of the anti-globalization attack is extraordinary. Indeed, it suggests to me that the attack is essentially misguided or poorly articulated. Where then are the problematic elements of economic globalization? Here I would submit that there are three major sources of problems:

(a)   First, corporate concentration and corporate power have by casual observation and by many accounts risen during the last several decades. To some extent, it appears that governments and society more generally have been swayed by arguments such as "large size is needed to compete internationally" and allowed waves of mergers and acquisitions to occur – indeed, perhaps contemplating the emergence of "national champions", such waves of mergers and acquisitions were even encouraged. Moreover, in a context where some nations encourage the emergence of large firms, other nations may feel obliged to follow suit. Whether or not there are true economies of scale or scope to exploit (which my profession argues in theory to be the case, other things being equal) – and whether such economies dominate diseconomies of scale and scope – appears not to have been particularly well scrutinized. Certainly, the wave of debacles in the last couple of years following the merger and acquisition feeding frenzy of the late 1990s suggests that the business case for some of the alleged "synergies" was less than solid. And the positive spin that securities markets analysts put on proposed mergers may have to be reconsidered in light of the questions of conflicts of interest now being raised by securities markets regulators about analysts promoting stocks (and this would include mergers and acquisitions that typically take place at inflated stock values) which their brokerages own or which support consulting and/or merger and acquisition under-writings by their firms. In some areas there has been a dramatic lessening of competition due to corporate consolidation. So there is at least a *prima facie* suspicion that rent-seeking behaviour by many in privileged corners of our societies has been at play. The fault, in this case, would seem to me to lie more with lax anti-combines policies, not with trade liberalization as its critics suggest.

(b)   Secondly, economic development and development more generally is simply not well understood and the adoption of what might be termed neoliberal policy prescriptions – including trade liberalization – by many developing countries in the hope of emulating the East Asian economic "miracles" (Korea, Taiwan, Hong Kong and Singapore) has often led to severe disappointment. Here it appears to be the case that context matters very much. The American economist Bradford Delong lists six past "crusades" for development, all of which failed in one way or another.[1] He counts the current neoliberal crusade as the seventh and – although he identifies himself as a neoliberal – gives the current crusade little hope of success. Given the fact that none of us really knows what drives development, there might be a case for we economists being extremely cautious about providing advice with such assurance: the economy, in fact, might be more of a biological than an engineering construct. It is quite possible that, in particular cases, trade liberalization may not have been beneficial to a country and that this was known to all concerned but disregarded. For example, it is not entirely clear that countries at a low stage of industrial development – a Papua New Guinea for example – benefit particularly from the entry of foreign multinational resource firms to extract gold, oil and diamonds. Unfortunately, it is often the case that local elites cooperate with foreign firms in what is effectively the stripping of a country's patrimony. On the other hand, a great deal of solid economic research over the past decade (such as that by Sachs and Warner) has found that developing countries with open trading regimes saw six times the economic growth of their closed contemporaries in the 1970s and 1980s: the GDP of open developing economies grew at 4.5% per year, while closed economies grew at 0.7% per year.[2]

This does not undermine the case for trade; but it does require a more nuanced case for trade than would be necessary if there were no risks of negative dynamics. At

1.   DeLong writes: "...this neoliberal crusade is not the first such crusade for economic development. Since World War II there have been at least six such crusades: the "building socialism" crusade, the "financing gap" crusade, the "import substitution" crusade, the "aid for education" crusade, the "oil money recycling" crusade, and the "population boom" crusade. All of them failed to spark rapid economic development." See J. Bradford DeLong, "The Last Development Crusade" http://www.j-bradford-delong.net/TotW/Easterly_neoliberal.html.

2.   Sachs, Jeffrey and Warner, Andrew, "Economic Reform and the Process of Global Integration" (1995), Discussion Paper, Harvard Institute of Economic Research, Harvard University, Cambridge, MA

the same time, it is not helpful to public policy formulation if the public criticism – which in democratic regimes often frames the basis for policy responses – is misdirected. In this regard, trying to shut down trade and investment liberalization, as happened in the case of the Multilateral Agreement on Investment (MAI) will not by itself put a spark in anti-combines policies; although it might reduce at the margin such additional competition as liberalization might induce.

The final observation in this regard concerns the role of the WTO dispute settlement body as a quasi-global supreme court. The record here is actually not very problematic at all for those concerned about the impact on local governance. The Dispute Settlement Body (DSB) has been sensitive to local politics (even if not every decision has been warmly received by everyone) and has even tried to bend to the pressure to allow amicus briefs – note that it was the consensus-based WTO membership that vetoed this. The issue here is not the WTO but the fact that the community of nations is not itself as enlightened as many in public groups wish it to be.

Third, the major source of problems both for macroeconomic management and for trade has been excessive and – in terms of economic fundamentals – hard to explain movements in exchange rates. The so-called "non-system" of exchange rates that has prevailed since the breakdown of the Bretton Woods system in the early 1970s has arguably been much less kind to emerging markets than was the Bretton Woods system. In the wake of the Asian Crisis, a new orthodoxy emerged in favour of either "robust" fixed exchange regimes (currency boards or outright dollarization) or pure floating. As Argentina has showed with the collapse of its currency board system, it is likely that even comparatively "robust" fixed regimes can be impossible under particular conditions – such as occurred when its major trading partners Brazil and the EU devalued substantially against the U.S. dollar to which Argentina's peso was fixed. This leaves only more or less pure floating as the option for emerging markets. The trouble is, we have not seen many markets "emerge" except in the context of quasi-fixed exchange rates – Mexico may be cited as an example, although the combination of massive financial support and a period of low valuation also played a role in Mexico's comparatively good exchange market performance of recent years (i.e., it is much easier to float up from a state of under-valuation than it is to float down from a state of over-valuation). There is much in the world of financial flows that is not well understood. The volume of trading of financial assets is far greater, for example, than predicted by the efficient markets theory. The behaviour of international portfolio capital remains skittish. And the behaviour of the G3 – (the U.S.A., the European Union, and Japan) – whose central banks have no mandate to ensure external stability of financial markets – has major repercussions in the emerging markets. The problems in these areas are, as noted, as severe for trade and direct investment as they are for macroeconomic performance in general. To put the blame on trade and investment is to entirely misunderstand the root of the instabilities.

Summary

Notwithstanding the enormous economic, social, and political benefits that developments over the past century or more have brought to most of us, there are real difficulties in the nature of the evolving global economy. But putting these problems at the feet of an abstraction called "globalization" does little good. A more refined targeting is required, in my judgement. I submit that refining the argument shows that trade and direct investment are not the source of the major difficulties, nor is the WTO as the "umbrella" body charged with administering that system.

Anti-combines policy, the economics of development, and the "coherence" of international finance with trade and direct investment need to be more carefully examined, however, to make our world an even more desirable place for us, and future generations, to live, work and play in.

· V ·

THE ROLE OF EDUCATION IN SHAPING COMMUNITY VALUES

Harvey Weingarten

As many of you may know, I am a relative newcomer to both the province of Alberta and to the role of University President. It has been just over eight months since I took office as the President of the University of Calgary.

In those eight months, I have learned many things. First and foremost, I have learned that University Presidents are often called upon to speak on topics which extend well beyond their scope of expertise and understanding. As a psychology professor specializing in eating disorders, I am used to speaking on a range of related topics, engaging in discussions based on research, and trying to add informed opinion to debates. Now as the President of the University, I'm called upon to speak on topics that go far beyond my realm of expertise and that certainly test the bounds of my own standards for what counts as "informed opinion."

Today's topic is no exception. I am certainly not an expert on the role of education in shaping community values. I come with little if any research to back up my claims. I have not done the requisite literature reviews or searched the annals for expert analysis.

So what you will hear from me this morning are personal views, the views of someone who has spent much of his life in education and someone who, like many of you here today, has a profound interest in the role education can play in the community and our society.

Let me begin with the premise that education plays a role not only in shaping values; it also is shaped by the values of the people and communities it serves. It truly is a two-way street.

That reality has become even more obvious to me in the months since I've moved to Calgary.

My experience with universities and the education system comes from places like McGill and Yale. Universities steeped in tradition. Universities which, by the way, both at one time had quotas on the number of Jewish people who were allowed to attend.

Calgary is different.

One of the reasons why I accepted the position with the University of Calgary is the very fact that it is not steeped in tradition. Instead it is brash, young, energetic, and full of potential. Just like Calgary. Just like Alberta.

Like all Canadians, Albertans value tolerance and respect for diversity. They value fairness, equality, and the right to be treated with dignity and respect. The same kinds of values that are explicit in Canada's Charter of Rights and Freedoms.

But in Alberta, there also is this strong streak of independence. It's a sense that people can tackle problems head on, go their own way, swim against the tide, and succeed. As some have said, Alberta is a place of great contradictions. A place where we value entrepreneurship, personal responsibility, and getting the job done. But at the same time, Albertans are keen volunteers, generous to a fault, and quick to step into the breach whenever people need help. There is an unwavering belief that anything is possible. And as I have learned in the months since I arrived, it is a place more interested in where you are going than where you have come from.

Those values and expectations shape the education system in Calgary and certainly shape the University I work for. The University draws great strength and character from Calgary. Just as Albertans and Calgarians value entrepreneurship, independence and innovation, Calgary's learning institutions are expected to reflect those values in how they approach their mandates, the role they play in the community, and the approach they take with students. Our university is not an institution steeped in tradition. We are more interested in where we are going than where we have been. And for our students, we are more interested in where they are going, in what they can become, and what we can do to give them the skills they need to succeed.

Turning to the role of education in shaping values, I believe most would agree that education plays a critical role. Not a role in isolation from families, communities, churches and other organizations in our society, but a critical role nonetheless. As teaching and learning institutions, our schools, colleges, universities and technical institutes have a captive audience of thousands of young minds. And we have a daunting responsibility not just to teach them facts and Information, but to open doors to ideas, to shape their views, and instill values that enable them to be positive and contributing members of our society.

The role of education in shaping values begins in the first few days in school when our teachers begin to instill in children some basic expectations: listen to others, treat your fellow students with respect, don't push and shove in line or force others to do what you want, but wait your turn, help each other out, be patient, and follow the rules. It extends to universities like ours where we challenge students to explore ideas, seek knowledge and truth, respect those with differing views, and use knowledge and skills not only for personal gain but for the improvement of our society as a whole.

As Samuel Johnson said, "The supreme end of education is expert discernment in all things – the power to tell the good from the bad, the genuine from the counterfeit, and to prefer the good and the genuine from the bad and the counterfeit."

The question, then, isn't whether or not education shapes values, it is how those values are shaped, and what values are included. Both areas have been the subject of considerable debate and discussion over the history of our country and countries around the world.

From my experience, schools and post-secondary institutions – aside from those with a particular religious orientation – have shied away from the explicit teaching of values. We are uncomfortable suggesting that there is a set of absolute values which must be taught to all students. We prefer the loftier approach of presenting ideas, encouraging debate, and assuming that, as Johnson puts it, in the end, our students will prefer the good and the genuine to the bad and the counterfeit.

I would argue that, aside from the "messiness" of this approach, it has produced the right results. Canadians are known for their tolerance of ideas, their willingness to listen, and their respect for diversity. We are not quick to judge others. We do not regularly jump on bandwagons or seek to impose our views on others. Instead we are thoughtful, sometimes slow to act, more willing to weigh ideas and options than to leap blindly into the fray.

Undoubtedly, this uniquely "Canadian" way of dealing with values is frustrating to some. There are those who believe strongly that there are absolute values, clear distinctions between right and wrong, and that students should not be exposed to ideas which clearly are unacceptable or run counter to commonly held views and values. Uncomfortable as it can be, I do not believe our education system's role is to indoctrinate students or to limit the ideas they are exposed to. Instead, I believe our role is to give young people the skills and the knowledge they need to assess ideas, to sort out truth from fiction, to expose the fallacies of arguments, and to make the right choices.

This isn't to deny that there are some values that

are fundamental to our society. Certainly there are. But if, in our learning institutions, we approach them as if there were no options and opposing views are not to be tolerated, we will achieve exactly the opposite of what we intend – a narrow society with a narrow view of what we believe to be important.

In fact, so often it is by being exposed to countering views that we come to understand why it is we hold certain values to be so important. When we are confronted with acts of intolerance. When we see atrocities committed against others. When we see the needless slaughter of people for reasons we cannot understand. When we listen to others whose views seem so wrong, so diametrically opposed to what we believe. It is in those disquieting times, when our very values and ideals are put to the test, that we are challenged to step back, to re-evaluate our positions, to understand the views of others, and to re-confirm why we believe what we do.

What values then, should our education system seek to instill in Alberta's students?

In the mid 1980s, the Government of Alberta established a Task Force on Tolerance and Understanding, chaired by one of the members of the Sheldon Chumir Foundation, the Honourable Ron Ghitter.

The Task Force report concluded that, "Our public education system is committed philosophically to encourage and facilitate the pursuit of excellence and truth by students, teachers and administrators by means of curriculum and attitudes reflecting the values of tolerance, rational thinking, freedom, esteem of self and others, independence, originality and honesty."

The report also referred to the goals of education adopted in Alberta as early as 1978. Those goals certainly shed light on what Albertans expect for their students and the values we expect to underlie their education. The goals include:

·   Intellectual curiosity and a desire for lifelong learning

·   The ability to get along with people of varying backgrounds, beliefs and lifestyles without sacrificing personal ideals and values

·   A sense of community responsibility which embraces respect for law and authority, public and private property, and the rights of others

·   An appreciation for tradition and the ability to understand and respond constructively to change as it occurs in personal life and in society

·   A sense of purpose in life and ethical or spiritual values which respect the worth of the individual, justice, fair play, and fundamental rights, responsibilities, and freedoms.

The goals also talk about developing an appreciation for the role of the family, an interest in cultural and recreational pursuits, a commitment to the careful use of natural resources and preserving our environment, and the development of self-discipline, self-understanding, and a positive self-concept through realistic appraisal of one's capabilities and limitations.

I don't know about the rest of you here today, but on reading those goals, I'm struck by how they have stood the test of time. Even though the face of our institutions of learning has changed and adapted to changing circumstances, the goals ring as true today as they did close to 25 years ago.

Speaking for the University of Calgary, I believe we have a responsibility to instill in all our students respect and tolerance – for others, for ideas and opinions, for differences, for history and traditions, for uncertainty and change.

We have a responsibility to encourage a relentless pursuit – a pursuit of excellence, of knowledge, of understanding and truth.

We have an obligation in everything we do to demonstrate fairness, justice, equality, fair treatment and a clear sense of "doing what is right."

We have a responsibility to show our students that education and learning are of little value if they are not used to improve our society and our world – if they are not used to shed light on the most challenging of today's problems and to seek better solutions.

Perhaps most important, we have a responsibility to remind students that the values and freedoms we take for granted here in Canada are things that are not readily enjoyed by millions of people around the world. There are countries in the world where a Jewish person like me, the child of Eastern European immigrants, could never aspire to be a University president. These are values we must never take for granted. And these are values we must instill in future generations of Canadians.

In my installation address in October of last year, I told the story of a young woman just graduating from Medical school. She approached me at the Convocation exercises and said, "Dr. Weingarten, I just wanted to say thank you." I confessed that I did not remember the woman and was baffled by why she was thanking me. She told me she had been a student in a class I had taught several years before – a class of about 300 students, so I guess it is no wonder I didn't remember her. She said, "When I took your course I became determined that I was going to try to help people. So I applied to Medical school and here I am today."

That story is a clear reminder of the purpose of education. It is not simply to teach courses, fill desks and libraries, or award degrees and diplomas. It is to change the lives of our students and, in that way, to change the world.

Let me conclude with some words from Ron Ghitter's report on tolerance and understanding in our schools. He said, "It is essential that all our children learn why our Canadian way of life is so very special, that they respect diversity without losing sight of the humanity which we all share, and that they possess the competence and skills necessary to participate in the continuing development of our dynamic and energetic society."

I couldn't agree more. It is our responsibility to instill values in young people, to reflect what our society values most, and to develop young people whose ongoing pursuit of excellence, ideas and truth will make the world a better place.

Stuart Walker

As a lifelong teacher at American Universities, I keep asking myself, where have we gone wrong in graduating so many obsessed with greed and self-centredness and devoid of a sense of ethics necessary for a democratic society to flourish? Should our curricula have included more emphasis on the good as well as the true and the beautiful?

Harold Morowitz. Entropy and the Magic Flute.

When one thinks of the word "community" what images, thoughts or associations come to mind? They naturally tend to be varied but on the whole they tend to be positive associations. One thinks of volunteers helping out in community campaigns, town meetings, democracy and personal responsibility. Others will talk of living in small towns or neighbourhoods where there is cooperation and a high quality of life. People think of commitment, team spirit and fun – of education where they are involved in their children's lives and experiences, and of helping to maintain a clean environment.

The word "community" has old roots, going back to the Indo-European base *mei* meaning "change" or "exchange". Apparently this joined with another root, *kom* meaning "with" to produce the word kommein: shared by all.

Therefore, what we are considering is the impact of

education in determining, fostering and propagating values which are shared by all. It is important to realize that a community will differ in size and composition in different circumstances. However, at the centre of most communities is an educational institution of some sort. This may be a child care centre, elementary schools, high schools, universities and numerous other learning communities, formal and informal. Indeed, in Victoria, British Columbia, schools are being clustered together into "families", or communities, of schools which consist of elementary schools feeding into a smaller number of middle schools (a renewed concept) which then feed into one high school.

In the past, powerful forces within society have determined both educational content and process. Boyd and Cooper (1994) argue that, broadly speaking, society has gone through several stages, each with its own priorities, and each with a different task for schools:

In the "Agricultural Era" the purpose of education was to promote common culture and citizenship. The metaphor of the schools was a Community Centre serving political and civic needs. Students were neophytes needing to be socialized and teachers were engaged in what was seen as a sacred profession. This call to service is dramatized in films such "Goodbye, Mr Chips" and novels such as "Tom Brown's Schooldays".

The "Industrial Era" saw a change, particularly in countries where immigration was a central part of the policy of populating countries like Canada, the United States and Australia. Education was used to "naturalize" the immigrant and prepare workers for the industrial society. The school could be viewed as a factory serving economic needs with an assembly line production mentality. Students were raw materials; products to be standardized, inspected and controlled while teachers were the supervisors, administrators and managers. In the "Social Era" of the 1960s and 70s (and perhaps the 80s) the purpose of education was one of social reform to meet the needs of all children. The metaphor for the school now is a hospital caring for victims of social injustice, meeting cultural and social needs. The students are seen as the vulnerable, with a need to be protected, while teachers are the caretakers. District staff diagnose and prescribe while administrators are the chiefs of staff.

The advent of environmentalism and the internet has produced the "Electronic/Ecological Era" where the aim is to teach individuals how to learn and love lifelong learning. The school now becomes a collaborative learning community engaged with the larger world. Students are explorers and constructors of knowledge, both producers and consumers. Teachers act as facilitators and coaches while administrators act as resource brokers and links to the community (Boyd and Cooper, 1994).

Within the last several decades, increased parent and student participation resulted in an increase in educational options. More and more, schools are responsive to the demands of those to whom they provide services. One of the ways schools have done this is to more clearly articulate the values that guide their policies and procedures, in order to attract like-minded students and their parents. Given the diversity of educational choices that we have in our society today it seems clear that different communities have different values, or perhaps articulate similar values in different ways. The values which differentiate schools, and the ways in which these values are articulated, will become one of the defining features of education and the communities in which schools exist.

One could characterize this era as the "Systems/Spiritual Era". The idea of "systems" recognizes that schools are now hubs of interconnected networks, the most useful metaphor being that of a living system. Here, students are creators of meaning, and teachers the co-creators. 'Spiritual' here does not refer to religion, but might be more accurately understood as referring to values that go beyond the mere physical sustenance. Increasingly, the foundational role of values is being recognized in many school curricula.

Thus, the purpose of education has been, and to some extent will always continue to be, to reflect societies' priorities and help fulfill their goals. However, the accountability and transparency demanded by increasingly involved interest groups, such as parents and students, as well as the recognition of the unifying force of an agreed upon set of values, has recently given schools the opportunity to play a more equal role in the development of those priorities and goals.

The need for reaffirming and instilling our collective values in an increasingly complex world brought on widespread reflection and introspection toward the end of the 20th century. Additionally, social problems and student attitudes are driving an awakening of the conviction that the institution of schools, along with the family, places of worship, and community, has an important role to play in helping students develop ethical behavior and core values.

Character education holds that certain core values form the basis of "good character," – the attitudes, beliefs, and behaviors that the school wants from, and is committed to teach to, its children. It means the school stands for these values and that it actively promotes them in school and the community. Rushworth Kidder, of the Institute of Global Ethics, suggests that there is indeed a core set of values which are universal. Indeed he uses the analogy of the school to ask us what those values are. He asks us to visualize the door that our children walk through each day into school. What words do we want inscribed into stone to remind our students what the core values are that validate this community?

Given the diversity of educational choices that we have in our society today it could be suggested that different communities have different core values or perhaps articulate the same set of core values in different ways. Different religious schools have a particular ethos while other educational methods identify other schools. Even within the state education systems parents are being given increased opportunity to choose which school their child attends rather than being mandated to attend a certain school based upon geographic location. The core values which differentiate schools, and the ways in which these values are articulated, will become one of the defining features of education and the communities in which schools exist.

Pearson College is a unique learning community. It brings together 200 students from over 80 countries for two years to study the International Baccalaureate curriculum. All students attend the College on a full scholarship and are selected in their countries by National Committees on merit alone. Merit can broadly be defined as having a strong academic record (however, this should not be the primary criterion), a strong interest in internationalism and a demonstrated commitment to community service. The mission of the College (and the United World Colleges) is through international education, shared experience and community service; the United World Colleges encourage young people to become responsible citizens, politically and environmentally aware, committed to the ideals of peace, justice, understanding and cooperation, and to the implementation of these ideals through action and personal example.

In 2000, students and faculty at Pearson College began a dialogue concerning moral values which led to the formation of the Pearson Centre for Global Values, now known as the Pearson Ethics Initiative (PEI).

The shift in emphasis from values to ethics reflected the intention of engaging in something other than the global promotion of a specific set of values. Rather, the vision was for a series of initiatives focused on the moral aspects of life at Pearson, within the UWC movement, in our local community and around the world.

While these initiatives have taken a variety of forms, they have all conformed to the definition of ethics used by PEI, "the practice of asking questions about how people should live, and how they ought to act, and supporting the answers to these questions with reasons."

As asking questions about how people should live and act requires asking what kind of lives they want, and what kind of people they want to be, this definition necessarily includes the activity of identifying values. Comparing and justifying answers to such questions requires critical thinking and reasoning. These two activities are largely intellectual – they require a variety of critical thinking skills, and are best achieved through dialogue. But having answers to such questions creates both an obligation and direction for action.

Aristotle did not say "happiness is the reward of values", but "happiness is the reward of virtue." There is a big difference. Values education is not enough to encourage a child to lead a productive and happy life. Neither sentiment nor ideals nor even conviction in the deepest truth is sufficient. Values alone cannot bring happiness. Good intentions have never been enough. In addition, the systematic development of good habits is needed. Otherwise we are condemned to a life where we aspire to do good but are constantly frustrated. Values remain in the mind, no matter how sincere the conviction. But we are beings of body and soul, of matter and spirit and therefore we need a psychology that recognizes this. Virtues make us better people; in some way they change who we actually are. Virtues are flesh and blood habits of action, habits that are part of us. Values are milky ideals, bereft of any power until they are translated into action.

In Victoria there are currently changes occurring in

the structure of educational delivery in the community. There are new middle schools being created in between the elementary school level and high school. This has proven to be a divisive debate within small communities. The Victoria School Board #61 has asked PEI to moderate discussions in communities where these new schools will be established. In essence the aim is to work with particular communities to develop a discourse to determine what the core values are which that community believes should underpin the operation of the new school. It is my belief that rather than simply being words students walk under each day as they enter school, values must form the foundation of the institution. They must be part of the fabric of everyday life and provide the basis for a common discourse in the community of a school to have real meaning. Ethics and values should, therefore, become the filter for everyday experiences in educational institutions.

The social, ethical, and emotional development of young people is as important as their academic development. It is critical to create school environments that simultaneously foster character development and promote learning.

In the United States, research shows that elementary schools that become more caring, responsive places better foster children's ethical and social development. In Japanese elementary schools, the three Rs are underlined by the three Cs – connection, character, and content. When school is a place of deep human connections, students are motivated to be the best people they can be. When values like cooperation, responsibility, and friendship are taken seriously, school becomes a better place for learning. When content is pared down so that students have time to see the meaning and importance in what they learn, students are more likely to develop a stronger connection to schools (Carter, 1999).

So, to be effective, values education requires a

comprehensive definition including the cognitive side of learning (thinking), the emotional side of learning (feelings), and learning manifested as character-in-action (behaviour).

Schools and teachers therefore need to understand that the moral framework for their mission, policies, curriculum, pedagogy, standards, assessments, discipline, and the conduct of daily school life must be comprehensive.

If one accepts the metaphor of the school as a living system, one can also then apply the principles of living systems to the school and in turn to the communities in which the school exists. The institution can never be separate from community pressure or influence. In fact, the school and the education that it espouses have the capacity to fundamentally change a community. The principles underpin the future viability of our communities.

Interdependence – All members of a community are interconnected in a web of relationships in which all processes are reciprocal. The success of the community depends upon the success of its individual members, and the success of each member depends on the success of the community as a whole.

Sustainability – The long-term survival of a community depends on a limited material resource base, shared talents and ideas, and sustained purpose.

Ecological Cycles – The interdependencies among the members of a community involve the exchange of energy and information in continual cycles.

Energy Flow – Human energy, experiences, and beliefs, transformed into meaning and knowledge, drive purposeful communities.

Partnership – All members of a community are engaged in a reciprocal interplay of competition and cooperation, involving countless forms of partnership.

Flexibility – Flexible communities give open rein to fluctuations and surprises from which they derive innovations and change.

Diversity – The stability of a community depends crucially on the degree of complexity of its network of relationships; in other words, on the diversity of the ecosystem.

Co-evolution – Most members of a community co-evolve through an interplay of creation and mutual adaptation. The creative reaching out into novelty is a fundamental property of life, manifest also in the processes of life and learning (Boyd and Cooper).

These principles provide the basis for understanding the benefit of including values as an integral part of an education. A healthy community, like a healthy living system, is based upon open communication and a shared understanding or common purpose which is based on a shared set of core values. Moreover it gives education the central role in helping shape the communities in which we live. However, talking about and understanding values, moral dilemmas or ethical situations is not enough. Rushworth Kidder, in a new book in preparation, argues that "moral courage" is required to take action in ethical dilemmas. He defines moral courage as "the quality of mind and spirit giving one the conviction to face up to ethical dilemmas and moral wrong-doing firmly and confidently, without flinching in the face of clear and present risk" (Kidder 2002).

When considering what role education has in creating community values, it is critical to understand what values the particular community shares. One of the most important legacies of public education has been to provide students with the critical capacities, the knowledge and the values to become active citizens striving to realize a vibrant democratic society.

Schools are an important indicator of the well-being of our democratic society. They remind us of the values that must be passed on to young people in order for them to think critically; to participate in decisions that affect their lives; and to transform inequities that close down democratic social relationships.

Education must be built on a strong foundation of relationships, human experience, and connectedness. Effective leaders will be expected to put words to the formless longings and deeply felt needs of others. They create communities out of words. At Pearson College one of the maxims used is "educating leaders for a changing world." Leadership is ultimately about virtues, strengths of character, and habits of right action. The Hitlers and Stalins, for all their capacity to get things done, were not leaders in the true sense of the word. Readiness to act in a manner that is ill-considered is not virtue, but its opposite, vice. To be a man or woman of action is not enough. Our society needs men and women of virtue.

Educators who work in our schools represent the conscience of a society because they shape the conditions under which future generations learn about themselves and their relationships with others and the world. The potential of education to have powerful impact on the communities in which we live is not new. The notion of values education has regained credence after a time when the focus might have shifted away from the collective to the individual. The future strength of our communities lies in the education of our children. The Chinese have always believed this is demonstrated most aptly in the proverb, "Sow a thought, reap an action; sow an action, reap a habit;

sow a habit, reap a character; sow a character, reap a destiny."

References

Boyd and Cooper, (1994) A GGSTeam Dialogue, Global Learning Communities, Tasmania.

Carter G.D., (October 1999) <u>Refocusing our attention on character education in the new millennium</u>, Israel ASCD.

Dalai Lama, (1999), <u>Ethics for the New Millenium</u>, Berkley, New York.

Kidder, R. (2002) Unpublished. Institute for Global Ethics, Maine.

Lickona, T. (February 1998). "A More Complex Analysis Is Needed." Phi Delta Kappan 79, 6: 454.

Lewis, C., and I. Tsuchida, (March 1998). "The Basics in Japan: The Three C's." Educational Leadership 55, 6: 32.

Morowitz, H. (1993) <u>Entropy and the Magic Flute</u>, Oxford University Press, Oxford.

Len Findlay

The Cunning of Education or the Democracy Staple? Which Should Canada be Promoting in its Communities and the World?

First a few words about my title, which appropriates two heavyweights, the political philosopher, G. W. F. Hegel, and the political economist and communications theorist, Harold Adams Innis, exemplars respectively of nineteenth-century European and twentieth-century Canadian thought. I use these two canonical figures to pose a challenge to Canada as an ethical state in the twenty-first century – a challenge which can best be met, I will argue, by education rather than the latest Canadian staple, democracy, which we export to the major neo-mercantilist powers for processing and more thorough commodification, and for the adding of geopolitical value so that their own overbearing, self-serving ways can be wrapped in the mantle of Canadian decency and reputable internationalism. Education I take to be the best source of ethical community, whereas democracy has increasingly become the creature of free market ideology and key to the latest phases of "structural adjustment with a human face" (Lewis, 27). The ongoing spats about softwood lumber, steel, wheat, health services, and water notwithstanding, and the eagerness of

Tony Blair to act as Washington's best friend to boot (see Wallace), Canada remains not only America's principal trading partner and ally in trade 'liberation' but also, to too great a degree, America's global beautician. The time has rarely been more propitious, therefore, for Canada to lead rather than follow, and to do so not via the muscular Chrétienité of the Prime Minister's Office, or the reduction of the national agenda to lasting-legacy syndrome and Cabinet successor wars, but via something closer to Lloyd Axworthy's human security agenda. It is time for Canada to act like the "clever country" (Dudley, 21) it is, but in a way more ethically grounded and nuanced than Australia's current government can lay claim to in its appeal to that notion.

To that end, my presentation will be academic, but, as I have already indicated, it will also evince a plain sense of the political jugular, in the hope that the book, planned to appear before the meetings in Kananaskis in June, may get the attention of government more effectively than its excellent predecessor (Daniels et al.) did last fall before the passing into law of Bill C-36 and related initiatives in the name of enhanced national security. In what follows, I will exercise my mind but also my academic freedom, and I fully expect instant, principled, and probing resistance to what I will argue and allege. Like the RCMP, however, in their recent, tardy response to the report of the Hughes Inquiry into the APEC meetings in Vancouver in 1997, I see no reason to apologize for my actions. In fact, I sprinkled a little pepper on my computer keyboard instead.

The Cunning of Education

I favour the word "cunning" as an antidote to current terms like Homer-Dixon's "ingenuity" or the ubiquitous "innovation" and "efficiency" (Stein). Cunning is a less pretentious as well as a less respectable word than the other three, but it more openly savours of human complexity, including a problematic but deeply interesting history, and a crisis of translatability which signals the broader crisis of mutual and collective comprehension and trust within modernity. Cunning implies knowledge but raises questions about the legitimacy of its acquisition, exercise, and outcomes, and about cunning's operational distinction between those who are in the know, and those who are not. Can cunning, then, by being grounded in education, become something other than elite interactions behind versions of Quebec City's wall of shame, or crony capitalism within the so-called knowledge economy? The need for such transformation is great, because it is not simply the West that wants in, but the world's poor, including Canada's disgraceful share of the indigent, the incarcerated, the apparently dispensable.

By the cunning of education I do not mean the low, animal cunning of popular cliché. Instead, I wish to invoke and depart from that cunning of reason which, in the second (1830) draft of *The Philosophic History of the World*, Hegel used to convey what he takes to be the privilege of the universal:

> for it is not the universal idea which enters into opposition, conflict and danger; it keeps itself in the background, untouched and unharmed, and sends forth the particular interests of passion to fight and wear themselves out in its stead. It is what we may call the "Cunning of Reason" (*die List der Vernunft*) that it sets the passions to work in its service, so that the agents by which it gives itself existence must pay the penalty and suffer the loss (89; German text 105).

This version of delegated agency and disposable particulars is the other and negative inspiration of Marxist praxis. (For the substance and implications of this opposition, see e.g. G.E. Parkinson.)

For Hegel, reason's cunning appears in the role of its cosseted favourite, the idea of the universal, the unmoved mover coolly insisting that the passions do its bidding and take all the heat for what they do. There is a promise of detachment here which continues to have a powerful appeal to academics, whether they know about Hegel or not. It conceals within formidable intellectual rigour that fantasy of uncontaminated eminence still readily encountered in talk about curiosity-driven or pure research, academic freedom, and institutional autonomy. Hegel's phrase seems, indeed, to enclose within a more encompassing and abstract scholasticism that trafficking in quasi-universals which theorists and historians of the university more usually encounter in Kant's *Conflict of the Faculties* (1798) or John Henry Newman's *Idea of a University* (1852, etc.), works which, like the open charters enjoyed by most Canadian universities, are unfortunately more mentioned than read, and too devoutly read when they are read at all.

Of course, an idea as enticing to intellectuals as the "cunning of reason" could not be left alone for long, especially in a century when the figure of the intellectual would be looked to increasingly both to mediate and to contest the benefits of the modern nation-state and its legislated freedoms. Accordingly, I could talk here about other scholars' play with the "cunning of history" (Mészáros, 443-59) or the "cunning of production" (Chryssis) or my own work on what Treaty Commissioner Alexander Morris called the "cunning of the white man" (cit. Gillmor, 17), and do so in order to counter the dominance of consumption and exchange value, and the relentless promotion of 'the' market as 'our' most compelling version of providence. *Laissez-faire* political economy tolerated a modestly anti-instrumental component of *laissez-étudier* alongside the academic disciplines freshly minted or re-commissioned in the interests of capital and empire, and did so in ways that show how capitalism shared with German idealism a common need for a providential principle and a capacity to justify its excesses as the energizing prelude to philanthropy.

I will get at some of these matters obliquely in what follows. However, I prefer on this reflective and interventionist occasion to link cunning to education, because education itself has fallen somewhat out of favour as a term with many academic leaders and government bureaucrats, or at least has had its application restricted to the K-12 system. Meanwhile, the broader culture seems to prefer information to knowledge, and both of them to wisdom, that embarrassingly positive or utopian counter to cunning. I invoke education also because it remains intimately connected to residues of the unmanageable and the unexpected, to dissent as well as conformity, to critical citizenship as well as economic agency, and to an ethical excess within a public good resistant still to what Janice Gross Stein aptly calls "the cult of efficiency." Education *cannot* function simultaneously as economic stimulant and sociopolitical sedative, though that would sometimes seem to be the hope of those who resort most eagerly to talk of training, accountability, and most of all, global competitiveness. Such hope for selective stimulation and sedation is, I wish to argue, a prominent sign of **un**ethical leadership in Canada today.

The cunning of education is, then, intended to offer a double disruption or "irritation" (as Maori scholar Linda Smith puts it) to our elite academic institutions in which pecking-order anxieties have led to the dominance of administrative discourse and priorities by the intertwined notions of excellence and research intensiveness, notions that require universities to define themselves by difference – from other educational players and from each other – though not by distance from elite donors and directive sources of government largesse (see e.g. Findlay, 1997). Universities tend increasingly to define themselves in effect as entrepreneurial entities rather than in an even-handed idiom of difference and connection, especially connection to the national, publicly funded education system and a broadly intelligible public interest. Yet a double emphasis on difference and connection seems to me the best way to resist tests of utility too narrowly understood and too punitively applied. Education's cunning is to be 'hors de combat' only in the sense that it provides a place for valuing that which cannot be known in advance and for enabling dissent from dominant orthodoxies both political and intellectual. This is not a matter of purity or detachment, and even less a matter of ethical décor; it is a matter of engagement, engagement in a different way from a distinctive site.

In so far as universities are seen as guarantors of democracy and the crucial rights and responsibilities of life in a free society, one is justified in claiming that **as higher education goes, so goes democracy**. At least that is the argument Northrop Frye finds in John Stuart Mill and redeploys himself in different registers and on innumerable occasions (as in *Culture and the National Will* 11-12). It is tempting, therefore, to infer from the current state of Canadian democracy, with decreasing voter participation and weak opposition to the federal Liberals, that universities have lost their way or become compromised, their faculties no longer (if they ever were; see Michiel Horn) the breeding ground for fearless tribunes and promoters of diversity, but rather hotbeds of cold feet, places where the funding chill is deeply feared, free inquiry a thing of the past, and unfunded research almost by definition less valuable than work funded by governments and the private sector. I exaggerate, especially in Calgary, the home of Flanagan, Bercuson, and Cooper, and close to the territory of those wonderful public intellectuals, Leroy Little Bear and Amethyst First Rider, but it is not much of an exaggeration. Let's have a quick look at Canadian democracy, then, before suggesting how it can be reinvigorated and exported by a recommitment to the cunning of education.

The Democracy Staple

I come to democracy these days via the democracy staple, a notion I have developed in order to help preserve the power of Innis's staples theory, that powerful story of development and dependency, as still key to Canadian foreign policy and economic history (for an analogous effort that also insists on the importance of social history, see Friesen 78-9) in an allegedly post-industrial, post-colonial era, and to affirm that any philosophical or theoretical formulation **must** be connected explicitly and critically to economic thought and practice if it is to disclose the full measure of its power as well as its limitations. For Innis, of course, Canada's commitment to the export of raw materials started with fur and fish, then developed on the basis of fur trade infrastructure, the lumber industry, and then wheat and mineral exports and so on, at each stage creating new regional economies while displaying a double dependency on Aboriginal resources and knowledge at home and strong demand in European and United States markets abroad. We are still living with this history, politically, economically, legally, ethically, under the principal and related headings of cultural diversity and economic diversification, and in the energies unleashed (or restrained) by a single world like "Kyoto." How we sustain diversity impacts powerfully on diversification, because investment follows political stability and educated workforces, while bridling at the environmental and other forms of regulation that make that stability and education possible in the first instance. And the fact that Canada tops the UN Human Index so regularly can be read in a number of different ways. This success can be read, for instance, as continuing shrewd management of our natural resources for the benefit of all Canadians, or as our successful marketing of ourselves as a poster-democracy which will sustain itself as long as the natural resources last, before removing its compassionate mask and exposing the realities of foreign ownership and transnational interests who, when they speak of fundamental freedoms, mean first and foremost the right of capital to free movement within a globally free market. Such economic visionaries resemble nothing more than a new flat earth society that "Strike[s] flat the thick rotundity o' the world" (*King Lear* 3.2.7) to make the planet one large and allegedly level playing field. There is some merit in both these readings, but the democracy staple at least requires us always to humanize and complicate these and other such readings and our calculations of prosperity, to wonder where the process of commodification stops, if indeed it stops at all, and to consider what might count as ethical nationalism and ethical internationalism today and tomorrow. But are we educated enough to do that, to face up to the challenges as well as the rewards of producing the democracy staple?

Paying wary and intermittent tribute to intellectual critique, the democratically elected Government of Canada shows a multiple dependency on academic knowledge and skills, in the form of a highly educated public service, an endless string of secondments and commissions for research and policy development, and high-profile intellectual cabinet presences like Stéphane Dion, Anne McLellan, and Pierre Pettigrew. The Government points, moreover, to independent and excellent public universities as guarantors of Canadian democracy. What the federal government does not seem to like are sharply critical intellectual challenges from separatist and aboriginal scholars, and from those disciplines aligned, however intermittently or residually, with generic activism and a concern for justice, and with communities of difference and dissent committed to an ethic of inconvenience. The political nation and the educated nation still overlap in substantial, broadly beneficial ways – the Canadian academic community serving a larger community of communities, if you will – but a new federal instrumentalism (and its only too faithful provincial echoes), as in its infrastructure and research chair programs, has dangerously fragmented institutional and national academic communities while tempting some scholars to dispense designer integrity and legitimacy on demand for the rich and powerful, and hence to simplify and travesty the notion of the public intellectual. Meanwhile, universities in general remain scandalously silent about, or too easily muted by, the treatment of a Sunera Thobani, too easily wooed by the Oprafying and Mapling of Nelson Mandela to insist upon that great man's political origins and continuing fidelity to a revolutionary project within a South Africa once again being made to fail when it does not dance to the tune of transnational capital and its instruments, the World Bank, the World Trade Organization, the International Monetary Fund, and the G7 which have relocated First World clout outside the fatiguing diversity of the United Nations. Behind the righteous outrage at Alliance MP Rob Anders' questioning of Mandela's fitness to become an honourary Canadian citizen, there lay all sorts of selective recall of the nature of Mandela's *Long Walk to Freedom* and evasion of its overlap with the struggles of Canada's First Nations.

And if we get the government we deserve, there is plenty of blame to go round. Within our democratic traditions and practices too many Canadians have allowed activism to become code for inconvenient or dangerous difference, largely ignoring the fact that activism has no opposite that any self-respecting scholar or citizen openly admits to – whether inactivism, or passivity, or indifference, or sycophancy, or feebleness, or age. To be a judicial activist or a community activist or, much more rarely in

Canadian public discourse, an academic activist, is to be depicted as utopian or seditious, or both – not a team player, never on side, difficult, irresponsible, or worse. And it is the nature and intensity of the activity in question, and its potential impact on the funding prospects of 'host' universities and the Canadian electorate, that leads to some forms of scholarship seeming worthy of discouragement or veiled dismissal.

The humanities disciplines in particular are positioned, roughly, with the eternal verities in a delocalized, dehistoricized zone – the spiritual arcanum of the private citizen as fully human being. Or, and usually simultaneously, the humanities are reduced to generic communication skills and critical and creative abilities tied to the challenges facing business. The arcane connections to the fully and mysteriously human plug into transcendental matters strongly marked as private, the exercise of conscience and freedom in matters of reflection and faith. At the same time they offer a modicum of the pragmatic, functionary, problem–solving, with something in reserve to meet Homer-Dixon's "ingenuity gap," and the rigours of competition in the knowledge-based, globalizing economy where brains are claimed to prevail over brawn, despite the military underwriting of competitive advantage – especially in the case of the United States. What this private-public distribution of humanities knowledge and values does is to squeeze the social and the political until it is capable of proclaiming only – or overwhelmingly – a liberal message. And part of this squeeze is felt especially strongly in the quarters of the academy where dissent and critique have their deepest roots. All that academic courage and candour was in the past, and not at all necessary, far less fundable, in Canada today, except as a retrospective cherishing of values and capacities now sacrosanct, safe as houses – or maybe only as safe as affordable housing or the drinking water in Walkerton or North Battleford. Decency and democracy, it needs to be said, have to be continuously earned rather than complacently inherited or systematically commodified, and no earnings index is complete without this kind of ethical and political accounting.

The academic humanities are a legitimating if currently diminished community within Canadian universities. But what do they legitimate? They are there in large part to ratify related illusions of institutional autonomy, academic freedom, disinterested inquiry, knowledge for its own sake, and a healthy and just democracy. They are strong signifiers, primarily because of their historical role, of defining freedoms we think we no longer have to fight for. There is a tyranny of presumption, a triumph of forgetting and spinning at work here, supported by a variety of tame humanists who have few problems with current federal policies and big ambitions for themselves within the academic edifice and funding engines of the current Canadian hegemony.

At the same time, the academic humanities have to find something for the less tame, more stubbornly feral portion of their members to do instead of acting up. And the answer of course is teaching – but without the lustre of federal sponsorship and with few of the institutional incentives and accolades that accompany it. The compromising and co-option of universities as deliberative democracies has led to the immiseration of dissent, the creation of an academic underclass discouraged from challenging the ascendancy of science and technology, the costly mystique of modern medicine, and the master narrative of the free, and increasingly emancipatory, global market. Ethics and environmental concerns are too often confined to afterthoughts or ancillaries to the main enterprise. Child poverty, racism, the rape of nature, food security, reproductive rights, are seen as the concerns of special interest groups, while Canada as a utopian construct, widely envied and emulated, is marketed assiduously inside and outside the country.

In light of such developments, perhaps the 'real' (or at least most salient) meaning of *Maclean's* rankings was and is to prepare the public for forms of competitiveness controlled increasingly tightly via federal programs in order to enforce compliance and elicit enthusiasm from the winners, and to stigmatize most forms of scepticism and critique as sour grapes, or intellectual mediocrity, the anti-competitive or warily competitive thereby reduced to the uncompetitive, collectivism and critique reduced to scurrilous escape from the bracing effects of possessive individualism. We can either continue to construct dubious hierarchies, dubious distinctions between winners and losers, new growth and deadwood, the one so much in demand as to have no need of tenure, and the other so deficient as to be undeserving of tenure's protections – or, we can affirm the need for de-polarization, reconnection, real communities, including especially communities of dissent inside and outside the academy. Fantasies of celebrity, fictions of distinction, are fed by governments via massive disinvestment and strategically targeted reinvestment that has the large majority of humanists waiting for the next blow to fall or the next inadequate pay cheque to arrive in the course of their just-in-time production of knowledge in the classroom. It is this apprehensiveness that needs to be mobilized and turned into something bolder and more effective in capturing public support. As a relatively meagre addendum to the current rash of academic hirings, and an almost total absence within all brain-drain talk, the humanities, like the reserve army of the unemployed, are made to represent an oversupply of the wrong thing, in part because that wrong thing includes a stubbornly inalienable, and hence invaluable, ethical sense.

I may not have Saskatchewan dirt beneath my nails or much of its scarce bison in my belly, but I do have its radical socialism and Indigenous solidarity between my ears and in my heart. Of course, some of you may see that as quaint, or dangerous, or just plain stupid, or all three. And of course that's fine. Less power to you, I say! But ethics of any sort requires a capacity to respect difference, to at least tolerate dissent, and to engage in the kind of debate that, if it is not always civilized, even and especially in political and academic fora, will nevertheless treat the category of the civilized itself as always potentially neo-colonial, while offering at least a glimmer of hope that we can do better, that deliberative democracies like universities can reconfigure where appropriate as talking circles where the eagle feather moves from one to another participant; or can mobilize in choric outrage when that seems warranted; or live up more fully to their responsibilities as public institutions committed to community outreach via institutional autonomy and academic freedom. And, of course, it is precisely because of the latter two traditions that people like me have been able to work for justice from positions of modest credibility and influence, and to use the classroom not as a place to politicize education but rather to expose the academy's existing politics and rampant bourgeoisifica tion through increased tuition and the supplement of scholarships for the deserving poor, a mix of extortion and charity only too familiar to students of feudal aristocracies or the industrial bourgeoisie.

Education Is Now Our Buffalo

Before he wrote his most famous work in which the connections of capital to the formation of the citizen of the world were articulated, and the dangers of capital flight underscored (see e.g. *Wealth* 847-8), Adam Smith had written important works on, for example, *The History of Astronomy* (incomplete in the 1750s; posthumously published in 1795) and *The Theory of Moral Sentiments* (1759), where, of course, modern capitalism finds its figure of providence in the market's "invisible hand": first in Jupiter's "invisible hand" undetectable in the natural behaviour of the elements but only in "irregular events" (*Astronomy* III.2; *Essays* 49); and then in the inescapable destiny of the rich:

> in spite of their natural selfishness and rapacity ..[to be] led by an invisible hand to make nearly the same distribution of the necessaries of life, which would have been made, had the earth been divided into equal portions among all its inhabitants, and thus without intending it, without knowing it, advance the interest of the society, and afford means to the multiplication of the species (*Theory* 184-5).

Smith's education, and his obligations as an educator, particularly when he returned to Scotland from his time as a Snell Exhibitioner at the somnolent and corrupt Oxford of the later eighteenth century, required of him range and intellectual connectedness, not narrowness and the right social connections (see Findlay 2001, 226-7). Is this a quaint fact of history with little or no bearing on the challenges facing the theorists and practitioners of global economics in 21st Century Canada? I think not, and the educating of myself and others as to why it is much more important than that is an example of how educators help build communities of scepticism and dissent through teaching, scholarship, and community service.

The division of labour which Smith did so much to understand and promote, when it became the academic division of labour serving industrialization at home and imperialism abroad, effected an uncoupling of political economy from philosophy, ethics, and aesthetics, and its narrowing into a reductive, stand-alone and truly dismal

science, as imperious in its promotion of laissez-faire policies at home as in its insistence on *terra nullius* and *carte
blanche* in colonies newly acquired or in need of more efficient exploitation for the good of the mother country and its
metropoles. The irony of a gifted and responsible academic generalist paving the way for functionary experts
who keep getting the little things right on the way to a big
mistake (as Karl Polanyi might say), including two world
wars – this irony is there to savour but, more importantly,
the damage is there to document in the eager acquisition
and reluctant relinquishment of territory, wealth, and power,
and there also to move beyond with the aid of new domestic and international instruments and a new vision of justice
that both recognizes and resolves to remedy the global distribution of poison and prosperity.

My small contribution to this process of exposure
and transformation here might be thought of as a sort of
countervailing rhetorical and intellectual duty levied against
academic silence and sycophancy in the U.S. and too
much of Canada, my outspokenness being enabled by
what some might term the unfair public subsidy of
Canadian universities. The floating signifier of structural
linguistics, the interpretative abyss of deconstruction, and
even the almost undetectable neutrino of modern physics
have a pre-Cambrian fixity to them compared with the
understandings of what constitutes a subsidy under
NAFTA. This is bad indeterminacy and the high cunning of
capital. But this can be effectively challenged by the good
cunning of education available in, for example, the radical
humanities and the Indigenous humanities at my university, new formations deriving from decolonization as an ethical and educational imperative, and the treaty process as
restorative and innovative humanism. Not *First Nations?
Second Thoughts* (as Tom Flanagan would have it), but
first nations/first-class, bringing cutting-edge education for
justice and good internationalism during and beyond the

UN's International Decade of Indigenous Peoples.

How much can law and self-regulation ensure that the current First World capitalist version of globalization is an ethical practice, respectful of international law and ILO covenants as well as local rights and realities? At the Monterrey Summit in Mexico in late March of 2002, it was Fidel Castro who most immediately attacked our Prime Minister, and not surprisingly, given the cogency of the Cuban leader's writings on these matters:

> Castro's speech tore to shreds the Monterrey Consensus, a document which many national leaders, as well as the United Nations, the World Bank and International Monetary Fund are promoting as the blueprint for a new, fairer world... 'The consensus draft, which the masters of the world are imposing on this conference, intends that we accept humiliating, conditioned and interfering aims,' Castro said to loud cheers from many of those gathered in the plenary room. 'In face of the deep present crisis, a still worse future is offered where the economic, social and ecologic tragedy of an increasingly ungovernable whole world would never be resolved and where the number of the poor and starving would grow higher, as if a large part of humanity were doomed.' His speech came just minutes after Chrétien spoke in favour of the consensus, calling it a 'compact for development whose ultimate goal is nothing less than ensuring that the benefits of globalization are truly global.' According to the consensus, rich countries are supposed to give more money and more influence in the international trading system

to poor countries, as long as poor countries show themselves worthy by stabilizing their governments and rooting out corruption. The consensus is based on the philosophy that democracy, investment and free trade will lead to greater wealth for all.... although Castro's performance was the most flamboyant, other leaders also criticized the Monterrey consensus or the international trade system. Leaders from one poor country after another called for real changes in rules of international trade which favour rich countries, instead of just the lofty words of the consensus document (Jaimet 1).

Castro's example of ethical leadership seems not have been seriously rivaled by any other figure in attendance.

After Castro's departure, the final day of the Monterrey event, President Bush made his much anticipated speech on the virtues of free trade while Canadians reeled under the realizations and fast-breaking realities of the 29% import tax on softwood lumber destined for the U.S. construction industry. The unembarrassable Bush did not look at all "fragile" (to use John Ralston Saul's moderate but contentious word describing Bush's appearance on September 11th of last year), and he could talk righteously about corruption in the developing world with nary a trace of Enronian self-consciousness. You may recall Bush's principal claim: "When nations close their markets and opportunity is hoarded by a privileged few, no amount of development aid is ever enough...To be serious about fighting poverty we must be serious about expanding trade... When trade advances, there is no question but the fact that poverty retreats."(Jaimet 2)   An ethic of risk beyond the boosterism and self-forgiving blunders of venture capitalists and their state functionaries – this is what Linda Smith joins our group at the University of Saskatchewan in locating in the Indigenous Humanities. The polarizing of too much of what we mean by risk between international currency speculation on the one hand and populations suffering domestically and internationally on the other, tends to conceal risks taken not on behalf of investors or communities but on behalf of all of us. Being a member of the Canadian academic community is, or should be, a very risky activity, as I will no doubt be made to realize by those who respond to my arguments and claims. But trying to be an ethical academic leader in the midst of globalization is for me not a matter of crossing the Rubicon in some neo-Caesarist way, but of not crossing the Lubicon – not crossing them and other Aboriginal communities but instead working with them in new coalitions of curiosity and exchange, new solidarities essential to the future of Canada as a just society, and hence important also to that world that looks to us still, and justifiably, for effectively ethical leadership. That look ought not to be disappointed.

Works Cited

Castro, Fidel. *Capitalism in Crisis: Globalization and World Politics Today.* Melbourne: Ocean Press in association with Editora Politica, Havana, 2000.

Chryssis, Alexander. "The Cunning of Production and the Proletarian Revolution in the *Communist Manifesto.*" In *The Communist Manifesto: New Interpretations.* Ed. Mark Cowling. New York: New York University Press, 1998.

Daniels, Ronald J., Patrick Macklem and Kent Roach, eds. *The Security of Freedom: Essays on Canada's Anti-Terrorism Bill.* Toronto: University of Toronto Press, 2001.

Dudley, Janice. "Globalization and Education Policy in Australia." In *Universities and Globalization: Critical Perspectives.* Ed. Jan Currie and Janice Newson. London: Sage, 1998.

Findlay, L. M. "Runes of Marx and *The University in Ruins.*" University of Toronto Quarterly 66 (1977): 677-90.

        "Academic Freedom, Theory, Autonomy, Duty." In *Pursuing Academic Freedom: 'Free and Fearless'?* Ed. L. M. Findlay and P. M . Bidwell. Saskatoon: Purich Press, 2001.

Flanagan, Thomas. *First Nations? Second Thoughts.* Montreal: McGill-Queen's University Press, 2000.

Friesen, Gerald. *Citizens and Nations: An Essay on History, Communication, and Canada.* Toronto: University of Toronto Press, 2000.

Frye, Northrop *Culture and the National Will.* Ottawa: Carleton University Press, 1957.

Gillmor, Don, with Achille Michaud and Pierre Turgeon. *Canada: A People's History.* Volume 2. Toronto: McLelland and Stewart for the Canadian Broadcasting Corporation, 2001.

Hegel, G. W. F. *Die Vernunft in der Geschichte.* Ed. Johannes Hoffmeister. Hamburg: Felix Meiner, 1955. *Lectures on the Philosophy of World History.* Trans. H. B. Nisbet and Intro. Duncan Forbes. Cambridge: Cambridge UP, 1975.

Homer-Dixon, Thomas. *The Ingenuity Gap.* New York: Alfred Knopf, 2000.

Horn, Michiel. *Academic Freedom in Canada: A History.* Toronto: University of Toronto Press, 1999.

Innis, Harold Adams. *Staples, Markets, and Cultural Change: Selected Essays.* Ed. Daniel Drache. Montreal and Kingston: McGill-Queen's University Press, 1995.

Jaimet, Kate. "Blueprint to help poor a capitalist sham: Castro." [Southam Newspapers] *Saskatoon Star Phoenix.* March 22, 2002. B8.

        "Bush outlines vision to aid poor countries." *Saskatoon Star Phoenix.* March 23. B8.

Kant, Immanuel. *The Conflict of the Faculties. Der Streit der Facultäten.* Trans, and Intro. Mary J. Gregor. New York: Abaris, 1979.

Lewis, Stephen. "Is This the End of History?" *Newsletter of Simon Fraser University Institute for the Humanities.* 4.1 (1990):1, 27-8.

Mandela, Nelson. *Long Walk to Freedom.* Harmondsworth: Penguin, 2001.

Newman, John Henry. *The Idea of a University.* Ed. Frank Turner. Rethinking the Western Tradition. New Haven: Yale University Press, 1996.

Parkinson, G. H. R. "Hegel, Marx and the Cunning of Reason." *Philosophy* 64 (1989): 287-302.

Shakespeare, William. *The Complete Works.* Ed. David Bevington. Fourth edition. New York: Harper-Collins, 1992.

Smith, Adam. *The Theory of Moral Sentiments.* Ed. D. D. Raphael and A. L. Macfie. Indianapolis: Liberty Classics, 1982.

An Inquiry Into the Nature and Causes of the Wealth of Nations. Ed. R. H. Campbell, A. S. Skinner, and W. B. Todd. 2 vols. Indianapolis: Liberty Classics, 1981.

Essays on Philosophical Subjects. Ed. W. P. D. Wightman, J. C. Bryce, and I. S. Ross. Indianapolis: Liberty Classics, 1982.

Smith, Linda. "Countercolonizing Methodologies: Indigenous Humanities and Research." Unpublished lecture, University of Saskatchewan, March 26, 2002.

Stein, Janice Gross. *The Cult of Efficiency.* CBC Massey Lecture Series. Toronto: Anansi, 2001.

· VI ·

MEDIA
DEMOCRACY
& RESPONSIBILITY

Bronwyn Drainie

Phnom Penh, the capital of Cambodia, suffers from a surfeit of newspapers – it had 218 of them at last count. Most of these papers sprang into being about 10 years ago, when the UN was overseeing the move towards democracy in Cambodia and wisely included an emphasis on free media in that endeavour. The trouble was that there were no standards or training to go along with that press freedom, so all these little papers became propaganda tools at best and instruments of lucrative blackmail at worst. A journalist would take a compromising picture of someone, then contact him and threaten to publish it in his newspaper unless the subject paid him off. The UN disappeared after the 1993 election, and the assassination of journalists began soon after that.

The current government, under its leader Hun Sen, took power by a coup in 1997. Hun Sen takes a pretty dim view of all this free media, especially when his wife appeared in one of these papers with a pig's head on top. So last year, he and his ministers drafted some new amendments to Cambodia's Press Law: these amendments decreed that you could only get a newspaper license if you were 1) over 25, 2) a graduate of a journalism school, and 3) in possession of a certificate from a doctor stating that you were not mentally ill.

I can think of a few media owners in Canada who might not be able to pass such a test, but let that pass. The good news in Cambodia is that these amendments have now been mothballed, and the even better news is that a Canadian NGO is largely responsible for this turn of events.

The NGO I'm speaking of is IMPACS, the Institute for Media, Policy and Civil Society. It's only 4 years old, it's based in Vancouver, it's an unusual and interesting organization, and I have the honour to sit on its board. IMPACS is all about strengthening the voices of civil society, and while our work in Canada concentrates on building up the media skills of charities and civil society groups, in our international work we focus much more on journalism itself and on the role it plays in hampering or promoting democratic progress. So I want to tell you about some of the places in the world where IMPACS is involved with free media projects and with the training of journalists – some of these are success stories, some are failures, and some – we really can't be sure.

Our clearest success has been in Cambodia, where IMPACS has been working for 3 1/2 years now. We run a radio journalism training project there, in a country where the Khmer Rouge devastated the media and wiped out virtually all its practising journalists, among the 2 million others it killed. We concentrate on radio because illiteracy is high in Cambodia and outside Phnom Penh hardly anyone reads newspapers. The TV industry is still in its infancy. But radio reaches everyone, through provincial stations, relay transmitters and often through loudspeakers set up in market squares. Radio is also something Canadian journalism excels at, and a steady stream of our producers and editors have taken the time to go to Cambodia to teach these training courses to journalists who previously ripped stories out of the local newspapers and read them on the air.

Most of these radio reporters are working with absolutely nothing: no telephones, no typewriters or computers, and only gradually with the tape recorders the Canadians bring with them when they fly in. Most of them don't earn enough to buy gas for their little mopeds, so they can't get out to investigate stories on their own. And yet, in the space of three years, a whole generation of reporters all over the country – about 550 of them so far – have learned the basics of developing story ideas, learning how to balance opinions from different sides, getting beyond government mouthpieces to interviews with the men and women in the street, plus how to edit tape, how to write clear, punchy scripts and how to deliver them on air. The first time one of his groups got up the courage to take a one-hour speech by the Minister of Information and boil it down to a two minute audio clip, our program director was really proud of his students.

When the government proposed those new restrictions to the Press Law, IMPACS responded by hosting a roundtable in Phnom Penh where many journalists and media organizations could discuss the possible impact on their freedom to operate. And that seemed to be enough to make the government back off. A recent story in the *Phnom Penh Post* reported that IMPACS' roundtable had motivated the government to shelve what would have been a ridiculous and unwise move.

On the strength of our work in Cambodia, much of which has been supported by the Canadian government through CIDA, IMPACS has now been asked to go into Afghanistan to work specifically with women. The plan is to create a women-run radio station and eventually a women's television network.

The women journalists we have talked to over there stress that women are still very afraid in Afghanistan. Many don't want to remove their burqas, and they don't trust the changes they see and hear about. The Taliban, they say, seem to have disappeared overnight, but they haven't really. All they did was shave their beards. Many women feel they are now living among an enemy they can no longer identify.

Because of all the security concerns that surround

the role of women in Afghanistan today, we are thinking about creating a two-pronged approach, with actual journalism training of girls and women going on inside the country, probably in Kabul, but with an independent women-run radio station located in Peshawar that can report on and focus on women's rights issues and whose programming can be broadcast throughout Afghanistan on government radio stations. There already exists a community of Afghan women journalists living and working in Peshawar that IMPACS could tap into for this very exciting but also very risky project. We're advertising right now for a Project Director for our first year in Afghanistan, if any of you are interested and have the rather steep qualifications.

In both the cases of Cambodia and Afghanistan, we're talking about rebuilding shattered societies and training a free and professional and responsible media as a key element in that rebuilding. But sometimes, and more and more frequently in these days of globalization, there are pan-national issues that arise that affect every country on earth, and the journalists of all those countries need to be brought up to speed quickly. Such was the case with the International Criminal Court, which was proposed in Rome a few years ago and which needed ratification by 60 countries to bring it into being. As you know, it was announced just two weeks ago that the required ratifications had been achieved, which means that the court will come into existence on July 1st , and will be able for the first time to try individuals for genocide, crimes against humanity and war crimes. IMPACS got involved by conducting a series of five workshops over two years, in Auckland in New Zealand, Windhoek in Namibia, Abidjan in Cote d'Ivoire, Yaounde in Cameroon, and in Kingston, Jamaica. The idea was that journalists from all neighbouring countries would be invited to these centres for three days of intensive training about the purpose of the Court, the history leading up to it, its impact on each of their countries. As it turned out, travel

costs were only being subsidized 50% and the vast majority of journalists working in Africa, for example, could not
begin to pay the other 50%. The result was that just 90 journalists from 41 countries got trained on the issues. Next
time the money might be better spent sending the trainers
to many more countries, where local journalists could reach
them at little expense. There is a lot of trial and error to all
these programs.

Elections are a source of tension in many countries,
and the media's role in election coverage can be crucial in
determining, not just the outcome of the election, but the
way the populace behaves leading up to, and in the after-
math, of the election. If the media are simply owned and
operated by the various political factions – if there is no
independent media in the country, in other words – the
chances of mature behaviour are slim. Take the case of
Guyana, a tiny South American country that no one up here
has given a thought to since the Jonestown massacre.
Again at the behest of the Canadian government, IMPACS
went down there two years ago to see if it could help stop
the cycle of hatred and ethnic violence that surrounds
every Guyanese election in recent times. 50% of the population is of East Indian extraction, and 40% of African ori-
gin. The blacks control all the government jobs, which are
shrinking, while the East Indians control the business sector, which is expanding. Newspapers split neatly along eth-
nic/party lines, using tactics like this to smear their opponents: the opposition leader's name is Hoyte, so the newspaper   headline,   "Hoyte   Charged   With   Molesting
Schoolboys", caught a lot of attention. Trouble was, the
Hoyte in question was a local teacher, no relation to the
politician.

IMPACS realized immediately that Guyana was not
a case of untutored journalists needing basic skills training.
Everyone involved in journalism there was extremely
sophisticated in the uses of the media to further their own

ends. Analysts we encountered there said that the level of
hatred being spewed out of news sources on a daily basis
was similar to the situation in Rwanda two years before the
genocide in that country.

What IMPACS did, in the run-up to the 2001 election, was to convene a series of three roundtables which
were attended by about 50 leading Guyanese media owners, managers, journalists and influential types like talk-
show hosts. Over the course of these meetings, a Media
Code of Conduct for election coverage was crafted and
signed by everyone. But it was an empty and cynical exercise. As soon as the election was over, the media lashed
out with biased, overheated rhetoric that clearly raised the
level of post-election violence and rioting, which went on for
six weeks: protests and demonstrations, roadblocks, burning of government and commercial buildings, tit-for-tat violence from one ethnically homogenous village to the next,
and an alarming increase in crime. Gradually things died
down . . . until next time. In spite of the failure, really, of this
initiative, our project director on the ground in Guyana
remained a little optimistic in his final report. He felt convinced that at least the communal drafting of the Media
Code of Conduct represented "a valid and vitally important
watershed." We simply don't know at this point whether
IMPACS will be returning to Guyana or not.

But on the other side of the world, in South East
Asia, a similar approach is starting to bear fruit. A group of
editors and media owners from seven countries – India,
Pakistan, Nepal, Sri Lanka, Bangladesh, the Maldives and
Bhutan – have come together in the last three years to create the South Asian Editors' Forum. They got in touch with
IMPACS and asked us to become their partners in an
extraordinary cross-border exercise in restraint and
responsible behaviour. Given the levels of hostility amongst
these various countries – especially India and Pakistan, of
course – these editors seem to like having a nice, non-

threatening, impartial Canadian in the room when they meet. These are the owners and publishers of enormously popular newspapers published in more than a dozen different indigenous languages around the sub-continent, and they have until recently seen it as perfectly normal journalism to fill their papers with ethnic slurs, character assassinations and outrageous rhetoric against their neighbours. But starting in late 1999, they began meeting twice a year, using English as the common language of course, developing personal relationships, debating coverage of controversial stories, organizing journalist exchanges from one country to another, even talking about creating a glossary of hate terms that they will all agree not to use. (That hasn't happened yet, but we're still hopeful.)

Are these meetings beginning to affect their approach to stories about each other? We have recent, startling, evidence that they are. Mohammad Aslam Kazi, the editor of *Kawish*, a major newspaper in Hyderabad, Pakistan, attends the Editors' Forum regularly. At its last meeting in Karachi, he told everyone that when the news came over the wire about militant Hindus on the rampage in the Indian province of Gujarat, burning mosques and killing Moslems, his reaction was that he didn't want to inflame the passion for revenge among his Moslem readership. Hyderabad, you see, is just over the Indian-Pakistani border from Gujarat, and in fact it has the largest Hindu minority of any province in Pakistan. Kazi ordered his editors to remove all speculation from the stories and to play down the religious context of the riots somewhat. There were no temple burnings in Hyderabad, no violence done to local Hindus. Kazi said, "I am convinced we saved the lives of thousands by the way we handled the story. This is a role we [editors] should be playing."

Think about that for a moment, and whether you think he did the right thing. There are many journalists – many very good journalists – in this part of the world, who would say he got it wrong. That it is never the journalist's job to strive for a certain outcome with his or her stories. That if we do that, we are engaging in the same kind of media manipulation that we claim to deplore when it's done by autocratic regimes.

This is something that we argue back and forth at our IMPACS board meetings all the time. On the one hand, maybe all we're talking about is doing good journalism, based on solid research, well-checked facts and the time and space to contextualize the story adequately. In that sense, I feel more comfortable with our projects in Cambodia and Afghanistan and with the International Criminal Court, which all involve basic training in good reporting methods. Our Guyana initiative and our work with the South Asian Editors' Forum is more contentious, because its ultimate aim is to change the behaviour and mindset of working journalists, and not only is that a really hard thing to do, I'm not convinced it's the right thing to do. Of course when lives are at stake, there doesn't seem to be any choice, does there? And yet I'm not sure we can take Mr. Kazi's claim at face value: how do we know that anti-Hindu riots didn't occur in Hyderabad specifically because he refrained from irresponsible reporting? Maybe there was some other reason.

Over this whole debate hang the ghosts of two of the bloodiest world confrontations of recent years: Rwanda and Yugoslavia. In both places, ethnically-based media were given free rein to spew the vilest sort of hatred against their countrymen, working their listeners and readers up into a daily froth of violence and revenge which obviously, ultimately exploded.

In Rwanda, it's interesting to compare what happened there and in neighbouring Burundi. If you recall, in the spring of 1994, a plane carrying the presidents of both Rwanda and Burundi was shot down. On Radio Milles Collines in Rwanda, a message designed to incite the population to kill was sent out, and people responded. In Burundi, on the other hand, UN leaders helped organize the politicians to go on national radio and plead for calm, and calm was what they got.

In Bosnia, just a couple of years ago and long after the war was over, a news item went out on a Serbian-controlled station reporting that Moslem fighters were kidnap ping Serbian children and feeding them to the lions in the Sarajevo zoo. The multinational military force that polices Bosnia has its own way of dealing with these preposterous news stories. In the words of one of the commanders, "We just go up the hill where they have the transmitter, and we find the switch and flick it up. Bingo! Turns everything off. And then we put a couple of sentries there so they can't go back and turn it on, and if they do, we blow it up. Quite simple, really."

Blowing up transmitters sounds amusing, but over the long haul, maybe it's better to encourage the media to act responsibly.

John Stackhouse

t is a great honour to be here, in the spirit of Sheldon Chumir. In reading about his life, I realized how we in the national media fail so often to tell each other about ourselves, and about the people that make this nation diverse, progressive and hopeful. Sheldon embodied all those qualities, and more.

What I want to focus on today is the global media, which also can be diverse, progressive and hopeful, and yet so often is not. In fact, I want to argue that the global media, while having a tremendous reach, is far from being globalized, and describe how much of a disservice that is doing to our world.

I gained some insight into the global media – I was very much a part of it – as *The Globe and Mail*'s correspondent in New Delhi from 1992 to 1999, when I travelled across and reported from much of Asia and Africa as the newspaper's specialist in development issues.

For all the places I visited that were off the beaten track, however, I enjoyed my greatest insight into how the global media really operate while staying in a tiny village in the mountains of western Pakistan. The hamlet was called Weria, and it was about two hours up the road from Quetta, the capital of Baluchistan province, near the Afghan border. This is now known as al Qaeda country, but back then Weria was about as far from the world's consciousness as you could get. Except for one factor: the village enjoyed a small check dam thanks to some Canadian development assistance. This was allowing the families to catch more rainfall, irrigate more land and develop new orchards for cash incomes.

As my hosts and I settled down for the evening, eating a freshly slaughtered goat and drinking tea, we talked a little bit about development and a lot about the world – their world and my world. We played card games and told each other about our countries. Actually, the evening was consumed with me telling my host Abdul Ghafoor and his brothers about my country, Canada. He had received Canadian aid. He had received Canadian visitors – whole delegations of them. But no one had told him about Canada. It's not that Abdul was cut off from the world. He had a radio, watched television in town and had gone on a recent hajj to Saudi Arabia. Yet whenever he encountered the media, it didn't tell him about Canada, nor did it tell the world about him. This confused Abdul. Why could we come to see him, he asked, while he could not come to see us? It is a fitting question to apply to the media. Why does it tell us about their world but not our world, the real world?

I don't think it is an inherent function of media to be narrow or parochial, or to become increasingly so as we, ironically, spread our reach around the world. It is more the result of recent trends in the global media. In Canada, those trends have been summed up in recent public debates by two terms: concentration and convergence. Ownership of our major media outlets has been concentrated in fewer hands, while the blending of different mediums into one outlet (convergence) has started to threaten the perceived independence of each medium from the other. Media diversity, it has been argued, is being lost.

It's important to consider the fact that concentration is not a new threat. In today's – *and Mail*, the small item devoted to news on this day, 25 years ago, mentions a protest by journalists in London over the merger of two newspapers, a sign of concentration they said threatened diversity. No one today, I dare say, would argue that Britain's media is less diverse than it was in 1977. Canada fretted so much about media concentration in those days that a Royal Commission in the early 1980s was launched. The Kent Commission did nothing really to change ownership trends, and yet, the Canadian media is in no obvious way less diverse in 2002 than it was in 1982.

Rather than concentration and convergence, I would prefer to focus on four other factors which, while hardly unrelated to the first two, wield a more profound influence on the way the media represent the world. These factors are the corporatization of news, commodification of news, commercialization of news and quickness of news. They have a lot to do with technology, a lot to do with economic trends and a lot to do with social trends. Let me outline them in this way:

1. Corporatization

News is now a major industry. Industrialists no longer start or buy newspapers, and broadcast outlets, to air their viewpoints or protect their interests. They invest in media because of the enormous profits to be made. Thanks to an expanding advertising universe, media conglomerates have also become very, very big. *The Globe and Mail*, a major newspaper by Canadian standards, is part of a media group that includes CTV and Sympatico that does more than a billion dollars a year in business, most of which comes from advertising. We are only a tiny holding for our ultimate owner, Bell Canada Enterprises, or BCE – just four per cent of its revenue. And yet BCE, one of Canada's biggest conglomerates, is only one-tenth the size of AOL Time Warner, a media company.

Despite some recent tumult in the industry, it's hard to see the trend reversing. Ownership of the media will continue to be controlled by large – very large – corporations.

A few decades ago, much of the media was run by family companies – Thomson, Torstar and Southam, for example – that were defined by fairly strong relationships between proprietors and journalists. Members from the controlling families often worked right in the newsroom. This was equally true in the United States. Today, by contrast, major media outlets are run by more impersonal corporations, with professional management teams, independent boards of directors and a diversity of shareholders dominated by institutional shareholders. The editor of *The Globe and Mail* is not likely these days to have much contact with the senior management of BCE, at least not like in the past with the Thomson family.

Is this bad? Not necessarily. Such corporate relationships can weed out unpredictable personal influences on journalism, allowing newsrooms to operate in more professional and accountable manners. But it can be very dangerous when the professional managers and shareholders see news as an investment, which must produce a return. In such a scenario, news carries no social value. It is merely a product, and must meet a pre-set financial hurdle to stay on the market. One noticeable result has been the increase in expected returns on revenue by newspapers. Corporate owners have demanded a greater return, in order to meet standards expected in the stock market, and journalism has suffered as a result. News holes are smaller. Newsroom budgets are tighter. It is only when the very basis of the investment is threatened – witness the current newspaper war – that financial standards are relaxed. Otherwise, the underlying asset value would be diminished.

2. Commodification.

In the information age, the amount of information available to every human has increased at such an accelerating rate that not only can few people comprehend all the information put before them, the marginal value of that information has been lost. Information, and news, have become commodities. A school shooting in Germany, a suicide bombing in the Middle East, a power struggle in the Liberal party – they all roll by like logs on the river. There are exceptions, of course, like September 11th – news that is so awesome in its impact that its value is clear to all. But for the most part, news has become little more than a data bit.

To make something of this news – to grab attention and make money – news outlets have had to brand themselves and their news, just as smart forest products companies do with all those logs. The clearest examples can be seen on television, where news now comes with personality. CNN stirred up attention after September 11th by hiring Paula Zahn from Fox News to anchor its main morning news program. Simply reporting the news – the task that made CNN a global force in the 1980s – is no longer good enough. Fox, MSNBC and scores of small cable news channels do that with all the news, all the time. Each news program must have its own character to differentiate it from the others, and thus add value. In Canada, you can see this trend with the redesign of CBC's flagship program, The National, anchored by Peter Mansbridge. Insiders jokingly call it The Peter Show, because most news clips begin with Peter calling on the reporter, by name, to give their report. When the piece is finished, the reporter signs off by saying, "Peter" – as in "back to you, Peter." While small in nature, these effects are important to adding a signature to the news.

TV has long been a personality-driven medium. In print, newspapers have taken a more radical approach to news by adapting the same techniques. This is most evident in the now common assigning of columnists, such as the *National Post*'s Christie Blatchford and *The Globe and*

Mail's Jan Wong, to provide the only news coverage those papers might bring to a subject. It's about much more than adding authority to a story with a regular photo by-line, or bringing some colour and flair to the news. In many cases, even in Blatchford's court coverage (and courts were once the sanctuary of objective reporting), the columnist's opinion and observations are as important as the news. In other words, the writer becomes part of the subject. How else can their reports stand out in a market that offers the average media consumer perhaps a dozen different reports on the same story?

I like to compare this trend in news to the breakfast cereal market. You can walk down a grocery store aisle and see scores of cereal brands, yet they all come down to a few common ingredients: sugar, one or two grains, and perhaps some fruit. The brand, the box, the image and the gimmick – turning milk blue, for instance – are what sell the product. Brand managers call it the promise and the payoff. McDonald's promises you golden french fries with a certain taste and suppleness, and no matter where you go in the world the payoff is the same. It's the same in reporting. We promise you a certain attitude with every Jan Wong article, and we give you the payoff, even when it's in the form of a news article. Otherwise, the report is just a commodity.

3. Commercialization.

When I mention the commercialization of news, I realize I am not treading on new ground. Mass market news has always been a commercial enterprise; that's how it reaches a mass market. What concerns me at this point is the new commercial values of the entertainment industry that are being adopted by the news media. Of course we make room for the lively, offbeat, even banal, as always. But there's a far greater change being influenced by

Hollywood, which now has an influence on almost every aspect of Western life. Very subtly, news values and entertainment values have blurred. The news now has character and drama. The Middle East, for example, is no longer a story about international law or national ambitions. It's about Arafat and Sharon. And the news has less and less to do with reality. It is not about life the way most people live it.

On TV, news has already been compressed past the limits of credulity. News cycles do not reflect the cycle of events and decisions in most of our lives, even of the lives of people always in the news. Yet we the consumers want events – news – to unfold faster than we know it actually will. And we want it to be told in terms of conflict and resolution.

After September 11th, the Bush administration spent almost as much time talking down public expectations as it did building a military coalition for a campaign in Afghanistan. Over and over, the White House told Americans, and the world, that the war against terror would take a lot longer than might be expected – even years!

If expectations were the enemy, where were those expectations formed? Think for a moment about the movie "Independence Day". With nothing less than the future of the planet at stake, the President of the United States was able to absorb a critical blow, assess the enemy, plot a counter-attack and wipe out the alien invasion force – in less than two hours. No wonder George W. Bush had to plead with Americans to give him months, even years, to wipe out al Qaeda.

The compressing of politics is a direct result of similar trends in the news media, and they both owe this new direction to Hollywood, where so many mass expectations begin.

4. Quickness.

For the sake of alliteration, I have referred to the fourth trend as quickness – the speed of news. In fact, the speed at which most information is now conveyed may be the most underestimated element of change, because it extends well beyond the mass media. Of course, we're so used to "live" coverage that few of us probably did not see the World Trade Centre collapse – live. From Princess Diana's funeral to a suicide bomb in Jerusalem, we expect to be taken to the scene within minutes, and we are. What happens anywhere in the world is now transmitted everywhere in the world in seconds.

But the digital technology that did so much to quicken quickness has also led to a diminution in the value of news. Just as news can become a commodity when too many outlets offer the same news, so too can it lose value by instantaneous transmission, because every bit of news can then be transmitted instantaneously with little to flag one item as being more important than the next. In effect, everything becomes "breaking news."

Nowhere is this more profound in its effect than in the form of email. The medium of email should be the most egalitarian ever known to humans. News becomes what you want it to be, and it is shared between groups of people, large and small, who join groups according to their preferences. In this new world, news is no longer mass market.

This very segregation of news, after it is transmitted so quickly, is what costs it value. Without the weight of a mass audience, news becomes a smaller form of information, like a stock tip or a bit of family talk. It is only news, and of greater value, when we know lots of other people will see the same thing. This is partly because the pressures of a mass market – one that is truly self-regulating – give us a stronger sense that what we are seeing must be true. Otherwise, some informed members of the same audience would stand up and object. But we also know our knowledge will be more valuable if others possess the same knowledge. Otherwise, we'd have no one to talk to about that suicide bombing, and would have to spend all our time explaining it to others – doing what the news media are supposed to do.

I like to think of a recent email campaign about peace activists stuck in apartments in Ramallah during Operation Defensive Shield, the Israeli military operation to re-occupy much of the West Bank. The news of one Canadian man trapped in an apartment, while not significant enough for the mass media to pursue, was bounced around the world many times by email, through several activist networks and their list-serves. It was instantaneous but no more significant than a chain letter. What is important, though, is how much time individuals, and not just activists, devote to receiving and analyzing such information. It has become one of their primary news sources. And yet it is very narrow. It is diminutive. It is the scaling down of news, even as it is sped up.

With all these changes, driven by technology, an expanding entertainment industry, economics and time pressures in Western society, the media have changed remarkably in how we operate in just one decade. We've also changed greatly in how we are perceived. We are no longer reporters. We are judges of history, and every bit as powerful, which I say with the greatest of reluctance, as the formal judiciary. To quote the media thinker Robert Hackett: "Media no longer reflect the form and ideas of dominant institutions. We are now the dominant force to which other institutions conform."

This is about something more profound than setting the agenda. This is about determining public discourse in a serious manner by forcing the other actors in any discourse to shape their views and behaviour according to media-set standards. Again, look at the Middle East and the painful effort by the Bush administration through much of 2001 and early 2002 to disengage from the conflict. In many ways, the conflict does not merit the great amount of attention it wins on a daily basis. Decades of war and tension in and around Israel have not, in the long term, determined oil prices, or pushed the world in a new direction, or even reshaped the Arab world.

And yet, because the Western media are so obsessed with the Middle East conflict, no politician, not even the U.S. President, can afford to ignore it. That's setting the agenda. The way in which we cover the conflict, with so much speed, personality and entertainment values, has as much effect, in that it becomes Hackett's norm – the one to which others must conform.

Now, how does this play out in terms of poverty? If the media pay little attention to global development issues, for instance, will other institutions conform and ignore poverty equally?

The huge public ignorance about poverty might indicate the answer is yes. Let me quote a straw poll conducted in British schools by Peter Adamson, a development communications expert who developed many of Unicef's groundbreaking reports on child poverty. He asked British students the following questions and got the following answers:

What percentage of the world's children do you think are starving – defined as "visibly malnourished"?
Common answer: 50 to 75 per cent.
Real answer: 1-2 per cent.
What percentage of the world's families live in absolute poverty – so that they cannot meet even their most basic needs?
Common answer: 75 per cent.
Real answer: 20-25 per cent.

What percentage of the world's six to twelve year olds start high school?
Common answer: 10-20 per cent.
Real answer: almost 90 per cent.

Ignorance indeed, and this was among children born in the information age with more information at their disposal each hour than what was needed to build the first atomic bomb.

It is probably fair to state that the media do a poor job of informing the world about poverty, especially when it comes to telling the North about the South. But that should not suggest, despite Adamson's findings, that the Northern media ignore the South. In fact, we pay it a great deal of attention. We just do it inadequately, for the reasons cited above.

The Northern media was paying significant attention to development issues as early as the mid-19th century, but it was in the classical role of reporting. The media conformed to other institutions, namely governments, churches and charities that were the forerunner of today's non-government organization (NGO) movement. In Britain, the building of the railroad gave citizens access to new rural areas, which quickly became popular for city-dwellers in search of bird life. By the 1880s, English wildlife and naturalist organizations had some 100,000 members. And the media followed, judging by the great number of magazines that emerged on naturalist subjects – National Geographic, in America, being the most noted.

The media also followed church groups to Africa and Asia as they embarked on early forms of development work. But the pattern began to change in the 20th century when a burst of state-led institutions began to set the world's agenda, with the media following. We followed armies into two world wars. We followed the United Nations into peacekeeping missions. And we followed the big bilateral aid organizations such as the Canadian International Development Agency, and new international financial institutions, like the World Bank, into poorer countries.

When there was an upswing in direct action, sparked by the 1960s zeitgeist, the media once again lagged. Even in its earlier decades, television allowed horrible situations to be conveyed to the world, but it remained NGOs and charities that led the media to the scene. Efforts like George Harrison's Bangladesh Aid and, before that, aid to war-torn Biafra consisted of NGOs leading the mass media.

The Ethiopian famine of 1984 changed that. Due to new broadcast technologies that allowed direct satellite feeds, and far bigger news budgets due to the growing commercial value of television news, the media became part of the story in Ethiopia – far more than any aid effort. On any given day, what the media chose to see and do became the famine. Pretty much everything else didn't exist. And aid agencies had to respond, not just with aid, but with their own new norms that would conform to the media's. The epitome (or nadir) of this was a French famine relief team that raced across the Sahara with emergency medical supplies for Ethiopians, and broadcast nightly news feeds updating viewers of its progress. It mattered little that only a portion of the original aid made it to Addis Ababa. The televised effort was what counted.

In 1991, the Persian Gulf War changed everything again. Thanks to CNN, the war became "all war, all the time" – as if we, the viewers, were part of the conflict. Beyond the new standard of immediacy set by reporters standing on Baghdad rooftops talking live during bombing raids, the Gulf War set a new expectation that anything of importance had to broadcast with the new buzzwords, "Live" and "Breaking News," to maintain that importance. Those terms became the new international standard, in some ways replacing Greenwich. The world could now set its clocks according to Wolf Blitzer.

From then on, the media would be seen globally as omnipresent and omniscient. No longer did governments or armies or NGOs set the agenda. The media did, and their norm is what the others would have to adhere to.

The result is profound, and perhaps best explained with examples.

In 1993, while covering the famine and war in Somalia, I met the great warlord Mohammad Farah Aidid at his headquarters town of Berdere, in the southwestern desert. Aidid's men had just looted a good deal of Canadian-supplied food and fuel to the town, in order to help their own cause at a nearby front, but the good General seemed to be scarcely ashamed. Instead, he put his pitch to Canada, through me, for more aid to help the starving children I had seen all over town and in its many feeding camps.

Even way out there, Aidid knew the importance of good press to anyone's war effort. But I soon realized I was just a warm-up act. The real media celebrity was circling over the desert town in a Lear jet, furnished by World Vision. It was the former Australian Prime Minister Bob Hawke, who was producing a documentary about the famine for Australian television and was being escorted around by the charity for obvious reasons.

I thought this was the ultimate convergence – a politician turned journalist being followed by a charity as he wondered through a war zone. But it was also important to look at World Vision. It used a media celebrity rather than aid to pry open a difficult door, because without Hawke the agency might have won no access to the warlord. In this situation, the media became a key actor.

Several years later, during the 2000 drought in Ethiopia, the British media, which focusses quite a bit on Africa, decided to make something of the story rather than ignore it until it became a famine. Led by a BBC crew that felt some guilt for missing the first signs of famine in 1984, the British and then American media reported on an emerging famine in Ethiopia in the summer of 2000. It soon became, in the media's words, a famine.

There was nothing much else in the news in those months to distract public attention. Kosovo had died down, as had the Monica Lewinsky scandal. And the media, being the media, needed a conflict or tragedy to report. Here it was.

Still, NGOs were not eager to rush into Ethiopia at that point in time, but they were seen as flat-footed by many of their donors, who expected them to be there. The donors had seen the famine with their own eyes on TV. But amazingly, as quickly as the media had taken up the Ethiopia story, they dropped it. Within weeks, a flood in Mozambique replaced the drought images for one very simple reason: A woman forced to stay in a tree because of the high waters gave birth in the branches. You could imagine the headlines around the world before they were written − and the nightly news clips. This disaster had all the drama of, well, a Hollywood film.

If you wonder what sort of impact this has, consider the earthquake that hit western India in 2001. When I was assigned to the disaster, and flew to the town of Bhuj, near the epicentre, an American woman sitting beside me on an airplane said she was from the relief agency CARE International and had come straight here from head office in Atlanta. Her job: media coordinator. The woman's task was to get as much media coverage as possible, particularly TV, for CARE staff on the ground, which is why she wore a green CARE t-shirt wherever she went. This struck me as the ultimate example of another institution, a charity, conforming to the institution of media. In the earthquake zone, it was actually behaving like a news organization. How else was the agency supposed to survive or grow?

And speaking of negative consequences, let me

cite one last case. The American journalist Daniel Pearl, who was murdered in Karachi, Pakistan, fell because the media is now such a central player that other actors sometimes feel the need to destroy it. Of course, they killed Daniel Pearl because he was Jewish. But there is no shortage of Jews in other professions in the region who could have been attacked or executed. He was killed because he was also a journalist – because his words were what others tried to conform to.

I came here to speak about the global media and responsibility. Here is what I think these ideas mean in terms of the responsibility many of you have assumed in fighting poverty: any organization that is going to work seriously in the world to promote human development is going to have to conform to the media, and that means finding ways to decommodify, commercialize, corporatize and quicken the issues and events they want to address. In short, they will become more like the media.

Consider the ones who are already successful. According to an Earnscliffe poll done a couple of years ago, 46 per cent of Canadians give to agencies that work to reduce poverty oversees. That seems to be not impacted by the media. But half of all such donations go to the big four overseas charities: World Vision (with roughly one quarter of all donations), CARE, Unicef and Canadian Christian Children's Fund. These are the organizations that have conformed most to the mass media. Whether it is their advertising and communications plans, their sponsorship efforts or their rapid mobilization in times of disaster, they act like they want to succeed in the media world.

I'm not sure this is responsible, for either the media or charities. I'm not sure it's democratic, either. But I do think it is the future.

Michael Valpy

The pursuit of journalism leads along forever-interesting paths. Which, by way of explanation, is why, some years back, I happened to be reading the transcript of a court hearing into how much of his assets Conrad Black's late brother Montagu would be required to share with his former wife under Ontario's Family Law Act.

One nugget from that transcript has remained indelibly in my mind. As I browsed enjoyably through the account of Mr. Black's 18 mahogany Muskoka pleasure boats and his collection of vintage Rolls-Royces, I came across this exchange between him and Mr. Justice George Walsh of the Ontario Supreme Court:

His Lordship asked: What happened when capital gains tax came in?

Mr. Black replied: Father couldn't be found for weeks. He was beside himself.

Father . . . was beside himself.

My purpose in telling that story, apart from prurient gossip, is to give you an idea of the state of my own emotions after reading Francis Fukuyama's *The End of History*, his proclamation of the eternal victory in human affairs of liberal democratic market capitalism. I read it, and thought, "Good God, the rest of my life is going to be depressing." Which, of course, is not the case because Fukuyama is on his way to being wonderfully wrong.

We are at a really fascinating point in history. The commanding ideology of unfettered global capitalism is coming to an end, or at least it has reached the beginning of the end. We are on the threshold of a political adventure as great as any in the past, moving beyond the nation-state, truly constructing the global village, constructing global democracy. Inevitably we're moving toward world governance. Inevitably in the process we've got to decide what should be in the commons and what can be left to the market; we've got to preserve local culture and protect the geography which we share not only with the rest of life but with generations yet to come. Not a lot of this is on the media's agenda to any significant degree and I don't know how we're going to accomplish it. But I wish I were 30 or 40 instead of 60, because I'd really like to be around to see how it comes out.

And before I go deeper into this topic I want to make one observation on the title of our panel, Media, Democracy and Responsibility. That last word – responsibility – makes me uncomfortable, never more so than with all the current furor about the 'Asperization' of journalism. The CBC's journalists have responsibility; the CBC has a statutory mandate to do this and that, X and Y. The rest of us don't. We work for private corporations which are entitled to put whatever product they want into the market place so long as it falls within the laws of the land. And I find the tut-tutting about the Aspers disingenuous.

However, if, on the other hand, Canadian journalists and the media corporations which employ them are not regulated by "responsibility", they might at least be guided by good and intelligent practices.

You've been listening for two days to the experts on globalization and democracy. We as journalists bring an expertise of our own to the discussion – or we are expected to. Our journalistic expertise is to test what mythologies about our society are authoritative, test what is valid about what Canadians believe to be true about themselves. The essential importance of a mythology is that so long as the people to whom it is applied believe the myth to be true, they will act according to it. Thus the American sociologist James W. Carey defines the role of the press as an agency for carrying on the conversation of the culture and cultivating certain vital habits of the community. I love those phrases: "an agency for carrying on the conversation of the culture", and for "cultivating certain vital habits of the community".

If we don't have a *responsibility*, we do have an important function – if we are doing our jobs intelligently. And Robert Hackett, a professor of communications theory at Simon Fraser University and a co-director of the media monitoring agency NewsWatch Canada, projects that definition of Carey's into an operational concept. In an essay he has written for a rather good book called *Democratic Equality: What Went Wrong* – a book edited by Ed Broadbent – Hackett states that what the news and information media do is to provide audiences with a mental map of the social and political world that is beyond their own, first-hand experience.

In a world of second-hand experience, he says, the mass media help to create the political reality that governs much of our political behaviour. What the media do, what the media are stunningly successful at doing – with their filters on first-hand experience – is not telling people what to think, but what to think about. They map the world for us, and they map its limits.

It is a very heated debate, both inside and outside Canadian journalism, about what journalistic values go into the cartography of that map. I'm going to avoid that debate – maybe – but I do want to take a few minutes to examine whether the map fits the reality of what is happening in Canada, whether the media indeed are carrying on the conversation of the culture and cultivating those certain vital habits of the community. I'm going to take a run at examining whether journalists have got the news agenda right, whether the second-hand images we're presenting are accurate.

There are two statements that can be made about globalization and democracy, statements amply re-enforced by what you've been hearing here the past two days.

The first is that there is an explosion of democratic engagement in Canada and around the world – but especially in Canada. The second is that the intellectual debate on globalization and democracy – here and elsewhere – is roaring down the highway and gelling on consensus to an astonishing degree.

Democracy's new pilgrims are ubiquitous, journeying in search of a new meaning, a new and venerated ideal, of something we all once thought we understood and did not need to worry about. They are travelling at the speed of light beyond the old manichaeisms of ideological zealotry. They are taking their politics to the street by the tens of thousands – in Seattle, Washington, Quebec City, Genoa, New York. They're going to be here for Kananaskis. They are in the universities, organizing conferences such as this one, teaching courses – as political scientists David Cameron and Richard Simeon are doing at the University of Toronto – aimed at ripping the old, tired, encrusted sediment off democracy and investing in it new meaning and understanding.

They are turning up for public lectures – 1,700 people a couple of months ago in Toronto to hear John Ralston Saul speak; hundreds more at a recent Simon Fraser University forum in Vancouver on public morality; hundreds more at a full-day public assembly in Toronto organized by the Maytree Foundation called Grazing on the Commons. They are holding private salons – as a young friend of mine in Toronto is doing, an MBA working in e-commerce at one of the chartered banks, of all places, who invited me the other day to her group's discussion on the future of political parties – a roomful of a dozen under-30 corporate lawyers, engineers, doctors, businessmen-and-women.

Democracy's pilgrims are to be found among those Canadians – the majority of Canadians, according to a survey by the Institute for Research in Public Policy – who put more faith in civil society advocacy groups than in their elected representatives, who put more trust in judicial interpretations of the Charter of Rights and Freedoms to defend their dignity and liberties than in their elected governments. University of Toronto political scientist Neil Nevitte – who has been tracking values in Canada, the U.S. and Europe for the past 20 years – has found Canadians more apt to engage in consumer protests, boycotts and grassroots political activities of all sorts than people anywhere else in the North Atlantic community – the evidence I would suggest we have just seen in public political ferment that led to the federal government's quiet withdrawal of Bill C-42, that intolerable legislation that grossly violated our Charter-guaranteed freedoms of assembly and expression.

Democracy's pilgrims are even to be found in Parliament and the provincial and territorial legislatures, where our elected representatives (and, indeed, our non-elected senators) are heard these days publicly declaring that formal Canadian democracy – old, tired, sediment-encrusted democracy – has become a shell for executive government and that political parties have ceased to function.

Democracy in this country is alive and well. The *content* is alive, if not the *form*.

What about the intellectual discussion and debate?

To begin with, the quality, the <u>presence</u>, of public intellectualism in Canada is exemplary – that presence of unfettered, scholarly public discourse, of speaking truth to power. If you doubt it, talk to some of Canada's academics who have worked across the border and seen the difference. Talk to people like Lewis Lapham, the editor of

Harper's magazine, who finds a sparkling, unleashed vibrancy in public intellectual debate in this country – particularly post-9/11 – that doesn't exist in his own country. The Tad Homer-Dixons, the David Schindlers, the Janice Steins <u>and</u> the John Ralston Sauls and the Mark Kingwells and many others – they're national treasures.

Second, there was a remarkable conference a few weeks ago organized by the University of Toronto's Munk Centre for International Studies and York University's Robarts Centre for Canadian Studies. It brought together some of the world's leading scholars and ranking international civil servants on globalization to examine and share thoughts on the future of the world trading system and international governance. These weren't the watchers-from-the-sidelines.

These weren't the Maude Barlows. These were the players, the backroom boffins and Richelieus at Doha and Geneva, the people who go to the World Economic Forum at Davos and New York so that the world's transnational corporate CEOs can hear what they have to say.

If anyone were to have showed up at that U of T/York conference expecting to hear hymns of praise for the Washington Consensus, expecting to hear civil-society opponents of the current structure of world trade liberalization trashed as "the young and the witless" – as one of my *Globe and Mail* colleagues memorably once termed them – if anyone had gone to that conference with those expectations they would have been disappointed to a faretheewell.

The experts' consensus was that the existing framework of global trade is not working in the planet's interest, that it can't work even in the interests of those who want it to work, that governments are aware it is not working, and that the global public – particularly in Europe and North America – is becoming increasingly hostile to corporate-driven trade liberalization. There was hardly any discussion about it. It's not working. Full stop. As someone said – it may have been Sylvia Ostry, Canada's former deputy minister of trade – if you were running a government, would you make your minister of trade or your minister of finance *also* your minister of the environment, your minister of labour and your minister of human resources? Of course not. The World Trade Organization is one wheel on a car. And the tire is flat.

What the experts at the U of T/York conference wanted to talk about was the effectiveness being demonstrated by civil society organizations – the people *New York Times* columnist Thomas Friedman described a couple of years ago as a bunch of flat-earthers in search of a Noah's Ark – the effectiveness they're demonstrating in forcing national governments and multilateral economic institutions to undertake public-consultation exercises, to implement measures for greater public transparency, to develop independent policy evaluations and – as Sylvia Ostry said – to alter the rhetoric, if not the policies, on the environment and Third World development. As she put it: "You couldn't get anyone at Doha to listen to you if you didn't throw something into your speech or your documents about building Third World capacity." What a change in two years.

There was discussion about how expertise-rich First World non-governmental organizations are increasingly functioning as secretariats for Third World governments on issues such as technical development, the environment and labour standards.

There was absolute consensus at the conference that civil society organizations had succeeded in denting confidence in ultraliberal market capitalism as the guiding principle for the global economy.

And there was considerable, at times almost fearful, discussion of what the future looked like for continuing civil society opposition. Let me report the observations from Dutch academic Jan Aart Scholte, who teaches at the University of Warwick's Centre for the Study of

Globalization and Regionalization and is one of the world's acknowledged experts on globalization movements:

Public opposition, he said, is tempered by at least five factors:

One. The principal civil society organizations that oppose unfettered global market capitalism face severe resource constraints; they also are disproportionately Northern, white, urban and middle class.

Two. The opposition movement is fractured, a situation unlikely to change in the foreseeable future – NGOs and trade unions, for example, have a long history of mutual suspicion, as do secular and faith-based groups.

Three. The vagueness and openness of the "globalization" opposition – and it's not an opposition movement; it's a corrective movement – has attracted what Scholte acknowledged as "many malcontents." But efforts to narrow, specify and impose agendas would drive away many of these people and keep countless more from joining in the first place. Meaning the civil-society movement is caught between a rock and a hard place: the malcontents obscure the message but the malcontents are needed as media bait.

Four. There is a prevailing climate of political passivity and cynicism in the advanced democracies inhibiting greater activism – something I believe is less true of Canada than other countries for reasons I've stated

And five – which brings me home. The mass media, said Scholte – while no longer quite as contemptuous and dismissive of the opposition movement as it initially was – remains supportive of corporate, neo-liberal, global trade objectives.

Is all this – Canadians' rip-roaring pursuit of democracy; the directions and focus of the intellectual discussion on globalization – is all this front-and-centre on the media map?

In general?

I don't think so. I think we're sucking wind. Running on a slow track. Not singing from the same page of the hymnbook that much of the country is singing from.

I think we do better than the American media. I think sometimes: thank God for the CBC and *The Globe and Mail*. I think what the U.S. media produces is astonishing. I've lived in the Third World: I know what state-run media propaganda looks like and that's certainly what I have been looking at across the border.

Nevertheless, I think our map, our media map in Canada, is out of whack. I think our media-produced map of second-hand experience in Canada is out of whack with Canadians' first-hand experience.

I mean, we have to all appearances a Quisling government sitting in Ottawa that has sold us into economic integration without political accountability, that is considering wiping out our southern border and that has sent our troops abroad to fight under foreign command, something we kicked and screamed against the British trying to do 60 years ago. Maybe this is the beginning of the post-nation-state narrative. I don't know. Whatever it is it should be bothering the media more than it appears to be doing. We may have moved beyond having a country to protect but we still have our culture to protect, our Canadian ways of doing things – something at the best of times the Anglophone media in Canada, the CBC excepted, have never been more than lukewarm about.

We have a pulsating, spirited, animated debate taking place in the country over what are collective goods, over what is the information commons, over what is the public role in services. This is a debate that transcends the electoral politics most of us grew up with and the electoral politics which still dominate the media's interest. We have a vibrant debate about governance in the country that is largely about the role of civil society actors and identity politics – a debate that totally messes up the left-right dramaturgy on which the mass media continue to excessively obsess.

One asks why. Why – if you accept this definition of contemporary Canadian mythology, of this conversation going on in Canadian culture – is Canadian media not entirely in sync?

I find Noam Chomsky's mad-dog/lap-dog thesis of mass media too simplistic – his five filters that ensure that media "manufacture" the subordinate population's consent to elite domination and muzzle and marginalize the voices of fundamental dissent. The five filters being: concentrated corporate media ownership; advertising; dependence on a few (a very few) elite news sources; political spin (analysis) from right-of-centre political think tanks and the so-called "natural religion" in the Anglo-American democracies of free-market fundamentalism. And I think he added a sixth filter along the way about the opiate of entertainment fluff. Or if he didn't, he should have.

In any event, I find all that somewhat simplistic. Whether or not Chomsky meant it this way or whether he was trying to describe an amazing synchronicity, his thesis implies too much intentionality, too much conscious manipulation and persuasion, and it ignores – as Simon Fraser's Hackett points out – the complexity of the processes by which news is produced and consumed (or interpreted), and the limits and daily pressures on the news-producing system. It's also too American. We have a Left that's mainstream. They don't. Which makes their Left paranoid.

I think the Canadian media, like the Canadian government, have got lazy. I don't expect corporate-owned media to go charging off to the barricades of civil-society protest. But neither do I expect it to marginalize itself in the greatest political adventure of half a millennium.

Like government, we seem to have lost the way. We navel-gaze; we focus-group; we do silly polls; we ponder why the under-35s aren't reading us; why women aren't reading us. We pay too little attention to how power is exercised and to who has power. There's a ribald saying about government that political journalists go haw-haw about in the parliamentary and legislative press bars of the nation, which is: "Never rule out stupidity as an explanation". It applies to us, as well.

· VII ·

GLOBAL GOVERNANCE
&
INSTITUTIONAL LEGITIMACY

Lloyd Axworthy[1]

Thank you very much for the very kind introduction, and thank you very much for inviting me to be with you this evening. I was kind of struck when I came in, and met an old friend of mine who's been at the conference – my brother Trevor had driven me up and was telling me about what a firecracker of a weekend it's been: tense discussion and incredible passion and emotion – and my old friend said, "Gee it's nice to see you. I hope you're going to quiet things down." I'm not sure I've made the best recommendation when someone knows I'll bring a dead calm to the proceedings at the end, but I feel like I'm here to do vespers or something. So at some point, if I do a benediction very quickly before the evening's over, you'll realize that I'm just living up to instructions.

But I have enjoyed this new found life of being out of government and being able to engage in the full and open and frank and candid discussion of the way that the world works. It was so candid that, a couple of weeks back, when I went back to my home city of Winnipeg, as I was getting off the plane this guy looks at me and says, "You look like Lloyd Axworthy." "Look like," I said, "that's 'cause I am." And he said, "Well, you retired from politics, right?" And I said, "Yeah, that's right." Then he asked, (there'd been an article in the *Winnipeg Free Press* one year after, where they'd showed me sitting on a log on Vancouver Island with my dog; I think it was titled 'A Bump On a Log With His Dog' or something), "Did I read somewhere that

---

[1] This chapter is prepared, with minor editing, from an audio recording of the Symposium proceedings.

during that time you'd participated in nine thousand votes in Parliament?" And I said, "Yeah, I made about nine thousand decisions." He said, "Well, Lloyd" he says, "I just want you to know that I've lived in Winnipeg all my life, and watched your career, and this is the first time I've ever agreed with anything you've done."

So here we are. It's a real opportunity, I think, to convene with you at the end of this session, because I think community dialogue is something that is becoming almost a phenomenon around the world. I was just in Washington, at the beginning of this week, and there was a story in the *Washington Post* talking about post September 11th. It was doing a reprise, six months after, and they were talking about how the people who were still feeling a lot of trauma, a lot stress, were single people, because they didn't have anybody to talk to, didn't have anybody to share this with. And they were talking about how some of the chi-chi little restaurants down in Georgetown that you go to were all of a sudden now filling up with people at lunch times and dinner times with total strangers talking to one another. Now, anybody who's spent any time in Washington, which I had to do in my career, knows that if Santa Claus walked across the street nobody would talk to him. All of a sudden people are reaching out; and I think there's a wonderful expression that our First Nations people have called the 'healing circle' – that after you go through a period of grief and tragedy and upset and stress, it's important to pull people together, to talk with one another, to share with one another, to be able to find a sense of reason, if there is one, and a sense of meaning through a common communion, to provide that understanding that I think we all personally try to reach out for. And one of the ways in which a healing circle works – and I see Kathleen Mahoney who is a good friend of my old friend Phil Fontaine who'd take me to the healing circles back in Manitoba – one thing they do is, they tell a story. That's one of the ways of trying to understand, not to deal in great abstractions but to simply tell a story. In fact you know there's a wonderful saying that the narrative of politics today is not the soliloquy of the state, but the human story.

So I thought tonight, just as part of my quieting down routine, that I'd open up with telling you a little bit of a story, which I came across in some things I've been reading recently about someone by the name of Raphael Lemkin. Now he's not somebody whose name comes easily to mind, but he is a fascinating man. He was a lawyer in Poland in the 1930s. He saw the impending threat that was taking place in that country, of the increasing authoritarianism, the reaction against the Jews, and tried to warn his friends and his family. His warning fell on deaf ears. People were not ready to believe that this incredible experience that was about to happen, would happen. So he left his native Poland and went to the United States, and spent the first couple of years at Duke University writing a book. It's a book called *Axis Rules In Occupied Europe*. It was the first time that the world had ever come across the word 'genocide'. You know, Winston Churchill, during the Second World War said this was a "crime that knows no name". Well Lemkin, who was a scholar and a lawyer, decided to write a book based on the remnants of evidence that were seeping out, the talking of friends, reading of letters, and he was the first one to actually put a label on this most horrendous of crimes. It was a rare example of scholarship as heroism, in effect, exposing the worst of all particular despotisms.

Writing about Lemkin, Michael Ignatieff, who is one of our great Canadian treasures, said that Lemkin's coining of the word 'genocide' was a leap of imagination beyond the realm of what common sense deemed possible. It happened two or three years before the world ever knew the names of Belsen or Auschwitz or Buchenwald or Dachau. Before anyone could even conceive of the terrible novelty of an industrialized mass slaughter of millions of people sustained by the desire to wipe a group of people from the face of the earth. But beyond this incredible leap of imagination that his book initiated, was this lawyer's determination to cause the word to circulate and not to simply let the book sit on the shelf. He undertook an activism. He took upon himself the almost singular task of drafting an international legal instrument to ban that crime and to hold people accountable for it. His ideal was a world made civilized by a rule of law, and he became the driving force in defining genocide as an international crime. He was successful in securing its inclusion in the Nuremberg trials that took place after the Second World War, and his final and greatest accomplishment was securing, in 1948, the passage in the UN General Assembly of a Convention, making the crime of genocide a matter of universal criminal jurisdiction.

There's a wonderful, poignant anecdote about the passage of that Convention. When the General Assembly finally passed the Act, Lemkin was found by himself in the back of a corridor weeping at the sense of relief after his years of activity. Lemkin's story does not have a happy ending – many of these stories don't. He died in 1959 quite disillusioned. The Cold War had created a stalemate in terms of the implementation of the law. His own adopted country refused to ratify the Convention. And yet as we all know, as we stand here many years later, we know that it was not a failed effort, that what people like Raphael Lemkin – and there were others but he was certainly one on the frontier and the edge – succeeded in establishing was a brand new commitment to the notion of humanitarian law that is now becoming a powerful and compelling standard to which we all adhere.

So what about the story – why did I tell it tonight? Well first because Lemkin was an ethical man, a moral man. He was a practical man who attempted to apply his ethics and it seems to me that, as many of you tonight reminisced about Sheldon Chumir, he was a Raphael Lemkin as well, a man who lived his morality and practiced his ethics and put it to work, not satisfied to sit back and let things happen. He wanted to make things happen, and we owe a great deal to people like that. They do not lament or wail or find themselves paralyzed by anguish or tied up in anger or indignation. They see an injustice and they attempt to correct it. They see a wrong and they attempt to right it. They begin to establish a sense of how civilization can conquer barbarism when it encounters it. That's why we're here ten years later to celebrate, in effect, the inspiration and leadership that Sheldon brought to so many of us, to so many people, and is still doing through the work of the Foundation. And we're here as part of a convocation, a healing circle, to ask ourselves about how you transfer and translate a sense of personal ethics, a sense of personal morality into a public ethic – something that begins to establish a standard, a norm, an institution, a practice, a convention to give it some good. In a sense we're celebrating two lives of two people who shared a great deal in common about that necessity of undertaking the very difficult thing to do, and that is: how do you combat evil through morality?

Since September 11th we've all heard a great deal about this challenge. We've all been mobilized to fight against the 'axis of evil', or we hear from the scholars about a "clash of civilizations". There's an incredible resounding call to arms, and we are now seized increasingly by a world full of certitudes and absolutisms and the truth as defined by one group of people. Teilhard de Chardin, the Jesuit theologian, had that wonderful phrase in his book where he said that we all know something important is happening to us but what is it? That's what we're trying to discover. What is it? Not only what is it, but what do we do about it? That's the key question. Because in a way we're seeing acts of sacrifice taking place. Watching television we hear about those who are involved daily with suicide missions, the fanatics who crashed into the World Trade Center, motivated by what they thought was their creed of belief. People who strap themselves with dynamite and kill people in the malls or markets of Tel Aviv; the fanaticism of a Timothy McVeigh. There's no culture, no society or region that isn't infected by that sense of what Nietzsche called the "nihilism of self-immolation" – you make a statement by destruction.

And, as I've discovered since being able to have a little more time and patience to spend with people, we're also beginning to discover our own vulnerabilities. We in North America recognize something that the rest of the world has known, that we do live in a world of insecurity. We don't know how privileged, how many prerogatives we had, living in this part of the world, compared to those who have faced that fear, never knowing the freedom of having fear not part of their daily lives, and realizing increasingly that the target of the fanatic, the extremist, the true believer, is not government, it's not institutional, it's other innocent civilians – commuters on an airline, shoppers, children. They're the ones who are paying the price. We grieved after September 11th over the three thousand lives lost at the World Trade Center. A hundred and fifty thousand people lost their lives in other kinds of civilian violations in the rest of the world during the same year – and it passes by. They were not soldiers or warriors or front liners – they were people who simply, with their families and their children and their villages, wanted to survive and prosper. And that's why the story of Lemkin is so crucial, because he identified that fundamental issue that increasingly, the crimes that we experience are not the crimes of nation-states, they're crimes against individuals, against people which become crimes against humanity, not against the state. And one of the legacies of the work of Lemkin as a lawyer was that we have now added to that list of crimes.

Rape and violation of women during civil conflict is now a crime against humanity. Ethnic cleansing is becoming a crime against humanity; so is abduction, starvation, kidnapping. And as we begin to torture ourselves through these kinds of understandings we're also seeing that equal crimes take place with the human smugglers who take people from one shore and move them to another for purposes of exploitation: the drug traffickers who kill thousands of young people simply for the sake of profit – fifty kids a month OD on the East side of Vancouver where I now reside; the arms traffickers who for diamonds or coltran or other forms of wealth, export vast quantities of weapons to various parts of the world. And the great mass weaponry of today is not nuclear or chemical or biological; it's an A-K 47 hustled by a thirteen year old kid in Northern Uganda. And so we have to recognize, I think, as we talk about globalization, that there is this underworld of a new criminal class, that's part of the global system. And what's frightening about it in particular is they're smart about it. They use the techniques of instantaneous communication, of high technology, of modern global management. All the things that itinerant lecturers have talked about in terms of the interdependence that I heard the young people in the street talking about. Well, international crime of a worse kind has also become interdependent. And if you begin to take a look at what happened in Afghanistan, it's no mystery that while the bombs were dropping, the Taliban and al Qaeda were running for cover, the trafficking in heroin was still crossing between the two lines uninterrupted, and that much of the anarchy and disillusion and violence that takes place even now is being fuelled by drug trafficking. It's no accident that the ability and capacity of those in that country to wage a war of terrorism was fuelled by an incredible amount of weaponry that was turned in, in the early nineties, simply as part of the last gasp and hurrah of the Cold War, when vast amount of armaments were put in to push the Soviets out of that country. And that underworld, that underclass of criminals who are interconnected and interdependent and interrelated and all the things that we talk about as globalization, is now part of the reality and we've come face to face with it. And the problem is, how do you cope with it? What's the answer? There is indeed a real struggle going on, and it's not a clash of civilizations. It's a clash of real values. It's a clash of those who see the world not in terms of absolutes or extremes, or singular truths – even though I think we're in danger of falling into that realm of the absolute – as opposed to those who believe that there is a different way to define humankind and enter the international community.

Since leaving government, I've discovered, amongst other things, a new technology – it's called reading. I picked up a book a couple of months ago by James Carroll, who's a well known American novelist, called *Constantine's Sword.* Now Carroll in his early life was a Catholic priest who left the priesthood for a variety of reasons. He said that he has been haunted all his life by the way in which anti-Semitism was a direct outgrowth of the early days of the Christian church, and asked how you trace that unfortunate legacy, because he felt, quite rightly so, that out of anti-Semitism has grown so many other intolerances and injustices. And I was captured by a reference he made in that book, *Constantine's Sword,* to what he called the "univocal community" where there's only one voice, a tendency to reduce everything, he says, every difference, to the unity of a sameness which destroys or eliminates the variety and detail of experience. And it's not the voice of the true believer, or the fanatic and extremist, waging holy war in the name of their own cause; because as Carroll said, we're up against that criminal class, that class of people who may not walk around thinking they're criminals, but by simply adopting a one-voice univocal view, are fundamentally changing the whole nature of human community. He comments that, if truth is by definition available to human beings only in partial ways, then we see life in a mirror only dimly, and the responsibility of people is to bring one's own experiences and one's own thought to a place where the community has its conversations – to offer and accept criticism, to honour the positions of others, and to respect oneself not in isolation but in a creative mutuality.

We in the Christian faith have called it the human spirit; our Aboriginal friends call it the healing circle – a finding a way of bringing all that together. And that's important because out of that sense of conversation, which is what you've all been having this past weekend, is the only way in which you begin to develop a public ethic, a sense of standards. And it is the toughest thing to do, because there is nothing more difficult than to turn an individual sense of morality, a sense of justice, a sense of tolerance into a collective identity that expresses itself through the state, through the government. And that's why, when I heard tonight that there's been a great deal of talk here in the rooms about the anti-globalist movement and the searching for "what do I do, how do I participate, where do I fit?", the reality is that as individuals you have to be able to translate and transmute that sense of individual morality into a public ethic. Otherwise it really is probably a futile crusade. And I'm not here to do any sort of recruitment for a political party, but I happen to believe strongly that that is what the public dimension is all about, in the sense that individuals may be moral in that they consider the interest of others before them, yet may find it very difficult to do in collegial action. Individuals have a conscience. States don't. And yet one of the great powers that we can acquire and derive is to slowly, surely, painfully, strikingly work out in that circle of conversation, in that acceptance of others' beliefs, work out what is, what becomes in a sense, the ability, the capacity of humankind to organize itself around an ideal, a moral, a statement. And that may sound awfully soft talk for someone who's spent twenty-eight years in the hard world of politics, but if you don't have that, if you don't have that as your inner core, it doesn't work.

And that's where I think the essence of Lemkin's legacy really lies, because he believed that, in terms of his own sense of outrage at what he and his family were experiencing in Poland, he had to find a way of translating it into rules and law and institutions and practices through the use of the state. It's Raphael Lemkin versus the terrorist, an act of self-affirmation versus self-destruction (of the bomber) – one a builder, the other a destroyer.

And that, to me, is the crucial question that we come down to: how do we translate that into the global community? I do not agree with some of the comments I think I heard, that we should sort of surrender to it. I believe that there is a capacity to bring it together, to make it work and I'll tell you why I believe that: because I've had the incredible privilege of being born and growing up and living in this place called Canada. I believe that we do have a vocation here. I'm not talking about some grand design of self-determination, that we are somehow the chosen people; but I do believe, I do believe of this particular community, as Felipe Fernandez-Armesto from Oxford said in *Millennium : A History of the Last Thousand Years*, that at certain times there are groups of people who can help make changes, who understand the trend lines, who become tipping agents, who begin to use their power to convene and their power to create to bring about something different. And I happen to believe that we are amongst that group of people – not exclusively so, not standing on some mountain top – but simply by dint of our history and our experience, by what we've done together in melding a public ethic in Canada, highlighted this month when we celebrated the twenty years of the Charter of Rights, in which we created a society in Canada built upon rights.

But now we have an opportunity to do the same thing, to make the same expression internationally. It's no accident, when I was Foreign Affairs Minister, that people from Eastern Europe, from parts of Africa, from newly forming countries would come to Canada to say: "Help us design a Constitution, a Charter; help us to develop a sense of how you can live in an atmosphere of calm and amity." There are many other models to draw from – the incredible outreach of our very powerful neighbour to the South, for example, which has globalized its own sense of values, chartered in the Declaration of Independence and other places. But people were coming here because they understood that we have a certain knack. It's also interesting, as some of you might have seen in the newspaper a couple of months ago (I think it was in *The Globe and Mail*), a report by *Foreign Affairs* that, in a way, Canadians are the most global people in the world. We rank at the top, I think, along with the Dutch and a few others, on a set of criteria: interconnected through the wire and information systems, level of organization, and political accountability. And most interesting is that we have more contacts, more links, more connections with other groups around the world than virtually any other country. People used to laugh that, as they's say, there isn't a club that Canada wouldn't want to join (whereas Groucho Marx asks, "would we want to join a club that would have us?") But the reality is, and it's true, is that our sort of "networking" if you like, was acquired partly out of our own self-interest, out of our own self-preservation – the academics call it "multilateralism". That has become, in part, our 'identity' – who we are, what we express. And we've learned, in a sense, that part of our preservation and enhancement as a country is to learn how to work within those networks.

Whether it's the United Nations or WTOs or whatever, we've learned not to simply passively accept them or to abuse them; and not to use our muscles, such as they are, to flex, not to push people around; not to use the elements of force. But we have the capacity – people used to laugh at what I called "soft power" – but it simply means to get other people to do what you'd like them to do. And there is, within this country, a capacity for doing that; and I have to tell you it's a capacity that is in deep, deep demand – far more than the supply allows. Now that doesn't mean to say, and I want to take a moment on this, that ultimately – and this is the toughest decision for moralists to make – that you may not have to use force from time to time. If you're going to have rules, if you're going to have standards, there may come a time when you have to enforce them. You have to be aware of the need and to become realistic in your attitude towards that fact: that there are evil people in the world, and that they have to be contended with. I think the hardest decision I ever had to make in close to twenty-eight years of public life was to advise, along with the Defense Minister and the Prime Minister, our cabinet in Parliament to use force in Kosovo, to defend a humanitarian intervention to protect against the ethnic cleansing that was going on over a period of time. It was tough, I have to tell you. There's nothing like putting your own soldiers in harm's way, realizing that there could be other civilians affected and having to balance in that area of judgment. What do you do about that – can you let that kind of crime against humanity that was being committed day after day go on? But it's also important that, if you're going to retain that ultimate resort, that you do so with the utmost sense of freedom and openness of debate and discussion, because nothing could be more corrupting of a democratic system like ours than to have those decisions taken behind closed doors without public expression, without parliamentary approval, without the attempt to explain your reasoning and have it justified. And that's where I think you stand here today in Calgary.

The G8 shows up in two months I'm told. And the

question is what you're going to do about it. I think the frustration many of us feel is, how do you react? I mean, here's this group of eight powerful countries hiding off in the mountain valleys. How do you address them? How do you influence that? What do you do? What do you say? What's the nature of what you do? Well, the first thing you have to understand is that the decisions that will be taken there are, in part, decisions that are grounded and rooted deeply in the politics of this country. Oxfam just released a report this weekend, noting that, for all the rhetoric about free trade and liberalizing trade that we are now engaged in – the Doha round and the WTO rounds and the Monterrey round (we're going through these incredible international convocations which will be repeated again at the G8 in Kananaskis) – for all that commitment, the only people who are suffering from free trade are the poorer countries, while countries like ours are getting rich. In fact Oxfam estimated that last year we robbed about a hundred billion dollars. Why? Because we have trade rules that exclude trade in agriculture and textiles and certain other commodities from poorer countries. We don't let them come into Canada because it's not in our self-interest to do so, as determined by decisions that come up through the playoff of interest groups and debate and so on; and anybody who suggests that we reduce subsidies or bring down those areas would find themselves in an awful lot of political hot water. I can say that now. You know I come from Western Canada. I understand what farm subsidies do. Now we're against them too, because the Americans have more of them, and the Europeans sort of are king of the hill.

Nevertheless, the Prime Minister has made an important statement that we have to come to grips with the problem of inequality in Africa, and he's going to get them joined. But will the end result be that Canadians, you, making choices as part of a political system, are prepared to give access to those goods that would provide a real shift in the problems of inequality? And so it's not a matter of some abstraction; and let's put the word 'globalism' aside for a minute. We're still talking in really hard tough terms about choices Canadians will make about whether we're able and prepared to have the freedom to make that choice internationally and globally that will really make a difference, and forget the communiqués and the statements and the rhetoric – that's the choice that is going to be deeply embedded in our political system. So don't throw up your hands, or necessarily go to the barricades, unless you're prepared to get involved with making changes in the political system here in Canada, to really bring equality about by making sure that it happens. That's the real issue.

And while we're on the subject, I'm glad – I couldn't be more delighted – that it seems a large part of your discussions with Bob Fowler and Stephen Lewis and many others who tried to focus on the problems and issues of Africa, because in a way it is neglected, it doesn't show up on CNN all that often. I've also had my own recent experience there. My Centre at the University of British Columbia is running a program up in Northern Uganda. Now Northern Uganda has never shown up on your TV screen, yet last month about seven hundred children were killed in a military action against the Lord's Resistance Army by the Ugandan army. I happen to know because I was there at the time. It's part of the war against terrorism because the Lord's Resistance Army, which has been fighting a rebellion in that part of the world for fifteen years, has abducted tens of thousands of children, kidnapped them, turned them into sex slaves, turned them into warriors. Ironically the LRA is now its own heir. Those kids who were abducted are now the new warrior class and the army's recruiting them. They worked out a deal. They've got tanks and they've got American advisors and they're doing their best. And on the other side of the world nobody's paying any attention. I mean if you really want to come to grips with international community, with interdependence, you have to ask yourselves are you then prepared to become an interventionist force in Northern Uganda? Are we prepared to put our own people on the line? Are we prepared to put our own resources on the line? Are we prepared to put our own reputation on the line to do something about the fact that, I expect, over the next six weeks, eight weeks, maybe two or three months, the LRA will be taken out? Despite the fact that along with it several thousand children will also be taken out? And the problem with that is not just the tragic loss of those children's lives, it's that the conflict will continue to fester. When I was up in those areas and I had the time to meet with the mothers and the camp people (there's a half million people, by the way, in the displaced persons camps – they've been there for twelve, fifteen years and they're asking for a thing called justice, the very thing Lemkin talked about fifty years ago) they were saying, "These are our children, and how do we bring them back, and how do we get them amnesty so that they're not going to be murdered as cannon fodder by a military action?" Which simply comes back to that question of how you use military force, and that has got to be something that isn't given carte blanche in this world. And they are desperately crying out for help to the rest of the international community to help them resolve that kind of issue. Well there's the old example of the tree that falls in the forest – if no one hears it, it hasn't made a sound, and maybe therefore it hasn't even fallen after all. I don't see much awareness – it doesn't have "the CNN effect", as we all used to say in politics.

No one's paying much attention to it and yet, you know something? We owe the people there a big debt, you and I, all of us in this room. I'll tell you why. Because when I was in that area, up around Galu there's a wonderful old hospital called Lachior, which was started twenty-five years ago by a Canadian woman. She died three years ago of

AIDS, treating people in that part of the world. But more importantly – I shouldn't say more importantly; that's pretty important – but more recently, a year and a half ago, because of the conflict, because of the war, because of the armies going back and forth, a strain of the Ebola virus was released out of the rain forests that were being destroyed, which is probably the most sort of ferocious, instantaneous killer you can possibly imagine. In this little hospital, now populated by African doctors and nurses, they had a choice to make. They knew that if that virus spread into the camps it would become a worldwide phenomenon. It would have the same kind of prairie fire reaction that the Black Plague did five hundred or more years ago. It just had that incredible potential to explode. And, as we know in today's interdependent world, you pick up a little speck on your shoe, or it gets in through a fly going into the air vent of an airplane, and all of a sudden it's worldwide. Well, those folks in that little hospital decided that they would save the rest of us, and they turned their hospital into a total isolation ward. They brought all the victims in and they knew that that was probably a death sentence on their own survival. And when I visited the hospital and was walking around the back I saw a little memorial down by a banyan tree with the picture of twelve doctors and nurses who gave their lives over a period of two months to stop the Ebola virus. And so when we talk about rights and obligations and debts and gratitudes they are heroes, just like Raphael Lemkin was, because they took a stand, they made a choice, they developed a position and they made a statement about their own willingness to turn a sense of personal morality into a public ethic in a very real way.

Those are the kinds of things that to me mean globalism. That's what I understand to be the interdependence that we live with. And our vocations as Canadians should be to provide the ways in which those acts, those individual acts of heroism, of morality, of ethics become part of a broader collective, collegial agreement and understanding, so that they are not simply random and ad hoc and capricious, but they become part of the way that we deal with the world. If it's a threat to public health, we are there for those people in that small hospital to give them the resources and the support they need; we're there for those kids who are being kidnapped today; we're there in terms of providing some relief in those displaced persons camps – not because we're going to get a plaudit on the Larry King show, but simply because it's the right thing to do.

Let me just close with this matter of the right thing to do because, on that wonderful video we saw I heard some words of despair, a sense of, "Ah you know it's failing, it's falling." Well, I'm not so sure. Sure there are unresolved issues out there; but let me just give another kind of statement that we can make as Canadians about two things that we've had real paternity in – that we've had a real role in creating. Joel, in his introduction, mentioned the Landmines Treaty, and we'll get into that, but I'm talking about something that will come into effect on July 1st of this year, called the International Criminal Court. A Canadian diplomat, Philip Kirsch, was the convener of the Rome Statute, and it was the government of Canada that put up the money and the resources and worked with a broad coalition of NGOs and other like-minded countries to get sixty-six ratifications for that, which were passed just two weeks ago. That's the real issue for Canadians. And let me tell you what it means for those of us who sometimes get down on ourselves, or doubt the effectiveness of what we can do. Let me just give you this example: that this is the first new international institution of this new century. And not only is it a new institution, but it fundamentally changes the nature of international relations because it declares that individuals are accountable for their crimes. They're going right back to the notion of Lemkin in 1945 at Nuremberg or the Genocide Convention. You can't hide behind sovereignty anymore.   You can't hide behind a nation-state and foreign ministers and generals and leaders and corporate executives who commit crimes against humanity will now be held accountable. It declares that justice will apply, and they can no longer say, "the devil made me do it, I was receiving orders, I'm hiding behind a national act." Now for the first time, if you commit a crime against an individual, you as an individual will be held accountable. Now, that fundamentally changes the very notion of an international global system.   Away simply from the maneuverings and the creations of the state, it gets it right back to the point of individual justice and accountability; and as that court comes into being I think we continue to have a role to make sure that we apply it, that we make it work, that we defend it, because there is opposition. A powerful friend to the South of us is deadly opposed to the International Court.   In fact, during the height of the Afghan war the Congress – Mr. Hemenway can verify this – Mr. Helms, one of those great minds of our last century, put forward something called the American Defensemen Services Act, saying that any country that supports or connects to the International Court will lose all American aid.   What he's saying is that any country that has the nerve to support or fight for justice is going to pay a price.   That's why it's very important for this country to stand up for those ideals and those moralities and those ethics.

So don't kid yourself.   There's a lot that we can do. And I'm going to make one further claim about a way to follow through – and again it's little known; these things are not the stuff of big media attention.   But in December of just last year, a commission that was established by Canada a year and a half ago, reported on the questions: how do you deal with the problem of humanitarian intervention, by what rules does a community of the international world come in and say to Milosovic that you no longer can attack a particular group? Or by what rules would we have the right to intervene in a Rwanda where genocide took place, or in many parts of the world today whether it's the Congo or Sierra Leone or other places, to make important choices? And the commission came up with, I think, a wonderful, incredible idea. You know something? Ideas are powerful. And that comes out of a sense of good. They said that sovereignty is no longer the right to hide behind your borders and do what you want to do behind your borders. Sovereignty, by definition, is the responsibility to protect your own citizens; and if you cannot protect your own citizens or if you're the perpetrator of the injustice then the international community has the right to provide that protection. That begins to fundamentally change the way the world works and once again it's an idea but ideas have to be turned into action. They have to be implemented, you have to fight for them, you have to organize, you have to mobilize, you have to go to the UN, you have to go to NATO, you have to go to Washington, you have to go to the G8 meeting in Kananaskis and say to Mr. Bush and Mr. Chirac and Mr. Blair, "look, you guys, we can't allow injustice and inhumanity to continue. We've come up with a good idea about how sovereignty can work. Sign on the dotted line." That's what, of importance, this kind of meeting that will take place in your community two months from now has to do. But it will only happen if Canadians themselves are prepared to do it.

The Parliament – a great forum – cannot be put to pasture. We can't be negotiating behind closed doors deals to become integrated with U.S. Northern commands because we know that automatically and ipso facto it would limit our freedom to pursue International Courts or Landmine Treaties or other protections; because when you're part of the same system you can't promote something which the U.S. disagrees with, and that's not being debated. That's not being discussed and there's only one way to get it discussed: you get it into the political system.

You make it work. You get that kind of thing out into the open, the same kind of thing that James Carroll talked about – that if you don't have a conversation, if you don't have a healing circle, you're not going to have democracy and without democracy you won't have a public ethic.

Let's not turn the buck back to somebody else. Let's not worry about them. I mean there are all kinds of things going wrong but the real choice, the real freedom, the real discussion is going to take place in this country if we're prepared to take our advantages and our capacities and our talents and our assets and our skills and put them to work to establish the kinds of institutions and the law and the rules that will help govern this new international community that we live in. And that's how we express our sense of ethics – the kind of thing that Sheldon Chumir talked about in his life, about taking his personal morality and turning it into a public good.

So I started with a story I'm going to end with the comments of a great story teller, the great Canadian story-teller, Carol Shields, who's just written a wonderful new book called *Unless* which my wife has made me read, again, along with James Carroll. As some of you who've read the book know it talks about the real disruption in a family's life when their eldest daughter, an accomplished, young, talented woman is found one day on a street corner holding a sign saying "Goodness", opting out in a sense, trying to make a statement but no longer in the mainstream, no longer running in the current, no longer participating, no longer making things happen. And I was listening to a commentary that Carol Shields gave on the Shelagh Rogers show a couple of weeks back. She said, "You know, when I was finishing *Unless* there was all kinds of talk, because it was early September, about evil being inescapable. But I was undeterred from writing about goodness because I think it's more interesting. It's a more important story. Evil is a minor corruption of this fundamental life force that we deal with. It seems to me," says Carol, "that evil is always something that's failed; it doesn't have anything like the force for good, and that's why" she said, "I'm going to write about goodness in my latest novel." To me that's a pretty good statement for Canadians to hold on to, advance and believe in: that there is a force for good and we can make it happen.

CONCLUDING REMARKS

The Honourable Ron Ghitter

Well, it's been quite a weekend.

With Dr. Benjamin Barber we examined the traditional role of the community of nation states, as they converged into the new global demands of interdependence, as our communities come under assault by global forces which we seemingly cannot control, and the growing irrelevancy, in some views, of the United Nations which, it appears, dramatically and drastically needs reform. Our panel of international, business, local and Aboriginal experts described the pressures of the new obligations that globalization imposes upon their areas of endeavour, and called for a new empowerment and a renewed engagement by all our citizens. Stephen Lewis, at noon yesterday, brought tears to our eyes as he wove his magic oratory to bring his wisdom and perspectives to the failures of globalization, in his view, in the underdeveloped world, and the failures of the developed world to face up to its moral obligations in alleviating poverty and disease, particularly in Africa. Our panel on Community Values and Democratic Participation examined the value of holding the G8 summit in Kananaskis country, and challenged us to understand the position of the activists, who will likely come to protest and express their deeply held concerns over the impact of globalization on women, the environment, children, and the impoverished nations of the world - a rather important topic as the Summit looms but a few weeks away in our community. This morning our panel of educators and humanitarians led us in a consideration of the important role of education in shaping community values, and the steps we must take to create a more tolerant and understanding community in a global world. This afternoon we convened with leading authorities from the media, to discuss the changing role of the media in a world of instant and often manipulated ideas.

Four featured speakers, nineteen panelists and moderators from all over the country as well as the United States, eighteen table leaders of discussions, ten volunteers and five staff all contributing to a weekend that, I believe, was like none other in Calgary before. And through it all the halls, the conference rooms, and, I'm sure, even the washrooms, were buzzing with discussion, with debate, as minds churned, as issues were explored in depth with new understanding, wisdom, and indeed, concern by those who took their weekend to be with us and to join in the discussions and share the knowledge that was passed on within these rooms. I don't know about you, but I'm mentally exhausted from it all, and I need a drink; so for one moment why don't you raise your glasses, have a drink, and let's relax and rest our minds for a moment: "to the resting of our minds".

But I observe that, when all is said and done, when all is finished and all the concerns are expressed, and all the problems are identified, a willingness to act comes to the forefront; and I sensed that throughout the rooms over the past few days. The answers that all of us are seeking seem to lie in raising a new empowerment of thinking globally and acting locally, and doing things in our own community that make a difference, in the hopes that they will move out with a momentum and that they'll have their impact elsewhere. And if I took anything from this weekend, it was the feeling that, if we do things within our local areas of involvement and move on from there, and think in terms of our global responsibilities, we will have captured, I think, the essence of what we heard this weekend.

I think it would be fair to suggest that Sheldon has a smile on his face this evening, for what has occurred this weekend, I believe, was the embodiment of his life, his commitment to critical thinking, ethical conduct in human relations, and the bringing together of citizens from all walks of life, to participate in the molding of a secure future for all the world's children, not just a chosen few. And how gratifying it would be for Sheldon to see the large numbers of enthusiastic and engaged young people who were a major part of this weekend, due in no small measure to the generosity of our corporate donors who paid for the entry fee and helped us open our doors to young minds and our future leaders.

For those of us who knew Sheldon - and that includes probably the majority of those in the room tonight - this weekend is particularly significant, for it brings back many memories to all of us of Sheldon's life. Last night Cliff O'Brien - a close colleague and friend of Sheldon, and one of the directors of our Foundation - and I were reminiscing about Sheldon, as I'm sure many of you do on a weekend like this. And I told Cliff the story of when Sheldon was considering running for politics. He took me to that lovely little Chinese restaurant in East Calgary - I forget the name - that he always liked to go to. And he told me that he wanted to run in Calgary Buffalo, my old riding, and said, "What do you think Ron?" And I looked at him and I said, "Sheldon, you can't win there. It's impossible." And he said, "Well I would like to run and I would like to win." And I said, "Well, go ahead Sheldon. But it's a Tory area. So go ahead." And while he was doing that he was also meeting with Cliff. And he went to have his oysters at The Ranchmen's Club and Cliff said, "You're running for the Liberals? Are you out of your mind? Why don't you run as a Tory?" And of course Sheldon didn't take the advice of either of the people whom he asked, as was usually the case. And of course as we all know he ran under the political banner as a Liberal, far from acceptable in this oil town, it seems, at any time, and he won handily, much to the joy and surprise of Cliff and yours truly - and maybe there was a little embarrassment, Cliff, in all of that, as he didn't take our advice. And as I and other Tories donated money to his campaign, I must say that we did so under the strict caveat that the donation be anonymous, for signing a cheque to the Liberal party at that time was tantamount to inviting lightning to strike your hand as you signed the cheque. No doubt many of you as well, are reflecting on Sheldon's remarkable life, as we sit here this evening, under the sponsorship of his Foundation.

And now, we move to the last formal portion of the weekend's program, and I will call on the Chair of the Foundation's Board to introduce it.

Joel Bell

I think you will agree that we have been exposed to a challenging array of important issues - and that we have had a most stimulating 48 hours. For that, we owe our great gratitude to one person in particular, our delightful, knowledgeable and effective President, Marsha Hanen. We are also indebted to a generous and committed citizen of this community - Sheldon Chumir. We are here because he willed it. As I have had occasion to say to some of our speakers, the Foundation is only as good and as worthwhile as the participation we attract. So, thank you all for the success of the weekend.

We have explored many concerns and ideas. We discussed the current means available to influence international actions to accord with our community values - and we found them lacking. We heard of credibility and performance gaps surrounding governmental and business institutions - giving rise to apathy and non-participation by many; producing protest by others; generating a felt need for change. We debated the techniques for capturing the benefits of globalization's economic potential while addressing the failings reflected in unacceptable results.

And, of particular concern for tonight's agenda we identified a discrepancy between the issues - which are trans-border and global; and, governmental and societal institutions - which are national in their ability to "civilize" legitimate but self-interested forces which need to be reconciled in a healthy society. We were told that we need new societal organizations and public institutions embodying global capacities - or methods of operating through existing trans-border and international entities to address these challenges; recognizing a greater degree of interdependence and relinquishing some domestic power or domestic self-interest to a greater global community consensus and harmony.

Quite deliberately, in order to keep your interest through the weekend, we saved the answers for tonight. And in order to deliver the answers, we called upon a man with very considerable international experience: the Honourable Lloyd Axworthy. Lloyd's life work has really been one of involvement in community concerns. He entered politics at an early age, rose very quickly to cabinet rank, and had responsibility over the years for what were the important societal issues of the day. He spent twenty-seven, actually twenty-eight years in public life, and he served in departments of Employment and Immigration, Transport, Human Resources Development and, latterly, Foreign Affairs. He entered the international scene as our Minister of Foreign Affairs, and brought to that job a fresh and strongly principled view. And in doing so, he really did Canada proud for the reasoned and principled interventions that, under his leadership, this country was able to bring. One of the examples that, I think, leaps to mind, is his taking on the challenge - under rather tough odds - of trying to develop an international consensus around the elimination of land mines that were maiming innocent people, often children, long after they served any military purpose. And he won a stellar victory, that is mentioned often: when I tell people that I meet, moving around internationally, that I'm from Canada, they remember Lloyd Axworthy and the Land Mines Treaty, and the leadership that this country showed, because of Lloyd, on that issue.

He stepped into the world of intellectual pursuit - and I don't mean by that, Lloyd, to disparage the intellectual quality of your role in government - but he stepped out of government and into a world where he continues to stimulate ideas and principles and pragmatic steps in the fields of international policy and human concerns. He became the Director and CEO of the Liu Centre for the Study of Global Issues at the University of British Columbia, and I think he's logged more miles since he left government than he ever could have as the Minister of Foreign Affairs. It's with a great deal of pleasure that I welcome Lloyd here. You can see in his biography the striking array of organizations that he's involved with where he continues to bring to bear his international experience, and from that experience I hope he will give us some ideas on some of the answers to the issues that we have been wrestling with over the weekend. It's our very good fortune to have a man of his experience here, and my very great pleasure to welcome the Honourable Lloyd Axworthy to the platform. [See Chapter 18]

The Honourable Ron Ghitter

L loyd, as we've moved through this weekend, and as we've discussed the various issues that have been so much in front of us, I think we've seen an element of cynicism, of "we can't really make a difference", of "these issues are much too broad, or much too expansive", of "what can we little people do as we sit around in a room in Calgary, Alberta," when we're hearing all of these matters relating to globalization and so on. But you've given us hope in your remarks, hope that we can make a difference, that we can do things in our community. Canada *has* made a difference, and we can continue to do so. Some of you may have heard Sally Armstrong - not at our Symposium, but last week when she came and spoke at the Women's Shelter evening. Having just come back from Afghanistan, she was speaking about apathy, and how one cannot sit back and do nothing, and how, in her view, apathy is evil. To stand by and just accept things and be silent and do nothing is just not acceptable. And in the book that you quoted - Mr. Carroll's book - the very first section of that book started at Auschwitz, as you recall - and was speaking about how people were silent at that time. But clearly silence is not an acceptable option. You've given us hope, and you've given us something to think about. We're very grateful for your remarks, and we thank you very much for being with us tonight.

And so, as we leave this evening, and this weekend, a couple of things come to mind. We have a big challenge. We've raised the benchmarks a little bit - the benchmark rises higher every year, as we bring in this wonderful array of speakers that we've had. It was just exceptional. We're very appreciative of those who came to visit with us and be part of our programme, and those who are here. And, for all of us who took part in the weekend, I guess there's a job ahead of us, a job to try and do something within our communities, and to think globally and work locally, and to make things happen; to try and overcome the difficulties and the challenges that we face in this new age of technocracy and globalization. So, good luck to you all. We'll look forward to seeing you again, at our next event, and we thank you again for being a part of such a great weekend.

Appendix

Luncheon
Discussion Tables

INTRODUCTION

During the third and final day of the Symposium, sand-wiched (literally) in between the morning and afternoon sessions, was an opportunity for Symposium participants to engage in a dialogue about some of the themes being explored over the weekend. The format was discussion tables over lunch. A list of topics and facilitators was provided to each registrant, and people were invited to sign up, on a first come, first served basis for their preferred topic. Various community leaders, academics, educators, and broadcasters kindly agreed to animate the discussion tables by preparing relevant questions and topics and moderating the debates.

The following is by no means an exhaustive account of what took place during the lunch period, but rather is intended to give the reader an indication of some of the issue – areas under consideration by those who attended the luncheon. The Foundation is deeply indebted to all facilitators and participants for their contributions.

At each table a participant was asked to take notes, in point form, of what was discussed. Afterwards the notes were collected and are reproduced here. Some notes were not available for publication. The facilitators were asked to prepare topics under four general headings related to the weekend theme of community values and globalization namely: the role of the media, education, local issues and national/international issues.

The purpose of the discussion tables was to provide an opportunity for the weekend participants to engage the issues raised by the speakers in a relaxed and open atmosphere. The Foundation hoped to have participants discuss, not just what the speaker said, but what action they might take as a result of the forum. Each session during the weekend included a question and answer period but these, by their very nature, could by no means hope to reflect the plurality of perspectives of the participants. The luncheon discussion table format was conceived as an additional opportunity for participation of all those attending the Symposium. We hope readers will find the notes stimulating and a helpful starting point for further discussions in the months ahead. Also included are various websites the participants recommended for further information about particular topics. As we shall see, the luncheon forum afforded an opportunity for group dialogue, local action, and informed exchanges.

Citizens:
Asserting their relevance in today's globalized world

Facilitator: Cesar Cala – Community Development

Practitioner and member of the Ethno-Cultural Council of Calgary.

Has globalization marginalized the role of ordinary citizens?

- Yes and No. The marketplace and profit have become paramount in globalization. They drive the processes of globalization to the detriment of civil society and the ecological basis of our existence. Consumerism has taken over citizenship.
- We are not irrelevant, although we can make ourselves irrelevant. Formal political processes, like voting, have become ineffective. There is a lot of rhetoric about citizenship and civil society but citizens are increasingly losing their power and say.
- Media has given us a connection to the world but it also has become unaccountable. The inundation of news has, ironically, made us less critical. Media has shaped people's view of politics and the world.
- Globalization has led to isolation and the constriction of public space. Neighbourhoods are fast disappearing.
- Communities have become more and more important as a countervailing space to globalization. People are trying to build or rebuild their communities as they define them.

What mechanisms and processes can ordinary citizens utilize to make governments, inter-governmental structures and corporations more accountable?

- Building critical thinking. People need to be more critical in their view of the world, in the way they look at the situations and problems of their communities, in their role as citizens and in their decisions as consumers. Education, both formal and informal, plays a big role in building critical thinking.

- Strengthening and expanding the public space. This includes making people a significant part in governance – not just as occasional voters but also as involved citizens. Ethical agencies of government are needed. Community development, and the expanded role of civil society in making governments and corporations accountable to the common good are ways to strengthen the public space.
- Building conscious consumers. Our consumption patterns and choices have considerable impact on the economy and the ecology of our communities and of the world. Wielding our power to consume can introduce significant changes.
- Building people-to-people solidarity and links. We can learn and exchange many positive things with people from other parts of the world. Making the connections between communities through sharing of experiences and tackling common issues build these links and make them possible forces of change.

THE ROLE OF THE MEDIA
IN AN AGE OF GLOBALIZATION

Freedom of the Press, Freedom of Journalistic Expression and the Public's Right to Know: Still Compatible in an Era of Free Trade and Deregulation?

Facilitator: Prof. Peter Desbarats – Journalist, Author, Playwright. Director and Chair of Research, Canadian Journalism Foundation.

Has the mainstream media become monolithic?
- There is too much politicization in the media now. Media have own agenda.
- Media and politics do not reflect the diverse com-

munities we live in.
- There is mis-representation in and by the media; not a sufficient range of views.
- The media create the news – an 'event'.
- The public's 'right to know' can intrude on an individual's privacy.

What is the effect of media concentration?
- Simplistic reporting, not censorship, rather a certain manner of reporting.
- The political bias of the media is accentuated.
- The poor state media in Israel means that people use BBC and CNN.

What are the alternatives?
- Publicly owned newspapers.
- The Internet is creating an open market place of ideas but offers fragmented information – it takes time to form an overall picture.
- The internet caters to specialized interests.
- Press councils play an important role in investigating complaints. This system works better in Canada than the U.S. with over 100 hearings in Canada every year.
- Community newspapers.

Media, Democracy and Globalization

Facilitator: Anne Petrie – Broadcaster and Writer. Host of Moral Divide on CBC Newsworld.

What is media?
- It is an information source. It is a driver of culture and values.
- The media communicates not only news but also cultural values. Values have changed from social

consciousness to acquisitive success and competition.

How does the proliferation of raw information through new 'Indy' media affect the democratic process?
- Information is now available to all, not just journalists – one can make one's own balanced judgement
- It creates a "know-nothing" population – people use information to validate what they want to hear. Can lead to ill-informed decision-making.

Is there a role for professional media?
- There is certainly a need for "an honest broker".
- There is much mistrust of the professional media because of its corporate/political connections.

Media literacy:
- People need to approach the media with the same responsibility that the media approaches the audience – the audience should have media literacy.
- The media reflects the views of the masses – it is not representative of the full spectrum of opinions.
- Conferences such as this are designed to give people the tools to 'unpack' and look through media filters.
- The problem is that people have so much to do in their lives – they cannot form their own in-depth positions all the time. People need to monitor the media, yet not all have the interest or the time necessary to do this.

Civic engagement:
- When issues are personalized connections are made and voter apathy declines.
- Need to put issues on the ballot, not just politicians.
- Money has not fixed AIDS, healthcare, Aboriginal

issues. Young people have not seen solutions to any of these problems – this has led to cynicism. We need to see change in line with the character of people. Just throwing money at a problem won't work.

What is ideal media? Media which:
- Teaches children civics/debate.
- Encourages collaboration and participation (i.e. neighbourhood run media).
- Focuses larger issues – shows how they affect us personally.
- Engenders trust.
- Introduces background sources – increases accountability.
- Gives people, especially the young, a voice.
- Shows possibilities for civic engagement – and successful examples of this.
- Shows diversity leadership – makes new Canadians feel at home.
- Doesn't have to take a position – there is a lot of 'grey' in issues – there is too much 'consumerism'. People should be required to think.

We Like to Watch: Breaking the Media Trance... and Getting a Word in Edgewise

Facilitator: Jennifer Williams – Journalist and College Teacher. 2001-02 Chumir Foundation Media Fellow.

- The existence of 400 channels does not mean that all voices are heard.
- The media in Canada is becoming concentrated and losing independence.
- We need to have an editorial stance that seeks the truth.

- 'Indy' media provides alternative views that are not given space in the mainstream.
- The media bombards us with sound-bites which doesn't allow for the connectivity of ideas.
- How can you create an interest in seeking alternative viewpoints?
- The internet helps the person who seeks an alternative view – but is this view heard in a world dominated by CNN?
- Schools do not prepare students to critically examine newspapers.
- Editors not able to find a balanced approach – they are always trying to find a sensationalistic 'hook' for an article.
- Freelance writers have to toe the party-line in order to get published.
- The editorial difference between Calgary and Edmonton newspapers reflects the different values in the two communities.
- Is the press just a business or does it provide a public service like education?

Websites recommended:

rabble.ca
commondreams.ca
straightgoods.com

EDUCATION IN AN AGE OF GLOBALIZATION

Education and Community Values:
The Case of Calgary

Facilitator – Dr. V. Nallainayagam – Instructor, Department of Policy Studies, Mount Royal College. President, Calgary Multicultural Centre.

How has Calgary changed in the past few decades in the face of globalization?

- Globalization should also be looked at from the point of view of the movement of people. There is greater mobility of people both within a country and between nations. There is greater migration of people from developing countries to developed countries partly due to increasing poverty and political upheavals.
- Calgary has become more and more multicultural with the influx of immigrants from different parts of the world. According to Statistics Canada in 1959, 1 in 350 was a member of a visible minority community in Calgary. In 1999 this ratio had changed to the extent that 1 in 5 was a member of a visible minority community. It is projected that by 2004 this will change to 1 in 4.
- Calgary has grown in the past few decades and this has brought about some other changes. An important change is the sense of alienation felt by many. This is compounded by the fact that people are caught up in their busy lives and there is very little time for interaction with others. Many do not know their own neighbours. Parents spend less and less time with their children.

What are the challenges that we face due to these changes?

- To integrate newcomers into the mainstream of society. We need to educate Calgarians about other cultures. We can achieve harmony and social peace only if we promote the values of respect for an appreciation of diversity in all its forms.
- Need to promote more social interaction and responsibility to bring about greater participation in the economic, social and political life of the city.

- Dealing with the increasing number of homeless people.

What values need to be promoted and strengthened in the face of these challenges?
- Respect for individuals and groups. This will imply an appreciation of diversity in all its forms.
- Respect for elders and teachers. The teaching profession has been devalued in the eyes of society.
- Absence of hatred towards people who are different
- Ethical leadership, virtue and moral courage. The ability to speak up against injustice.
- Family closeness.
- Compassion and social conscience. The need to create a caring and sharing society.
- Empowerment. People should feel that they have a voice in the society.

How can education help shape and promote these values?
- Teachers should be encouraged to teach not only the subject but also impart values to students.
- Schools should be more in tune with the community. Parental and community input should be obtained in identifying important values.
- School curricula should address issues such as: respect for diversity, good citizenship, and social responsibility.
- Team activities like sports and drama are important in helping to promote the values of sharing and caring.
- Training at school level is necessary to promote ethical and principled leadership and moral courage

Aboriginal Education and Community Values

Facilitator: Pat Loyer – Consultant, Aboriginal Education,

Calgary Catholic Separate School District

What is Aboriginal education? What should it be?
- There is currently a 'one size fits all' approach to teaching.
- The first step is to develop an element of trust.
- Need multiple curricula – Aboriginal issues don't just belong in social studies.
- Need the presence of Aboriginal authorities – where there are authorities there is power and knowledge
- Need to increase the self-esteem of Aboriginal students – this will help them to stay in school.
- Aboriginal education is important for both Aboriginal and non-Aboriginal people. It is important for adults as well as youth.
- Both formal and informal education needed. There is a need to get away from 'confined' learning and sharing environments – we need more opportunities to exchange knowledge in public spaces.
- Need to value teachers. Ignorance is expensive.

Should Aboriginal youth be in separate Aboriginal schools?
- There are positives and negatives. At an early age these schools can encourage self-esteem which doesn't happen in the public system. It is crucial to catch children at an early age – make them enjoy school.
- On the negative side it can encourage separation.
- We need multiple sites of involvement – there is not one answer (either separation or inclusion). Need to seek the best practices – sometimes separate schools will be appropriate, other times not.

What actions can we take as a community?
- Need to acknowledge that this is a problem that we as Calgarians need to address.

- Accept that mistakes will be made, but still be prepared to take the risk – there is a danger of getting stuck in just talking about the need for tolerance and understanding.
- It is important to promote a public discourse that does not marginalize and stereotype Aboriginals. Encourage non-Aboriginals to support such a discourse.
- Vital to co-ordinate efforts and resources – 'Aboriginal education' should be dealt with by whole communities as well as schools. Again, multiple sites of involvement are necessary – First Nations, schools, NGOs, charities, corporations, governments – all have a role to play and a responsibility to get involved in building a more understanding community.
- Demand better teacher training – students can graduate from the University of Calgary's education program without knowing anything about Aboriginal issues

Education and Community Values: The Impact of Globalization

Facilitator: Dato' Professor Gajaraj Dhanarajan – President and CEO, the Commonwealth of Learning

"Living together in harmony must be the ultimate goal of education in the 21st Century" (Myoung Won Suhr in "Learning, the Treasure Within" – a UNESCO report). However, whether in school or at home, at the level of the community or the nation, this idea does not percolate far or deep enough to impact on our daily lives. At the international level this is even more difficult where school systems are especially nationalistic in character. Does this mean that in a globalized world, the ethno-centrism that exists in

our educational world is among the greatest barriers to world peace and understanding?
  · Education is being treated as consumerism.
  · Children are not being shown any more respect in Canada than in other countries.
  · Family is a myth; families in this era are broken.
  · Value is a verb, not a noun; need to link values to what is happening in the classroom.
  · Conflicts occur between tradition and religion.
  · A country cannot be constructed by formula.
  · The system needs to adapt to the children, not vice-versa.

The challenges to community values in an economically globalized world are great where multiculturalism becomes the norm. The reconstructing of economic relationships between countries and corporations means workers spend a lot of time dealing with people who are different. Therefore it would be disingenuous to believe that these changes will not have any effect on personal values; sometimes to the detriment of indigenous values. How should the curriculum respond to this?
  · There are expectations for high academic achievement in different cultures, like the Chinese culture. It appears that immigrants have influenced the Canadian educational system.
  · Charter schools are like faith communities with different ethnic groups setting up their own schools.
  · If too many Charter or private schools are put in place, what will happen to the values of citizens of different countries? Public schools will end up with the leftovers.

The rapid expansion of communications networks has effectively spread Western, urban-industrial, middle-class values to billions. There is sufficient concern about the disruptiveness of this when they become the standard of lifestyles against which local populations, especially the young, measure their achievements. Is there a contradiction here when on the one hand we would wish to see values education develop internationalism and multiculturalism and on the other, decry the threat of cultural colonialism?

- Need to recognize there are different values and aim for cohesiveness.
- Use more intuitive words and more sensitive ones when speaking of values.

Education and Community Values: Our Responsibility, Our Possibility

Facilitator: Maria Kliavkoff – Director of Education, EPCOR Centre for the Performing Arts.

Education should be about 'lifelong learning'. Lifelong learning involves teaching students how to ask critical questions. As students learn this skill they become lifelong learners. Education requires teaching the skills of values and ethics:

- Respect
- Global communication skills
- Critical thinking skills

The realities of classrooms today make teaching these skills a challenge:

- Large class size
- Closing of small schools
- Focus on the traditional 3 Rs instead of the 3 Cs (connection, commitment, and content)
- The values of the community we live in are often at odds with ethical values.
- Ethics used to be taught in the family – as families

are breaking down it is becoming the job of the educators to teach values.

What is our responsibility?
· As educators and as community members to be willing to educate all ages in values and ethics
· To recognize that it takes a community to raise a child.
· To recognize where we are not acting as a community, but rather as individuals and encourage interdependency.
· To not allow governments to off-load their responsibility for education in the name of low taxes.

What is our possibility?
· For each individual to own up to our responsibilities as discussed above.
· For each individual to be accountable for their actions (ethically speaking).
· To be willing to work more on community building (i.e. look for ways to bring our small and successful programs together). Act more in community.

GLOBALIZATION: LOCAL ISSUES

Applying Human Rights
to Build Healthier Communities

Facilitator – Marilou McPhedran – Founding Director, York University International Women's Rights Project and Executive Coordinator, National Network on Environments and Women's Health, co-founder of LEAF, the Women's Legal Education and Action Fund and METRAC, the Metropolitan Action Committee on Violence Against Women and Children.

Members of this group were from a number of different communities in Alberta, Ontario, and Saskatchewan. Participants built their discussion around three key questions:

- If the quality of life has declined/improved in your community in the past 5 years, is the cause primarily local, regional, national or borderless?
- If you had ten million dollars to spend to increase participation in your community in strengthening Canada's democracy, would you invest primarily in the NGO or the governmental sector? What would your priorities be and what results would you expect within 2 years, within 5 years?
- Linking to the questions above, what are the strongest drivers of democratic development, in your experience?

There was consensus in agreement with Hannah Arendt's assessment that a society must be measured by the treatment of its most vulnerable members. This group looked at indicators such as child poverty and homelessness to confirm our impression that the quality of life – overall – in communities across Canada has declined. Growth in gated communities, there are now two in Medicine Hat, follows attempts by wealthy people in the U.S. and developing countries to ignore the less fortunate and protect their privilege by building insulated communities.

Here are the group's answers to the ten million dollar question. Some members opted to support another's recommendation so we end up with seven recommendations. Note the emphasis on youth, women and democracy strengthening.

- Expand the Pearson College model to make it more accessible to mid-level kids and less elitist.
- Invest in a model for more effective co-ordination

among NGOs so NGO democracy building and training at the local level can be increased.

· Build stronger programs for intergenerational leadership training, using special measures to ensure participation by younger community leaders.

· Strengthen communities across Canada by creating in them an "open, safe space" focused on local democracy.

· Partner Canadian communities with local economic development projects run by women in Sierra Leone and Haiti. For example, purchase a satellite dish and provide internet access, including computers to these groups to conduct distance education and improve co-ordination of projects.

· Conduct a survey among young people in Calgary to determine which organizations are trusted by young people then give the ten million to those organizations through the Calgary Foundation.

· Invest in "evidence-based advocacy" in Canada – invest in NGOs such as the Women's Legal Education and Action Fund so that equality rights in Canadian democracy are strengthened – use some of the money to build an "international arm" of Canadian NGOs that contribute to healthier community building in Canada, such as Democracy Watch, The Canadian Coalition for Gun Control, LEAF – make sure that what Canadians have learned is available for NGOs in other countries such as countries in Eastern Europe and Asia.

Recommended websites:
World Health Organization (WHO)
www.who.int/hpr/archive/cities/index.html.

Healthy Cities documents can be downloaded at: www.who.int/hpr/archive/cities/docs/index.html   and obtained from the WHO Collaborating Centre dedicated to healthy communities in Quebec City. There are more than 100 Quebec communities that use the WHO healthy cities model in local governments.

The major United Nations human rights treaties, with clear language about social, economic, cultural, civil and political rights as well the Convention on the Elimination of All Forms of Discrimination Against Women (CEDAW) can be found through www.un.org/publications.

Globalization and Democratic Participation: Local Perspectives

Facilitator: Dr. Diana Hodson: Past-President, Canadian Council on Social Development. Member of Board, Parkland Institute

There is not enough engagement across different sections of the community. Business does not engage with the social development sector. Economic and social development are not linked.

How do we engage in local activities that will have a positive impact on the problems created by globalization?
- People are tired – they are working harder and longer.
- Media limits debate – many sources present one single message and therefore people are not involved.
- People should be active in NGOs, community associations, neighbourhoods
- The next Chumir Foundation event might consider the challenges to local engagement and help to identify strategies.
- Could the Chumir Foundation fund a local initiative to reclaim the public sphere?

· Calgary should develop a social planning council that would create an alternative to local government driven research.

What can we do after this weekend?
· Join a voluntary organization.
· Send a letters/emails to politicians.
· Create a new alliance.
· Become an advocate.
· Plan a neighbourhood party.
· Learn how to approach others in a non-confrontational manner.

Globalization and Democratic Participation: Local Perspectives

Facilitator: Madeleine King – Alderman, City of Calgary

Examples of how globalization has impacted locally:
· Cell Tower issues – local experts dealing with federal issues.
· Nature of community is changing – there is a shifting sense of place and time
· Food security – where does it come from? Food industry is owned by a small group of firms. Where does organic food come from?
· The legalization of doctor assisted suicide in many communities around the world is an eye-opener for North America
· Globalization too slow to halt the deviation and inefficiency that is festering in government and politics
· The growing cultural diversity is an upside to globalization.
· The mythology of the West is destructive to its residents.
· Hysteria is whipped up by the criminalization and

marginalization of dissent.
- Globalization is having a negative impact on the environment – the growth of traffic, global warming, the spreading out of Calgary, hosting the G8 in Calgary is bad.
- The internet is a positive aspect of globalization.

Has your definition of community values changed because of globalization?
- It is offering us more hope.
- No – more and more people are feeling hopeless and left out.
- Globalization will strengthen the role of the city.
- This community's values are changing for the better – an acceptance of others' beliefs will enhance the community.

Does globalization make local participation more or less important?
- More important, local issues are manageable, but national levels for trade discussions are still necessary
- Cities and towns will become more of a force nationally because of globalization.
- Need to promote the importance of special interest groups – we have to stop marginalizing them.
- Need mechanisms at the local level to resolve disputes.

GLOBALIZATION: INTERNATIONAL ISSUES

Globalization and its Economic, Political and Social Impact

Facilitator: Michael Embaie – President of the African

Community Association of Calgary. Part-time Instructor, University of Calgary.

What is globalization?
- Some people define it in specifically economic terms.
- The main problem is that of marginalized communities trying to find a place in the world.
- Corporate globalization is a quest for expanding markets.

What has globalization achieved? What needs to happen?
- Institutions such as the IMF and World Bank have not helped development – they don't do what they say they will. The World Bank is immune from prosecution. If such institutions do need to exist, they need to have an enforceable mandate.
- We are missing the perspective of people from poor countries. We hear from people who have traveled there, but rarely people who live there.
- There are positives to globalization – it has opened the world up.
- While Mexico realizes that the U.S. takes advantage of it, Mexico still gains some benefit.
- Structural adjustment programs have caused nation states to lose power.
- Nation states still have power, but can be quashed by larger trade agreements such as NAFTA.

As citizens, how can we change things?
- Perhaps spending time on blaming others is not the most productive.
- There are many problems of poverty in Canada and the U.S. – involvement becomes a question of where best to invest the time and energy.
- Governments need to consult with the public more.

- Power comes from shareholders (and their votes) more than from the actions of national governments. If shareholders don't like the direction the company is taking they can pull their money out.
- The difficulty is the capacity to buy shares – a dollar a vote will be marginalized.
- One suggested action is to remove the protection of corporations under a Bill of Rights. Recognize that corporations are not citizens and should not be afforded the same rights/protections.
- Citizens need to use the media to get their message out.
- Because of media concentration people need to be informed about 'Indy' media.
- Organize conferences (opportunities) for people from the North and South to come together, this will help to build a global community.
- Need to make sure that we don't just talk. Need to vote. Need to make sure that the networks that are being built around issues like the G8 continue on into the future
- Developing a common 'activist' front is difficult but necessary. Need a leader for the movement.

Globalization and Democratic Participation: International Perspectives

Facilitator: Dr. Bob Ware – Professor of Philosophy, University of Calgary. Member of Board, Parkland Institute

- It is important to share information globally – "understanding each other by knowing each other".
- Examples include: sister communities; farmers in Mexico and Alberta sharing cooperative experiences. The National Farmers Union allow for ideas to be exchanged internationally.

- It is important to educate people about the groups that already exist.
- Exchanges between communities and organizations which may not be specifically community-focused.
- The internet has made information more readily available. Previously the Arusha Centre was the only source for such information (in Calgary). Perhaps these centres of information may no longer be needed?
- It is important to earn our democracy through action.
- How can we recognize global interdependence? People feel powerless. We need to encourage a feeling of belonging in people.
- The media should portray protesters as 'pro-community' rather than 'anti-globalization'.
- The G8 has prompted a lot of debate. That is an indication of change. For example, *The Calgary Herald* approached the organizers of the G6B about running some pieces on the alternative conference.
- Why must protest have to center around the G8? Why don't protesters create their own (positive) event? The G8 is protested because it is symbolic – need to have events in concert which raise awareness

What do developing countries want/need?
- Opportunities to discuss and share ideas.
- Ideas are generated locally – we need to provide developing countries with platforms.
- Importance of globalization 'from below' – Canada needs to ask what it can do rather than dictate what it will do.
- Need an umbrella organization like the United Way extended to the international level.

- Need to break the barriers of silence in the international disorder.
- Thoughtful participation is less difficult than people think.

Globalization and Democratic Participation in an International Context

Facilitator: Brian Long – Vice President, the Commonwealth of Learning

- The response to globalization should be miniaturization.
- The government is fearful of deconstructing protests.
- Protesters need a legitimate forum to raise concerns.
- Must work locally to improve our own government before examining others.
- Protests need solid documents/concepts to support – must do more than just raise voices.

Global Governance and Democratic Legitimacy

Facilitator: Dr. Stephen Randall – Dean of Social Sciences, University of Calgary

What is democratic legitimacy? Do we have responsibility to vote or just the right?
- Need for an effective opposition and more faith in the present system of government.
- Parliamentarians feel frustrated – everything happens outside parliament.
- Party discipline – is this an issue that should be investigated?
- There is no accountability at a global level.

· A tension exists between local interests and global interdependence.
· Legitimacy in democracy depends on strong grass-roots connections.
· The individual and his/her government need to be constantly re-connected.
· Need capacity for dissent to make a difference (i.e. Tiananmen Square).

Notes unavailable:

– **Local Spaces in a Globalized World?**
Facilitator: Dr. Roger Gibbins – President and CEO, Canada West Foundation.

– **The Global Justice Movement: Local Organizing for Kananaskis and Beyond.**
Facilitator: Sarah Kerr – Activist and Educator.

CONTRIBUTORS

Joel Bell is Chair of the Board of the Sheldon Chumir Foundation for Ethics in Leadership. Mr. Bell was trained in law, economics and business at McGill University and Harvard University. He has extensive experience in the public and private sectors. While in government, Mr. Bell served as principal economic advisor to Prime Minister Trudeau and was a founder and Executive Vice-President of Petro-Canada. He also helped set up the Canada Development Investment Corporation and served as its President and CEO. While in the private sector he worked as an investment advisor and business consultant. Mr. Bell also has experience in the telecommunications field which includes a stint as head of Power Direct TV. His community involvement includes service on the Board of the Calgary Philharmonic Orchestra. Most recently he has been participating in several Canada-U.S. cross-border organizations.

Benjamin R. Barber is the Gershon and Carol Kekst Professor of Civil Society at the University of Maryland and a principal of the Democracy Collaborative. Mr. Barber has written and lectured extensively on issues related to democracy, politics, culture, citizenship, and education. He consults regularly with political and civic leaders in the United States and Europe such as former President Bill Clinton and President Roman Herzog of Germany, as well as with institutions such as the United States Information Agency, the National Endowment for the Humanities, UNESCO, and the European Parliament. Among Mr. Barber's honours are the Guggenheim, Fulbright, and Social Science Research Fellowships, an honourary doctorate from Grinnell College, and the Berlin Prize of the American Academy of Berlin (2001). He holds a certificate from the London School of Economics and Political Science and an MA and PhD from Harvard University. For television, Mr. Barber co-wrote with Patrick Watson the prize-winning CBS/PBS ten-part series *The Struggle For Democracy* and the companion book. Mr. Barber's fifteen books include the renowned *Strong Democracy* and the international best-seller *Jihad vs. McWorld*. His most recent work, *The Truth of Power: Intellectual Affairs in the Clinton White House* was published in 2002.

David Schneiderman is an Associate Professor of Law at the University of Toronto Faculty of Law. He completed his BA at McGill University his LLB at Windsor University and his LLM at Queen's University. He was called to the Bar of British Columbia in 1984 where he practised law As well, he served as Research Director of the Canadian Civil Liberties Association in Toronto, and was Executive Director of the Centre for Constitutional Studies at the University of Alberta. Professor Schneiderman has authored numerous articles on Canadian constitutional law and history, comparative constitutional law and economic globalization. He has edited several books, including *The Quebec Decision, Charting the Consequences: The Impact of the Charter of Rights on Canadian Law and Politics*, with Kate Sutherland, and *Social Justice and the Constitution: Perspectives on a Social Union for Canada* with Joel Bakan. He is founding editor of the quarterly *Constitutional Forum Constitutionnel* and founding editor-in-chief of the journal *Review of Constitutional Studies*. Professor Schneiderman is currently completing a book manuscript entitled *Reigning Authority: The Constitutional Order of Economic Globalization*.

Gretchen **Mann Brewin** retired in May 2001 from a lengthy career in municipal and provincial politics. Ms. Brewin was first elected to the British Columbia Legislature in 1991, representing the riding of Victoria-Beacon Hill, and was re-elected in 1996. Before that, she was Victoria's first woman mayor, serving two terms in that position after three terms as a city councillor. She established Victoria's first Social Planning Committee, the position of Social Planner and a City Task Force on Violence Against Women, Children and the Elderly. As a British Columbia MLA, Ms. Brewin was a key member of the presentation team that brought the Commonwealth Games to Victoria. She went on to serve as Attaché to Team Canada and on the Board of the Commonwealth Games Association of Canada. Ms. Brewin was the province's first woman Deputy Speaker and was elected Speaker of the Legislative Assembly in March 1998.

Lynn F. Foster is currently the Coordinator for the G6B: The People's Summit, which is the counter-conference to the 2002 G8 summit, having taken early voluntary retirement in 2000 after a thirty-one year career in the federal government. She is also the co-founder and Executive Secretary of the International Society for Peace and Human Rights and has been a volunteer with Amnesty International for over twenty years. She completed a BA at the University of Calgary in Psychology and an MSW at the University of British Columbia. From 1972 until 1996, Ms. Foster has served in various capacities for the government of Canada including District Director and Program Officer with the Departments of Multiculturalism, First Nations, Disabled Persons, and Women, in Vancouver and in Calgary. Other work for the government of Canada has included service as Regional Coordinator for the Status of Women in Calgary and Edmonton and as a social worker for Indian Affairs in Prince George.

Russell Hemenway has been National Director of the National Committee for an Effective Congress since 1965. The Committee, based in Washington, D.C., identifies and supports progressive candidates for public office. Mr. Hemenway was educated at Dartmouth College and l'Institut d'Études Politiques in Paris. He has served as the Director of the New York State Department of Commerce and was the national presidential campaign manager for Adlai E. Stevenson. Mr. Hemenway is also Chair of The Fund For Constitutional Government and President of Citizens Vote Inc. He serves as director and executive committee member for both the Fund for Peace and The Population Institute. He is the Board Chair of The National Security Archives and a trustee of The Mott Charitable Trust.

Brian F. MacNeill is Chair of Petro-Canada and a Director of Enbridge Inc., The Toronto Dominion Bank, Dofasco Inc., Western Oil Sands Inc., West Fraser Timber Co. Ltd., Veritas DGC Inc., Telus Corporation, and Sears Canada Inc. Mr. MacNeill holds a Bachelor of Commerce degree from Montana State University. He earned a Certified Public Accountant designation in the U.S., and a Chartered Accountant and FCA designation in Canada. Mr. MacNeill retired as Chief Executive Officer of Enbridge Inc. on January 1st, 2001, having led Enbridge since 1990. He is a member of the Alberta and Ontario Institutes of Chartered Accountants, and the Financial Executives Institute, a Fellow of the Canadian Institute of Chartered Accountants, and Chair of the Board of Governors of the University of Calgary.

Stephen Lewis is currently United Nations Special Envoy for HIV/AIDS in Africa. Mr. Lewis has extensive experience as a politician, diplomat, and humanitarian. In addition to his fifteen honourary degrees from various Canadian universities, Mr. Lewis is the former Deputy Executive Director of UNICEF, former leader of the Ontario New Democratic Party, and former Canadian Ambassador to the United Nations. In 1993, he became coordinator for the international study, known as the Graca Machel study, on the "Consequences of Armed Conflict on Children". That report was tabled in the United Nations in 1995. In 1997, in addition to his work at UNICEF, Mr. Lewis was appointed by the Organization of African Unity to a Panel of Eminent Personalities to Investigate the Genocide in Rwanda. Throughout his career Mr. Lewis has been a tireless advocate of the rights and needs of children worldwide.

Robert Fowler is the Personal Representative of the Prime Minister for the G8 Summit and Personal Representative of the Prime Minister for Africa. In addition Mr. Fowler is Canada's Ambassador to Italy, where he is accredited as High Commissioner to Malta, Ambassador to Albania and San Marino and Ambassador and Permanent Representative to the United Nations organizations based in Rome. Prior to his appointment as Ambassador to Italy, he was Canada's Ambassador to the United Nations in New York. He has held various senior positions in Ottawa, including Assistant Secretary to the Cabinet (Foreign and Defence Policy) at the Privy Council Office, and Assistant Deputy Minister (Policy) and then Deputy Minister at the Department of National Defence. Mr. Fowler was born in Ottawa and has a BA from Queen's University.

Naomi Klein is an award-winning journalist and author of the international best-selling book *No Logo: Taking Aim at the Brand Bullies*. Translated into 22 languages, *The New York Times* called No Logo "a movement bible". *The Guardian* short-listed it for their First Book Award in 2000. In April 2001, *No Logo* won the Canadian National Business Book Award, and in August 2001 it was awarded Le Prix Meditations, in France. Ms. Klein writes an internationally syndicated column for *The Globe and Mail* in Canada and *The Guardian* in Britain. For the past six years, she has travelled throughout North America, Asia, Latin America, and Europe, tracking the rise of anti-corporate activism. She is a frequent media commentator and has guest lectured at Harvard, Yale, and New York University. In December 2001, Ms. Klein was named *Ms. Magazine*'s Woman of the Year.

John M. Curtis is Senior Policy Advisor and Coordinator, Trade and Economic Policy, and Director of Trade and Economic Analysis, Foreign Affairs and International Trade Canada. As the Department's de facto chief economist, he is responsible for trade and economic policy advice, analysis and research, particularly with respect to emerging trade issues, the evolution of the world trading system, and links between Canada's domestic economic structure and international economic developments. Having completed his BA at the University of British Columbia, and his Doctorate in Economics at Harvard, Dr. Curtis has maintained formal teaching and research links with both Carleton University and the University of Ottawa. Over the past several years, Dr. Curtis concentrated on all aspects of the Uruguay Round of GATT negotiations, including its relationship to existing and emerging regional trading arrangements in Asia, Europe and Latin America. He has also played a major role in the Asia Pacific Economic Cooperation forum over the past decade, serving as the founding Chair of the Economic Committee for its first four years (1994-1998). Prior to that, he participated in the Canada-U.S. Free Trade negotiations, was the federal government's first coordinator of regulatory reform at the Treasury Board, served in the economic policy secretariat of the Privy Council Office and before that with the International Monetary Fund in Washington, D.C.

Len Findlay is Professor of English and Director of the Humanities Research Unit at the University of Saskatchewan. Educated at Aberdeen and Oxford, he came to Canada in 1974 and has served as President of the Association of Canadian College and University Teachers of English, Vice-President (External Communications) of the Humanities and Social Science

Federation of Canada and Senior Policy Analyst for the Universities Branch of the Saskatchewan Department of Post-Secondary Education and Skills Training. Professor Findlay has published widely in nineteenth-century studies, literary theory, and the nature and role of universities and the humanities in Canada. He was last year's Northrop Frye Professor of Literary Theory at the University of Toronto and is at work on a book on intellectual and artistic freedom.

Stuart **Walker** is currently Director of Lester B. Pearson College of the Pacific. The college has two hundred students, aged sixteen to nineteen, from over eighty countries. All students attend on a full scholarship. Mr. Walker grew up in South Africa but was educated in Australia. He received his BA at Royal Military College, his Diploma of Education at Monash University, and his Master of Educational Administration at Deakin University. Mr. Walker served as Founding Headmaster of Snowy Mountains Grammar School in Jindabyne, Australia from 1996 to 1999. Prior to that he was Deputy Head of Timbertop, Geelong Grammar School in Mansfield from 1989 to 1995. Mr. Walker is also an experienced sailor who has participated in ocean racing.

Harvey P. **Weingarten** is President and Vice-Chancellor of the University of Calgary. A distinguished scholar in the fields of psychology and medicine, Dr. Weingarten came to the University of Calgary from McMaster University, where he served as Provost and Vice-President (Academic) from 1996 to 2001. Dr. Weingarten holds a BSc from McGill University, and a M.S., MPhil, and PhD from Yale University. He joined McMaster University as a member of the faculty in 1979, and went on to become Chair of that university's Department of Psychology in 1989, Full Professor in 1990, and Dean of McMaster University's Faculty of Science in 1995. He also serves on the Board of Trustees for the Alberta Heritage Foundation for Medical Research, the Board of Directors of the Calgary Canadian and Chinese Economic and Cultural Foundation, and the Board of Directors for Calgary Technologies Inc.

Bronwyn Drainie is one of Canada's leading cultural journalists. She is the author of two books *Living the Part: John Drainie and the Dilemma of Canadian Stardom* and *My Jerusalem: Secular Adventures in the Holy City.* From 1988 to 1996 she was an arts columnist for *The Globe and Mail* and from 1996 to 1998 was Chair of Media Ethics at Ryerson Polytechnic University. Ms. Drainie has worked for many years as a broadcaster for CBC-Radio, hosting such programs as "Sunday Morning", "Celebration", and "New Releases". She won an ACTRA award as Best Host-Interviewer on Radio for 1980. She has written for all of Canada's top magazines such as *Saturday Night, Chatelaine, Report on Business, Toronto Life, Elm Street, Canadian Forum,* and *Books in Canada* and has written position papers, opinion and discussion papers for civil society organizations such as the Canadian Council on International Cooperation and the Canadian Centre for Philanthropy.

John Stackhouse is Foreign Editor of *The Globe and Mail*. He was previously the newspaper's Correspondent-at-Large, and from 1992 to 1999 its development issues correspondent, based in New Delhi. He previously worked for *Report on Business Magazine, the Financial Times, London Free Press* and the *Toronto Star*. His work has won five national newspaper awards and a national magazine award. He sits on the boards of World Literacy Canada, Canadian Journalists for Free Expression and the University of Toronto's International Development Studies program. His first book, *Out of Poverty*, was published in 2000.

Michael Valpy currently writes on religion, spirituality and ethics for *The Globe and Mail*. His previous work for that newspaper has included being a member of its editorial board, an Ottawa national political columnist, its Africa correspondent, and a national columnist on social policy and urban issues. He began his journalism career at *The Vancouver Sun*, eventually becoming that newspaper's Associate Editor and National Affairs Columnist. He has co-authored two books on the Canadian Constitution entitled *The National Deal* and *To Match a Dream*. In 1997, Trent University awarded him an honourary doctorate. He has won three National Newspaper Awards - two for foreign reporting and one for an examination of how schools cope with children of dysfunctional families.

The Honourable Ron Ghitter is a former Alberta MLA and former member of the Canadian Senate. He is currently a Board Member of the Sheldon Chumir Foundation for Ethics in Leadership. Well known as a person deeply committed to human rights, Mr. Ghitter received the Alberta

Human Rights Award in 1990, and an honourary doctorate from the University of Calgary in 2001. First elected to the Alberta Provincial Legislature for the riding of Calgary Buffalo in 1971, he sponsored the Individual Rights Protection Act in 1972 and was Chairman of the Ministers Consultative Committee on Tolerance and Understanding, structured to provide Alberta's Minister of Education with recommendations on how the school system can better encourage tolerance and understanding in the province. He was a founding director of the International Centre for Human Rights and Democratic Development, chair of the 1990 Mayor of Calgary's Task Force on Community and Family Violence, member of the Federal Advisory Committee on Violence Against Women, and co-chair and founder of the Dignity Foundation, a non-profit organization established to encourage support for human rights in Alberta.

The Honourable Lloyd Axworthy is Director and CEO of the Liu Contro for the Study of Global Issues at the University of British Columbia and holds positions on several boards and companies. He joined the law firm of Fraser Milner Casgrain as a consultant on trade and international affairs, and is a board member of the MacArthur Foundation, Human Rights Watch, Lester B. Pearson College of the Pacific, University of the Arctic, the Institute for Media, Policy and Civil Society, and the Conflict Analysis and Management Advisory Board at Royal Roads University. He graduated with a BA from United College (University of Winnipeg) and received an MA and PhD from Princeton. First elected federally in 1979 as a Liberal Member of Parliament for the riding of Winnipeg-Fort Garry, Mr. Axworthy was re-elected in 1980, 1984, 1988, 1993 and 1997. He held several Cabinet positions, notably

Minister of Employment and Immigration, Minister Responsible for the Status of Women, Minister of Transport, of Human Resources Development, of Western Economic Diversification and Minister of Foreign Affairs. Mr. Axworthy left politics after twenty-seven years in the fall of 2000.

Sheldon M. Chumir

Sheldon Chumir was, by anyone's standards, an outstanding human being. Born in Calgary on December 3rd, 1940, he excelled at virtually every endeavour he undertook. As a Rhodes scholar, tax lawyer, rock concert promoter, politician, civil libertarian, public interest advocate, hockey player, businessman and many other things, Sheldon worked and played with passionate intensity. His life was characterized by intelligence, humour, hard work, decency, and fairness. As a student, Sheldon achieved excellence in sports, academic pursuits, and student activities. After completing a law degree at the University of Alberta as his class's gold medallist in 1963, Sheldon was awarded a Rhodes scholarship to study at Oxford. When he returned to Canada in 1965 he pursued careers in the law, business and politics.

These accomplishments were impressive, but Sheldon wished to help those whose civil rights had been infringed and so he left his practice as a tax lawyer in 1976 and set up his own firm to defend the rights of the powerless. His commitment to civil liberties was unmatched; typically, he worked *pro bono* for causes that he felt were important. He also taught civil liberties at the University of Calgary Law School.

Sheldon loved to debate issues, recognizing that principled and respectful disagreement was vital to the democratic process. His approach to issues was characterized by careful reflection and independence of mind. His educational and legal experiences turned him into a vigorous supporter of public education, civil rights and individual freedoms. Whatever the issue, Sheldon could always be found acting for the underdog – for the person or group he felt needed his help.

As a politician Sheldon was convinced that voters wanted political leaders to strive for fairness and honesty in all of their dealings. He rejected the notion that politics was a blood sport where only the ruthless could survive. His political instincts helped him to get elected in 1986 – the first Liberal elected in Calgary in over fifteen years – as a Member of Alberta's Legislative Assembly for the riding of Calgary-Buffalo. He was re-elected in 1989.

In addition to his unique personality, Sheldon also had a unique perspective in that he was familiar with the internal dynamics of both the public and private sectors. He was, therefore, able to conceptualize and to criticize the strengths and weaknesses of both systems.

Sheldon sensed that our society suffers from a crisis of leadership. Both in government and in business, he perceived that people had lost faith in the capacity of established institutions to meet the needs of those they served. The first sign of this loss of faith was the public's increasing reluctance to spend time reflecting on issues relating to the public good.

When he died at the age of just fifty-one in January of 1992 following a brief illness, there was an enormous outpouring of respect and admiration not only from his many friends, but from people from all walks of life who felt how keenly they would miss his integrity, his dedication to humanitarian causes, his gentle humour and sense of fun, and his genuine warmth toward people from every corner of the community. Following his death, Sheldon was recognized by the Law Society of Alberta and posthumously awarded the Distinguished Service Award for Service to the Community. The inscription on the award reads in part:

> Founder of the Alberta Civil Liberties Association, he was a tireless champion in *pro bono* work for various unpopular causes and wrongs to be set right. His spirit lives on through the Sheldon Chumir Foundation for Ethics in Leadership, created as his last wish as a legacy for Canada.